This book is due on the last date stamped below.
Failure to return books on the date due may result
in assessment of overdue fees.

SEP 2 5 2015		
SEP 2 5 REC'D		
FINES	.50 per day	

DAKOTA
CROSS-BEARER

DAKOTA CROSS-BEARER

The Life and World of

a Native American

Bishop

BY

Mary E. Cochran

WITH AN
INTRODUCTION BY

Raymond A. Bucko

AND

Martin Brokenleg

University of Nebraska Press
Lincoln & London

Publication of this volume
was assisted by The Virginia Faulkner Fund,
established in memory of Virginia Faulkner,
editor-in-chief of the University
of Nebraska Press.

ⓧ

Library of Congress Cataloging-in-Publication Data
Cochran, Mary E.
Dakota cross-bearer : the life and world of a Native American bishop /
by Mary E. Cochran ; with an introduction by Raymond A. Bucko and
Martin Brokenleg.
    p. cm.
Includes bibliographical references and index.
ISBN 0-8032-1511-8 (cl : alk. paper)
    1. Jones, Harold S., 1911– . 2. Santee Indians—Biography. 3. Santee
Indians—Religion. 4. Santee Indians—History. 5. Episcopal Church—
Bishops—Biography. 6. Racism—Religious aspects—Episcopal Church.
7. Christianity and culture—Great Plains. I. Title.
    E99.S22 J65 2000
    283'.092—dc21
    [B]   00-023544

CONTENTS

⚛ + ⚛

ILLUSTRATIONS

� + ✶

PREFACE

※ + ※

This book is Harold Jones's story as he told it to me in a series of tapes and conversations. To the facts, conversations, and happenings remembered and recounted on the tapes, I have added my interpretation of what he might have been thinking and feeling. Harold Jones and his wife Blossom gave their consent to this amplification of the story, and Harold has had the opportunity to verify my interpretation.

In 1966 my husband and I moved to Standing Rock Reservation on the borders of North and South Dakota, where he was called to minister to the Dakota people. During our mutual years in the Dakotas, we became good friends with the Joneses. We regretted their move to Navajoland and joyfully welcomed them back after Harold's election as Suffragan Bishop of South Dakota.

The tapes and this book are the result of a conversation I had with Harold, a fine storyteller. "Your story should be written down," I said. "Will you write it?" he replied. "Using my own experiences, I would like to show how Almighty God stays with us through both our hardships and our good times, never letting us down." I have tried to convey this conviction of Harold's in the book. His story also gives a picture of the joys and pains of growing up as an Indian, and of how he later dealt with the cultural conflicts he faced both within the church and in the larger society.

I am grateful to the many persons who gave encouragement and critique at various stages in the writing of this book, especially to Virginia and

Jim Sloan for their proofreading and helpful comments; to Ed and Carolyn Bryce, who generously shared their expertise in publishing; to my husband David for his editing (and nagging); and to Wanda Cartznes, who did the word processing with care and enthusiasm.

INTRODUCTION

≫≪ + ≫≪

Raymond A. Bucko
Martin Brokenleg

Frank Fools Crow, a prominent Lakota spiritual leader, was buried on December 4, 1989. His wake and funeral were moving events attended by many people from Pine Ridge and neighboring reservations as well as individuals from across the country. The ceremonies were covered by a large contingent of reporters and photographers. Fools Crow's body was brought to rest by a horse-drawn wagon at St. Barnabas Episcopal cemetery on the Pine Ridge Reservation. At the burial site, the Lakota spiritual leaders separated into two clusters at either end of Frank's grave. At one end was a group of Lakota Episcopalian clergy as well as one white Catholic priest, all wearing black pants and clerical collars. At the other end were traditional leaders, most wearing blue jeans and Western shirts but a few with classic Lakota feathered headdresses and ribbon shirts. Both groups prayed as Fools Crow was solemnly laid to rest. In order to record the ceremony, the news photographers positioned themselves with their backs to the Episcopalian priests and deacons and pointed their cameras toward the traditional leaders. In the process they excluded from view an important part of Lakota reality, focusing only on what they had deliberately selected for their perspective. Outsiders have commonly used this strategy of selectivity when viewing the reality of Indian life, thereby reducing complexity to simplicity and oftentimes to mere stereotype. In the nineteenth century the cameras could well have pointed in the other direction, focusing only on the Christianized Indians. Rarely have the two realities been integrated into a single picture.

For this reason, *Dakota Cross-Bearer: The Life and World of a Native American Bishop* is a unique contribution to a fuller understanding of the complex interrelations of Christianity and Native belief as well as of Indian and white cultures. Mary Cochran composed this biography of the first Dakota Episcopalian Bishop, Harold Jones, from hours of his recollections, which were carefully taped, transcribed, and then transformed into a literary narrative that was checked by Jones and his wife Blossom for accuracy and fidelity. The author structured Jones's life story as a traditional European biography, beginning with birth and childhood, providing genealogical background, tracing his life through adolescence, college, seminary, and ministry as an ordained priest, and finally culminating in his elevation to the rank of bishop in the Episcopal Church. At the same time, the work is faithful to the style and organization of a Dakota storyteller, spinning out associations among persons, places, and events, relishing relationships, and using stories to teach, encourage, and entertain the audience. This dual structural style allows us to appreciate the intricately intertwining histories of Jones's roots and associations among Dakotas, Lakotas, and later European immigrants. The portrait presented in *Dakota Cross-Bearer* draws upon the deep perceptions of a man who has lived a rich, full life among many different cultures and peoples. As such, it offers a precious treasure of family and tribal histories. This tale is not simply a romantic idyll, however. Much of its wealth, paradoxically, lies in impoverishment and hardship, while triumphs are set against a long history of injustice and tragedy.

Harold Jones's biography unfolds in a warm narrative style that considers harsh realities but does so with a genuine and unique Dakota humor and understanding. Jones and his family were surrounded by a white population that wanted them to assimilate and at the same time wished them to remain romantically "traditional." In addition, the Jones family dealt with a church that strongly desired a native clergy but was often ill equipped to negotiate cultural differences in both educational styles and communal responsibilities for Native priests. The church was also unable to support the clergy and their families sufficiently in financial matters.

Thus the title of the work presents an irony that, as the reader will see, is clearly present in Jones's life: a cross-bearer is both one who leads the people in liturgical procession and one who follows Christ in his sufferings.

Dakota Cross-Bearer provides an apology for Christianity alongside a healthy critique of church policies and practices. At the same time, it steadfastly maintains a respect for traditional religious practices and beliefs. Jones strongly connects his Christian faith with the larger contemporary Dakota belief in and respect for Wakan Tanka (the Great Mystery). Rooted in a traditional culture, the early Dakota converts respected the integrity of this new Christian tradition that was brought to them. The narrative also demonstrates how an individual as well as a group of people can actively create their own history and transform their own culture. The Jones family did so with perseverance and integrity.

The book is a chronicle of Dakota family relationships, both genetic kinship as well as relations based on church membership. It is also a work of biographical geography. The Niobrara Convocation, a large annual gathering of Native Episcopalians for prayer and social activities, is a key element in the life of Jones and his family. These meetings take place at various locations around the Dakota and Lakota country and are primary social and religious events for Episcopalian Dakotas and Lakotas (see Sneve 1977, 216–17). Bishop Jones clearly savors the memories of these events as he uses geographical locations as mnemonic devices for recollections of the individuals with whom he was reunited, the foods he enjoyed, and the deep friendships he developed. While a map generally shows geographical positions in relations to other physical locations such as roads and geological formations, Jones's biographical geography, mapped out by means of his own narratives, associates place with the rich social interactions that are an essential part of Dakota and Lakota culture.

A few comments here may help readers become familiar with the rich texture of Native life described in *Dakota Cross-Bearer*. While European and American scientists believe that the Native peoples of the Americas migrated from Asia by way of the Bering Strait thousands of years ago, many Dakotas and Lakotas hold that they have always lived in North America. Europeans and Americans referred to the Dakota and Lakota people collectively as the Sioux, a word derived by the French from an Algonkian term for the Dakotas (*nadouessi*), which originally meant "snakes" and thus "enemies." These people increasingly avoid using this foreign term for themselves as they assert the right to determine their own identity and future. The term Dakota was also used for both the Dakota and Lakota groups during the nineteenth century (see Powers 1975, 3–11). These groups are similar in many ways and count themselves as relatives, but they also exhibit distinct cultural and linguistic features. Today Native peoples refer to themselves using terms from their own languages, and they wish others to do the same. The terms *dakota* and *lakota* mean "ally" or "friend." They also refer to the spoken languages of the respective peoples, just as the term English can refer to both a cultural and a linguistic group.

The Dakota and Lakota are divided into seven groups known as the seven fireplaces. The easternmost group, the Santee, consists of four subgroups: the Wahpekute (Leaf Shooters), Mdewakanton (Spirit Lake Village), Sisseton (meaning unclear, sometimes translated as Fish Scale Dweller), and Wahpeton (Leaf Village). These peoples call themselves Dakota. The central group, the Yanktons, consists of two subgroups: the Yankton (End Village) and Yanktonai (Little End Village), both of whom also refer to themselves as Dakota. The westernmost and largest group, the Teton, refer to themselves as Lakota. The Teton are subdivided into seven groups: Oglala (They Scatter Their Own), Hunkpapa (End of the Circle), Sicangu (Brulé in French: Burned Thighs), Itazipco (Sans Arcs in French: Without Bows), Oohenumpa (Two Kettles or Two Boilings), Mnikowoju (Planters by the Water), and Sihasapa (Blackfeet) (Powers 1975, 13; DeMallie 1986, 20). Bishop Jones, himself a Santee Dakota, has a long career ministering to the Lakotas on various reservations in western South Dakota. As is quite apparent in the text, these groups see each other as relatives and have maintained close contact with one another.

Although Europeans knew these people by reputation since at least 1640, French explorers in 1660 provide the earliest European record of contact with the Dakotas. As the United States established itself as a power in a multinational North America, it sought to secure its borders as it rapidly expanded west. The first official contact between the United States and the Dakota people occurred in the fall of 1805 when Lieutenant Zebulon M. Pike signed a treaty with some Dakotas. This treaty marked the beginning of a very difficult relationship between the two polities (Meyer 1993, 24–27).

Years of white immigration into their territory had steadily eroded the Dakota land base and resources, but the group's condition worsened radically after the signing of the Traverse des Sioux Treaty in 1851. This dire deterioration coupled with the abrogation of treaty commitments precipitated the Dakota Conflict of August 1862, which resulted in the execution of thirty-two Santee participants in the conflict and the exile of the Dakotas from their homeland. The displaced Dakotas were dispersed and settled on reservations in Nebraska, North Dakota, Montana, South Dakota, and Canada (Meyer 1993, 133–54). A similar process of restriction of land and other resources began somewhat later for the Lakotas, culminating in the Wounded Knee massacre in December 1890, when over 150 innocent and defenseless Lakotas were slaughtered (Utley 1963, 227–28). These tragic events loom large in the historical consciousness of Jones as well as of the Lakota and Dakota people in general. Many Lakotas and Dakotas today are still able to name their relatives who were lost in these conflicts.

While this history of division and devastation is clearly part of the fabric of Jones's life, it is counterbalanced by memories of good relationships with whites established through trade, Church ministry, and friendship even during this early period. Many of these alliances resulted in intermarriage. Indeed, at the time of the Dakota Conflict, some Dakotas risked their lives in order to warn, protect, and even rescue their white friends and relatives from hostile bands. Jones himself recalls one of these incidents in his narrative, which serves as an important corrective to the stereotyping of events as well as persons.

Missionaries first visited the Dakota country with French explorers in 1680, but American missionary efforts did not begin in earnest until the 1830s when the Pond brothers, Gideon and Samuel, arrived at Lake Calhoun (S. Pond 1893, 38). Independent of any organized church mission group, they began learning Dakota and translating the Bible into that language. Two years later the American Board of Commissioners for Foreign Missions sent their own missionaries to establish churches and schools. Among the early missionaries were Dr. John P. Williamson and Stephen Return Riggs, who continued the study of the Dakota language and eventually wrote a grammar and dictionary. Episcopalian missionaries did not arrive until 1860, when Henry Whipple, bishop of Minnesota, sent Samuel Hinman to Dakota Territory to open a mission and a school (Sneve 1977b, 17). Missionary visits by Catholics to the Dakotas and Lakotas began in the 1830s (Duratschek 1985, 3).

The early missionaries did not meet with much success except among some of the mixed-blood population and a few of the Dakota women. Only after the Dakota Conflict did many Dakotas adopt Christianity. While a multitude of motivations—religious, social, political, economic, and cultural—prompted the Dakotas to make this transition, Bishop Jones's narrative focuses on the spiritual dynamism of Christianity that helped the people to reconstruct their shattered lives.

An essential question became more and more pressing as new settlers surrounded the Dakotas and economic, ecological, and political changes made adherence to old lifeways increasingly difficult. Jones raises this question in the context of his narrative, and it remains important in contemporary Indian life: Why should the Dakotas and Lakotas, who have often been betrayed by the new settlers, accept these people's religion and cultural ways? The great irony here is that while the early missionaries wanted the Dakotas and Lakotas to fully assimilate European and Christian ways and consciously renounce their own culture and religious beliefs, the Natives themselves were content to incorporate the best elements of the two cultures and religious systems. Today, when the Churches have become more tolerant and respectful of traditional beliefs and practices, a growing number of Native peoples are drawing a rigid line between the two belief systems and insisting on adherence to one or the other.

Clearly not all Dakotas and Lakotas chose the Christian path. Those who did sometimes incurred the wrath and prejudice of both sides. Bishop Jones and his family see Christianity not as belonging to white people but as a universal religion, one that the Dakotas and Lakotas were prepared to accept as part of their own spiritual heritage. In his understanding, the sufferings of Christ are joined to the suffering of the Indian people. Jones worked among very poor people and his family struggled to survive on the small salaries provided for church ministry. It is important to note, however, that the Dakotas and Lakotas mark wealth not by monetary assets and material possessions but by the richness of family relationships and friendships. In these aspects, Jones and his family are clearly wealthy, caring for others and incorporating outsiders into their family through both tribal and church affiliation.

While this biography is filled with pathos and struggle, it also contains joy and great humor. Despite the stereotypical stoic image etched into popular consciousness by movies, television, and novels, Dakotas and Lakotas have retained a glorious sense of humor and irony, particularly when times are most sacred or circumstances most tragic. Thus in chapter 8 Bishop Jones provides a comic retelling of a Christmas pageant in one of his parishes with a compassionate look at the deep problems of alcoholism, using humor to embrace, accept, and heal human weakness and tragedy rather than to dismiss the problem or condemn the person.

Dakota and Lakota humor is largely verbal. Events become funnier in the telling and retelling, and comic embroidery is always appreciated, with friends and family members frequently substituted as the heroes of the story to add to the humor. These people delight in verbal confusions within their own language and between their native language and English. As Jones's narrative illustrates, the Lakotas and Dakotas use humor to redeem and transform many situations. There is also is a great fondness for humorous self-deprecation. Jones delights in a story in chapter 3 in which a clergyman's verbal mistake produces hilarious results during a very solemn event, as well as an account of his own linguistic befuddlement in chapter 8. To understand Bishop Jones's linguistic plight, one must understand something about Dakota (Santee) and Lakota as related languages.

Lakota and Dakota represent two dialects of a closely related language. Jones tells a story on himself about one such confusion that involves the often humorous difficulties one can encounter in switching from one dialect to another. The predominant sound in Dakota is *D* (sometimes Native speakers refer to it as the D dialect) and in Lakota, *L*. Thus the word for friend in Dakota is *koda* and in Lakota *kola*. Translating from one language to another, however, is not always a simple matter of consonant switching as each language has certain unique words. Lakotas and Dakotas both tell jokes involving switching between the Lakota *L* and Dakota *D* while speaking a foreign language, English. In one story a boy from Rosebud travels east to the Dakota country for a basketball game. While he is there, he falls in love with one of the Santee cheerleaders. He really wants to impress her, so when the time comes for him to leave the town he stands next to her, looks down at the ground, and says, "I dove you." In another story a Dakota comes out to the Pine Ridge Reservation to attend boarding school and is picked up by some relatives at the train station in Rushville, Nebraska. He has been told back home about how his relatives to the west talk different. When they get to Pine Ridge, he notices that he has left a bag back in Rushville. Remembering the *D* and *L* differences, he says to his relatives, "I forgot a bag back at the . . . at the lepot!"

In addition to his personal and familial relationships, Jones's life also presents a portrait of the inner workings of the Episcopal Church. Like other Christian denominations among the Lakotas and Dakotas, his church raised up leaders within Native communities to help spread the Gospel message and incorporated these communities into the existing church structure. In a diocese that is non-self-supporting (such as South Dakota) and thus designated as "missionary," the bishop was elected by a council of bishops and exercised semiautonomous authority. By the time Jones was ordained bishop, missionary districts had been abolished, both clergy and laity elected their bishops during conventions, and these bishops exercised their authority through a conciliar process in consultation with other church members. In mission areas, superintending presbyters or archdeacons supervised the clergy. Unlike in the Eastern Orthodox and Roman Catholic Churches, married men are eligible for the office of bishop. Formal offices for ministry in the Episcopal Church also included deacons, lay readers, and sisters, women dedicated to the ministry. Jones was ordained at a time when women began to gain greater access to hierarchical ministerial roles in the Episcopal Church.

Bishop Jones makes frequent allusions to hymns throughout his narrative. Church music (generally European melodies with lyrics translated into Dakota or Lakota but sung in a distinctive style) is very important in the lives of Christian Dakotas and Lakotas. Like persons, geographical locations, and specific foods, hymns also engender webs of remembrances. The adoption of specific hymns by individuals who later become identified by those hymns is consonant with traditional Dakota and Lakota uses of

sacred songs. Christian Lakotas and Dakotas, especially the older generation, identify themselves and others with favorite hymns. So too departed
members of congregations are memorialized with certain hymns, and the
singing of favorite hymns are an important part of both funerals and the
memorial rituals held one year after a death. It is not uncommon for elderly individuals to sing a cappella every stanza of a hymn from memory
(and these hymns can exceed five or six stanzas) to honor a specific relative
at church events such as Christmas gatherings. Thus the musical honoring found in traditional settings such as feeds (a reservation English term
for feasts that provide extra food for families to take home) and dances are
continued in church life.

Ecumenism is also an important element in the life of Dakota and Lakota Christians, although early in mission history it was more often practiced by the Natives than by the churches that they joined. This important
dynamic is brought out in Jones's narrative in the context of his ordination
to the episcopacy. While the early missionization of the Dakotas and Lakotas was marked by interdenominational competition, the Lakotas and Dakotas recognize each other first and primarily as relatives and then as
members of certain churches or traditional religion. The government tried
to control denominational rivalries and use church personnel to manage
the reservations through what was called the Grant Peace Policy. Each reservation was supervised by a single denomination, and rival groups were
forbidden to maintain churches or to proselytize on reservations from
which they were excluded. The Episcopal Church was charged with mis-
sionizing the Pine Ridge, Rosebud, Cheyenne River, and Yankton Reservations. The Quakers were assigned the Santee Reservation, the Presbyterians Sisseton and Flandreau, and the Roman Catholics were placed on the
Standing Rock Reservation. This policy of denominational allotment began in 1869 and ended with the last allotment in 1875. In 1881 the government at last gave all religious groups free access to proselytize on the reservations (Prucha 1976, 30–71; 1979, 2; 1984, 513, 516 n.4).

The terms *mixed* and *full blood* are used in this work, and indeed are
part of contemporary Lakota and Dakota discourse. While some Indians
do occasionally joke, "If he had a nosebleed, he wouldn't be Indian anymore," the notion that culture is joined to biology is an artifact of nine-

teenth-century European and American racial and cultural theory. These faulty ideas unfortunately remain with us today. The government used the idea of "blood quantum" to determine who was eligible for treaty rights and payments. In Lakota, however, the word for someone who was of mixed European and Indian heritage is *iyeska,* which means "white (European language) speaker," and the term often used for Lakota is *hca,* meaning "authentic, true, real," or as one Lakota translated it, "through and through Sioux." Being Indian is a matter of behavior, not blood. Thus to honor one's relatives, to be generous, to open one's home to strangers are all marks of being Lakota and Dakota.

We are fortunate to have this rich narrative to help us understand the tragedies and triumphs of an individual who remained part of his family and community as he struggled to live among many worlds. In reading about Bishop Jones's life, we may be inspired to grow in compassion and understanding for others. Moreover, this book extends an invitation for reconciliation among peoples and their beliefs—despite and perhaps even because of past conflicts and misunderstandings.

❧ † ❧

The authors of this introduction wish to express their gratitude to Christina E. Burke at the Heritage Center, Holy Rosary Mission, Pine Ridge, South Dakota, and to the author, Mary Cochran, for thoughtful critiques of their introduction; to Jim and Bernice Green for help with the linguistic elements of Bishop Jones's narrative; to Mark G. Thiel of the Marquette University library for help with bibliographical and archival sources; to the staff at the Le Moyne College library, especially the research librarians Inga H. Barnello (and her trusty National Union Catalog) and Gretchen Pearson; and to the interlibrary loan staff at the Le Moyne library, particularly Mary Lee Shanahan and Wayne A. Stevens, for their hard work and perseverance, for without them and this facility this kind of research would not be possible.

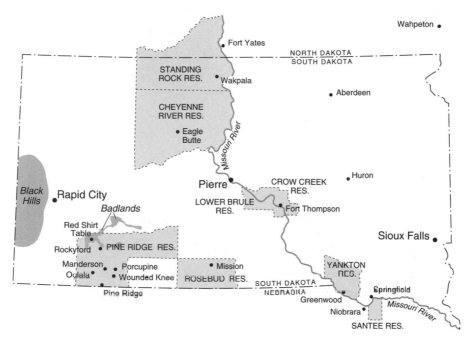

The Dakotas of Harold Jones

DAKOTA
CROSS-BEARER

PROLOGUE

❧ + ❧

The Dakota Sioux tribes, living on lands that the U.S. government had appropriated for the new state of Minnesota, looked forward to July 1, 1862. They had been instructed to come on that day to Fort Ridgely to receive the long-overdue payments for their land, payments that had been delayed, they were told, because of the Civil War. Five thousand hungry men, women, and children gathered in vain to receive the promised food and money. In desperation, some of the men broke down the warehouse doors and distributed food to their people.

Most of the families then returned to the homes they had been forced to leave. However, four restless Santee youths went on a rampage and killed the families of two white settlers. Soldiers subsequently arrested some three hundred Indians, and the cry of the enraged whites was: "Kill them all!" President Lincoln finally consented to the execution of thirty-two of the men. He also ordered the removal of all Dakota Indians from the territory.

These events cast a deep shadow over the lives of the survivors and their families for several generations. In the summer of 1863 the Dakotas began the long journey away from their homes in Minnesota. They traveled first on foot, guarded by mounted soldiers, then by boat down the Missouri River to the territories of Dakota and Nebraska. Their destination was Crow Creek, South Dakota, a desolate place, dry in summer, bitter cold in winter with barren land unsuited for farming. Their first task in their new home was to bury the dead who had succumbed on the small, crowded boat, on which the Indians had lacked space, sanitation, and food.

The Dakotas remained at Crow Creek for two years but were forced to move when the government found them a better location in Nebraska Territory, at the mouth of the Niobrara River. Several white settlers had been displaced to make room for the new Santee Reservation, so the Indians arrived as unwelcome intruders. A young missionary from the East, the Reverend Samuel Hinman, was one of the few whites friendly to the Dakotas in their new home. Mr. Hinman had been with the Dakotas in Crow Creek for two years and relocated with them to the Santee Reservation. Concerned for the Indians' well being, he called on some of his friends in the East to send contributions during the first months after the move. The friends not only sent money and food for sustenance but also provided funds to build a small church. When the converts outgrew it, they built a larger church, named Chapel of Our Most Merciful Saviour.

One small boy who survived the long journey from Fort Ridgely, Minnesota, was William Holmes. His three aunts took turns carrying him on their backs when his short legs were not able to keep up with those walking. His mother, Wicanpiata-win (Woman Who Gazes at the Stars), died during the imprisonment at Fort Ridgely. His father had fought in the Civil War and never returned, his fate unknown.

William Holmes grew up as a Christian and watched with interest as the new church was built, never dreaming that someday he would be its priest. As a young man, William taught at the Moreau River School on the Cheyenne River Reservation. While there, he was prepared for ordination by the Reverend Edward Ashley, who was training Indian men for ministry among their own people. One day while he was serving on the Pine Ridge Reservation, he went back to his Niobrara home for a visit, and there he met Rebecca Hobbs, a young white woman who was teaching in the Niobrara Indian primary school. She was the sister-in-law of the first resident white doctor on the reservation. In spite of the strong objections of the doctor and Rebecca's sister, the two were married and for many years brought the wisdom of both their cultures to the several communities they served. When their own children were grown, they raised a second family, the two young sons of their daughter Ida, who had died giving birth to the younger. The boys' names were Harold and Kenneth Jones.

1

CHILDHOOD

☙ † ☙

The Dakota wind whistled and moaned with sudden force across the prairie, lifting tumbleweeds from their shallow roots and sailing them across the road. It was a familiar and invigorating sight to Harold Jones. The sights and sounds of the prairies also evoked many memories, for much of his boyhood had been spent in this country.

Ranchers, accustomed to sudden changes in the weather, planted groves of trees to break the force of the wind near their homes. Harold looked for one of these windbreaks close to the road. His arms were stiff from holding the wheel steady as the wind buffeted the car, swirling eddies of sand on one side and nudging him toward the shallow ditch on his right. Those strong gusts, bordering on hurricane force, didn't last very long as a rule. Harold decided to rest awhile and wait it out. Since he had retired as bishop, the frantic days of rushing to meetings were over. Only recently had he been called back to temporary service after the bishop of South Dakota had resigned. Today he had plenty of time to get to the church to meet the confirmation class.

He found some shelter beside a large haystack, just on the other side of a fence where the road widened enough for him to park. He turned off the ignition, clasped his hands behind his head, and relaxed.

☙ † ☙

How many memories welled up with the sound of the wind and the sweeping view of this wonderful prairie! He closed his eyes and felt again the grip of his grandfather's hand over his as they walked from the warm kitchen to the barn. It had been long ago, near the beginning of the twentieth century, when his grandparents had allowed him to face the fury of a winter storm for the first time. Harold had felt very proud and very frightened by the howling winds and the biting cold of the snow, which stung his face and took his breath away. But the animals and the chickens needed to be fed and watered, and Grandfather thought he was big enough to help.

Inside the barn, it had been bitterly cold. The two horses stomped restlessly, breath steaming from their nostrils. Harold had watched while his grandfather led the cow into the horse's stall, close beside the gentler horse. Then Grandfather lifted the lantern off the hook, lighted it, and then suspended it again over the animals' heads. The chickens were huddled together on their perches, too frightened to come down for the grain Harold poured out for them.

The trip back to the house was easier, with the wind almost tumbling them up the path to the steps. Grandmother was waiting at the door to welcome them into warmth and light. She removed the wet scarf wrapped around Harold's neck and brushed the melting snow from his cheeks.

Harold and his younger brother, Kenneth, owed their lives to their grandparents. Harold's memories of their mother were faint. One strong recollection, his last of her, was the memory of her holding him and hugging him a bit longer than on other nights as she tucked him into bed. The next morning he was catapulted into a world of confusion and loss. Instead of his mother, a neighbor woke him with the news that he had a new baby brother and that his mother had gone to heaven, so he wouldn't see her any more. Overnight his father changed from a loving, playful man into an absentminded, distant, and morose person. He seemed to forget his two young sons, burying himself in the work of the YMCA as he traveled from reservation to reservation in the Midwestern states.

William and Rebecca Holmes, Harold's maternal grandparents, lifted him out of his emptiness and carried him and his baby brother back to their home on the Santee Reservation. The Holmeses lived in the rectory of the Church of Our Most Merciful Saviour, just across the river from the white settlement of Springfield, South Dakota. The rectory family had a parcel of land for farming, as did each of the other families who lived on the reservation. Other children of Rebecca and William Holmes lived nearby on their own allotments, close enough to help with the heavy work on their parents' farm and to be on hand when the Reverend Holmes traveled around the reservation and occasionally to Washington DC, when he was called there to represent his people. When the boys joined the Holmes family, Grandfather Holmes had already served his Indian people for many years as a clergyman. After years on other reservations, he had returned to his own Santee Reservation as priest-in-charge, living in the rectory of the Church of Our Most Merciful Saviour, the same church that he had helped to build as a boy.

Harold's paternal grandfather, whose name was Mahpiya (Cloud), lived nearby. He had changed his name to Jones, the name of a favorite white friend. He was blind and did not seem to be aware of his small grandsons' presence.

Soon after the boys' arrival in the Holmes household, their grandfather held Kenneth in one arm and lifted Harold onto his knees with the other. He explained that they were gifts from their mother and father and, more importantly, they were also gifts from the Father in Heaven. "You are Harold and Kenneth Jones," he said. "Your Grandmother and I are Rebecca and William Holmes, but we are one family and we thank God for you."

✿ + ✿

Harold was not immediately aware of any differences between his grandparents. One summer day, however, he noticed that he and his grandfather had turned red brown, while his grandmother remained pink and white and wore a sunbonnet when she worked in the garden. When he asked her about this difference, she laughed and told him it was a long story, which she would tell him someday when she was not busy.

She related that story one late autumn day, while the wind moaned and flung falling leaves against the windowpanes. Harold had an earache and so was not allowed to be outside. His grandmother gathered him onto her lap to rock him.

"Now tell me," Harold urged, stroking her white arm with the motion of the chair.

"Tell you what?"

"Why you are so white," he said.

Grandmother began her story with an account of her early childhood in Massachusetts, where she had been born. Her grandfather had been a shipbuilder, and her father worked with him building ships that sailed between England and the United States. When she was still very young, her father had moved his family to the new Nebraska Territory. A faraway look filled his grandmother's eyes as the rocker continued its squeaky song. Harold patted her arm, prompting her to continue the story. "Tell me how you met Grandfather, Grandmother."

Her gaze turned back to him, and she laughed. "After your great-grandmother's death, we children grew up quickly and left home. My sister married a young doctor named George Ira who had just been appointed the first doctor to live on the Santee Reservation. She asked me to come and live with them and help teach in the Santee Boarding School. So I came.

"Your grandfather was helping his cousin Amos Ross, one of the first Indian clergymen, on the Pine Ridge Reservation. He knew Grandfather spoke several Sioux dialects as well as English, so he taught in the boarding school and often acted as an interpreter.

"Santee was Grandfather's home, and he came back for visits. He loved to sing and play the organ, and so did I. I was happy when he visited. I brought my classes and all the people who worked at the school together, and we gathered around him to sing.

"Grandfather was a very handsome young man. He was teaching, and so was I. We both were sad because we had lost our mothers. We had lots to talk about. One day he asked Uncle George Ira if he could marry me."

"I'm glad," Harold said, and his arms traveled around her waist.

Grandmother laughed. "So was I, but Uncle George wasn't."

"Why not?"

Her laughter shook them both. She laughed so hard she had to unclasp her arms from Harold to wipe the tears from her eyes. Finally, she went on. "It wasn't funny then. Uncle George frowned. He said, 'William, you can't be serious. You and Rebecca belong to different races. Your people and hers are very different in the way they live and think.'

"But we planned our wedding anyway, and when they saw that they couldn't stop us, Uncle George arranged to have some of his friends kidnap me out of my room and carry me away so that I'd miss the wedding. But Grandfather got wind of it and warned me, so I locked my door. After that, nobody bothered us, and the next day we both arrived at the church and were married. Grandfather's family came to the wedding, but Uncle George and my sister didn't. They never came to see us, so we were glad when Grandfather was called to O'Kreek to teach in a day school there." Grandmother ended her story with a hug, as she slipped Harold off her lap to go prepare lunch.

Almost word for word, Harold would recall that story in later years. When he had been a small boy, the story seemed like one of the fairy tales his grandmother told. The tale lost its luster later, however, because of his personal experiences with racism, and he came to feel a special, warm sympathy for his grandparents.

🌿+🌿

As far back as Harold could remember, life had been punctuated with services every Sunday in the Church of Our Most Merciful Saviour. Cousins, aunts, uncles, and friends filled the pews along with Kenny and himself, under the watchful eyes of his grandmother. Most Sundays his grandfather served as the preacher, but sometimes he traveled by buggy or on horseback to visit other missions on the reservation.

Some of Harold's friends and their families told him that life for the Dakotas had been different in the past. Before the missionaries came, Wakan Tanka, the Great Spirit, spoke to those who listened for him, not in a church, but in all of nature—wind, the sun and moon and stars, the birds and animals. Everybody listened in those days. Older boys went up in the hills alone on a vision quest to wait for a special message from Wakan Tanka, delivered by a bird or an animal. When the boy received the message, he changed his name to the name of the messenger and gained its special qualities. Harold wondered about these differences between the old ways and the ways of Christianity. When he discussed this matter one day with his grandmother, she told him he was now old enough to join her Sunday school class and that Kenny should come too.

Every Sunday afternoon at two o'clock, Grandmother met with the children in the parish hall. Her pupils numbered seven: Andrew Trudell, Steven Moose, Charles St. Claire, cousin Nelson Jones, Cliff Johnson, Kenny, and Harold. They always began the class with the Lord's Prayer and the Apostles' Creed and then moved on to the Catechism and *Instructions for Little Ones*. The older boys learned faster, and Harold felt their restlessness when he or Kenny stumbled over the creed and they all had to begin again. Though careful not to let the teacher know it, Steven and some of the other older boys teased and mimicked the younger class members.

One afternoon Grandmother asked the class, "Who made the round world and all that is in it?" She looked right at Harold, whose mind had wandered to other things. Feeling himself growing hot, he dropped his eyes before her steady gaze. "I don't know, Grandmother," he murmured. The silence around him thickened. Others knew the answer but, in keeping with the Dakota sense of polite behavior, would not give it. If he were stupid, they would act as if they were all stupid. Grandmother knew this too. She pursed her lips.

"We will go on to another question," she said. "But by next Sunday I want you all to know the answer to that question."

After Sunday school, Harold and Kenny followed the other children outside. When they had walked down the hill some distance from the parish hall, Steven Moose turned to Harold. His voice was accusing. "You don't know who made the world and all that's in it? Well, I'll tell you who! It was Steven Moose."

He gripped the back of Harold's collar and turned him around to face him. "Remember that, Nephew Harold," he said menacingly. Although only a few years older than Harold, Steven was, in fact, his uncle, and uncles, as Harold knew very well, must be obeyed. "And you too, Kenny, and everyone else. When Aunt Rebecca asks next time, 'Who made the world and all that's in it,' you just better tell her Steven Moose!" He gave Harold a strong shake before letting him go. Steven ran down the hill, waving his arms wildly as he whooped and laughed.

That night Harold's grandmother went over the answers. Before prayer she hugged both grandsons. She laughed a little, as she said she knew Harold hadn't been listening. Clearly, Harold should know it was our Heavenly Father who made and cares for all his world. Harold nodded uncertainly, wishing Grandmother would forget about it. He wanted to tell her about Steven, but he didn't dare bring it up. As a good Dakota, he would have to obey his uncle. But how could he say something that wasn't true, even though he knew it was a kind of joke?

The following Sunday Grandmother told her class briskly, "We will all say the Lord's Prayer and the Creed. Andrew, will you lead us, please?" Over the top of Andrew's bowed head, Harold caught the piercing gaze of Steven just before he too bowed his head.

Harold was gripped with an unfamiliar feeling of tension. His grandmother must certainly understand that, by Indian rules, they all must stick together. The class had been silent on his behalf last week, and this time he must go along with Steven. But Grandmother's skin was white, and that factor went along with seeing some things differently.

"My dear children," she went on cheerily, "we come to the question we failed last week. All together now, who made the round world and all that is in it?"

One loaded moment of silence followed. Then the voices answered her in a chorus, "Steven Moose made the round world and all that is in it."

Grandmother's smile froze on her face; then it disappeared altogether. "I hope you are ashamed of yourselves," she snapped. "And Steven, I can see your influence in this! The answer is: 'Our Father in Heaven.'" Steven bowed his head, but behind his lowered lashes, Harold caught the glitter of triumph. The next question was asked in a no-nonsense tone, and it was a meeker class that responded immediately.

※ † ※

One evening, Harold's grandmother shared her dream of a school for Indian boys. "It would be a church school, not like the agency school that teaches you how to read and write and do sums. This one would teach those things, but it would also help you to grow in the knowledge and love of God. There could be instruction in farming and carpentry and ranching and maybe running a business."

Harold felt dismayed. He didn't need that school—his life was fine the way it was. Nonetheless, Grandmother sounded so happy when she talked about it that he nodded in response.

His grandmother continued. "This year when the bishop visits us, I will talk with him about this dream of mine. One way to help him remember is to give him some money toward it. There are many things you can do to help. It will be good training and good fun too. But now, our prayers."

Dutifully, Harold and Kenny knelt beside her. The familiar prayers ended this time with a new request. "If it be thy will someday soon, may there be a school for our dear Indian boys to bring them up in the fear and love of the Lord and prepare them for Christian living. If such be thy will, give us the strength and vision for its accomplishment. Amen."

By morning, his grandmother had planned her first step toward the goal. "Uncle Ray and Uncle Guy are out in the back field plowing a special corner for us. We can plant popcorn, and when the late summer comes, we can harvest the crop. I'll pop it, and you boys can sell it at the baseball games."

When she shared her hopes with the Sunday school class, Harold felt relieved. She seemed to have forgotten the incident with Steven Moose. Harold and the others nodded enthusiastically as she told of her plans and asked for class support.

"There are ways we can all find to raise the money. We can sell copies of the magazine the church uses to promote mission activity, *Spirit of Missions,* and I am sure you all have other good ideas." Again, Harold nodded vigorously. It was hard to imagine why she wanted another school, but she must have a good reason. Thus began a project that stretched from Harold's early childhood through his youth.

❧ ✝ ❧

The warm winds of May were sweet with the scent of the wild plum and chokecherry blossom as Harold Jones carried water to his popcorn patch. He heard the geese, winging overhead. What message did the leader of the geese give that transformed those straight lines into a kind of dance, curving and sweeping through the sky like a ribbon in the breeze? The ribbon became two strands, then magically one again. Not a bird in that straight line wavered. They pressed on with joyous sounds. Harold watched them until they were only black dots in the sky. Then picked up the bucket and trudged on.

While the ensuing long, hot summer days ripened the corn crop, Grandmother packed the ice cream freezer with ice from the icehouse and filled the canister with cream from the cow. In the shade of the woodbine that grew over the porch roof, she spread paper and set the freezer pail on it. The boys—Harold and Kenny as well as their friends—needed no urging to crank it. When Harold's turn came, his arms would ache as the cream gradually changed from liquid to mush and then to a smooth, white mass.

That part of the procedure was fun, but Harold dreaded what followed. Very little of the finished ice cream stayed at home; most of it was reserved to sell at the baseball games in the Santee ballpark. With the sun pouring down and a hot wind blowing, business was usually brisk. Kenny would tag along, giving Harold a hand with the delivery when he felt like it but more often just watching. Hard as it was having the sun melt the precious ice cream into a sticky puddle as he scooped it into a dish, the worst part was raising his voice and calling out: "Ice cream, ice cream, ten cents a dish!"

"But I can't do that!" Harold had protested. His gentle grandmother had looked at him sternly and said, "Nonsense, Grandson! All your life you will be with people. While you are young, you must get over the fear of speaking to others. Remember, you are doing this for the new school."

When the popcorn was harvested at last, Harold stuffed the popped corn, flavored with home-churned butter, into twenty-five neat bags. The popcorn sold even faster than the ice cream. With a pocketful of nickels, Harold could then sit beside his empty basket and give his full attention to the ballgame.

By the time Bishop Burleson arrived for his annual visitation, a small replica of a bank building was packed to the top with dimes and nickels, and Grandmother was as pleased as she could be. The bishop would be staying with them for the night, before he made the round of the other churches on the Santee with Grandfather. There would be no Sunday school class that day because a reception was to be held at the house with everybody invited to meet the bishop. People were busy bringing cakes and cookies, and Grandmother had worked all week turning eggs, butter, milk, and flour into wonderful things that kept the kitchen smelling so good that the boys had to find ways to sneak samples.

On Sunday morning the bishop arrived. When the boys heard the sound of the carriage wheels, they hid behind the curtains upstairs and peeked out. They watched Grandfather come out of the house, take the horse's reins, and hold out his hand to the tall man who stepped from the carriage. Grandmother hurried from the kitchen, untying apron strings on her way.

The boys left their secure place behind the curtains and ventured to the top of the stairs. From that vantage point, they could see the bishop's dark head nodding and bowing and his hands reaching out to grasp both of Grandmother's. "My dear Rebecca," he was saying, "how good to see you after so long a time! You do manage to keep looking well in spite of the busy life you lead!" They moved from the door, and only the murmur of voices reached the top of the stairs. Grandfather came back from the barn, where he had unhitched the bishop's horse, and his voice joined the others.

Harold sighed and punched his brother. "I guess we're prisoners up here until time for church, Kenny," he said.

"Nope," replied Kenny. "I'm going down."

After Kenny had gone downstairs, Harold listened to the momentary silence and then to the chorus of welcome.

"This is my younger grandson, Kenneth," Grandfather was saying proudly below. "I think someday he may grow up to be a clergyman too!" Harold could picture the big man taking Kenny's hand and pumping it.

"Good for you," the bishop boomed. "The church needs you all right, and I hope you grow up to be just like your grandfather. Where is that brother I hear you have?"

"If I know Harold, he's found your horse and is feeding him a lump of sugar." Grandfather laughed. "Like his Indian ancestors, he loves the freedom of the outdoors." Pride filled his voice. "They're both good boys."

"And that brings me to a subject very dear to my heart, Bishop," Grandmother began. "I long for the day when there can be a church boarding school for Indian boys . . ."

Harold backed away from the stairs and wandered into the bedroom. It wasn't a bad idea feeding the visitor's horse a lump of sugar. Maybe it was worth a climb down the tree to do it. But just as he raised the window to step out on the roof, the church bell rang, and a flurry of activity erupted below. He watched as his grandfather and the bishop headed in the direction of the church. Grandmother followed them, rounding the corner of the house for the barn and calling for him.

Harold leaned out the window. "Here, Grandmother."

"Mercy on us! What are you doing all by yourself up there, Grandson? But stay there, I'll come up. Today you must wear your best suit."

Grandmother hurried into his room. As she took his white shirt from the drawer to wear with his best knee pants, she told him about her talk with the bishop. "He likes the idea of the school," she said, "but just as I expected, he said he thought it would be impossible to raise enough money for it. So now, dear Grandson, is the time to surprise him with your bank! I have told him that with prayer and hard work we can do it! This morning, in church, you must go up and hand him your bank when I give you the signal!" Grandmother's eyes were bright. "When he sees how much one small boy has earned, he will see that it is possible!"

There was no time to think. The church bell gave second notice, and by the time Grandmother, Kenny, Harold, and his bank reached the front steps, the church was almost full. It was confirmation Sunday, and family members of the girls and boys who would be confirmed had gathered from miles around. The group to be confirmed was sitting in the front pews, and Grandmother drew the two boys into a space in the second pew from the back. Harold, who, as a member of the minister's family, was usually seated in the front row, studied the backs of peoples' heads and tried to guess who they were.

Grandfather Jones had arrived earlier then usual. He sat with two hands resting on the head of his cane, facing straight ahead and listening very hard.

"I wonder if the Bishop knows that my Grandfather Jones is blind," Harold thought. "Grandfather looks as though he's staring a hole through him." Harold glanced up at Bishop Burleson, who was sitting in the big chair in front of the altar. Beams from the morning sun filled the chancel, but the bishop's black robes and his white sleeves seemed to have a shine of their own.

Harold poked Grandmother urgently. "Grandmother, let Kenny take the bank," he whispered.

Grandmother shook her head. "It's your bank, Grandson," she murmured. "You must have the honor of taking it up. Grandfather will explain about the gift just before the offering is taken, and that's when I will start you on your way."

Harold sighed. Though young, he was learning to accept the irrevocable. He heard his dog barking from far away outside. In contrast, the church was filled with the kind of silence that rooms have when they are full of people sitting still, punctuated only by an occasional cough or the scraping of a foot on the floor. The bishop's voice drifted across the congregation as he addressed the confirmation class. When he finished speaking, the group went up to kneel in front of him. The bishop placed his hands upon each of their heads. As the class returned to their pews with hands clasped, Harold watched for any discernible difference in their appearance or bearing. Well, they did look pretty solemn now.

Turning suddenly, Harold caught Grandmother wiping away a tear. He straightened and looked more intently toward the front, but what was happening in the chancel didn't make him feel like crying at all.

A hymn followed, "Soldiers of Christ Arise." Grandfather Jones's voice rang out over all the other voices, and the bishop looked out to see who was singing so vigorously. Harold filled with pride. Grandfather Jones didn't know people looked at him when he sang. He just loved to sing, and he seemed to pour himself into the song.

When the hymn was over, Grandfather came forward. While he talked, Harold contented himself with following the graceful waving of his long white sleeves in the breeze that came through the sacristy door. He wondered idly what would happen if a big wind were to come up suddenly—would Grandfather's sleeves stand straight out and hide his face?

A hand clutched Harold's shoulder, interrupting his thoughts. "Now, Grandson," Grandmother whispered.

Harold grabbed his bank and stumbled over the kneeler on his way to the aisle. It looked a very long way to the chancel steps. He wished now that he had listened to what Grandfather had been saying. As Harold walked toward the chancel, the silence settled down again on both sides of him, and he could sense rather than see the smiling eyes of friends and relatives. At the steps he paused; his arm shot out with the bank in his hand. Grandfather motioned him to the top step and then guided him over to the bishop, who was again sitting in his special chair. The bishop rose. Harold's eyes slowly traveled from the large blackness of the bishop's robes to the gold pectoral cross and finally to the face above it, which was looking down at him and smiling. Again Harold thrust out his arm, and this time two large hands at the ends of billowing white sleeves reached out to receive the bank. Suddenly, he was picked up bodily and kissed on the forehead. When his feet touched the floor once more, Harold dropped his eyes, gave a jerky bow, and then turned to make his way down the long path of eyes.

As Harold stumbled over the kneeler again and sat down beside Grandmother, she brushed another tear from her cheek. "You have made this a historic day, Grandson," she murmured.

❧✛❧

From one season to the next, Harold passed his childhood contentedly. His grandfather had wonderful tales to tell—Indian legends of Iktomi, the trickster, of the Sun Dogs, and of animals who gave gifts to humans. Grandfather also told stories of vast buffalo herds that had roamed through these plains. "They were a dark, moving blanket, spread across the green prairie in the spring," Grandfather would say. "And in late summer hunters stalked the buffaloes. The pounding of so many hooves reverberated through the earth and could be felt across many miles."

Harold explored the riverbanks with other boys and learned to shave off the red willow bark that, when mixed with tobacco, becomes *kinnikinick,* which both grandfathers relished. In early summer when the rivers over- flowed their banks, the boys would take gunnysacks to the small inlets and catch by hand the catfish, bullheads, and carp trapped there. Grandmother would stop whatever she was doing to clean the fish, burying the entrails to fertilize the rosebushes and preparing the fish for their dinner or for friends. If there were too many fish for immediate use, she would send them off to market, and the money would be added to the offering for the school.

By July and early August, there would always be berries to pick in the low places, where bushes grew in profusion. Groups of women with bas- kets on their arms would spend the day picking the berries. The young children went with them, sometimes helping with the picking but more often playing scouts or looking for quail and pheasants, foxes and coyotes, whose whereabouts they reported back to older brothers and fathers for fu- ture hunting trips.

Before summer was quite over, school began. Fall arrived, bringing with it cool winds and dazzling silvery sunsets behind swirling brown leaves and bared branches. Fall meant bringing in the pumpkins, digging pota- toes, and toasting sunflower seeds. It also meant a tugging at the heart as the geese flew serenely and unwaveringly down the river, seeking a warm- er place. Fall was time for Grandmother to take from the cedar chest the mittens, scarves, and caps that had been buried in mothballs. Grandfather, Uncle Guy, and Uncle Ray worked hard to stock the woodpile. Working be- side them, Harold learned to use a hatchet and later an axe.

The first swirling snowflakes were always an occasion for glee. They were carried on the wind like thousands of dancing milkweed seeds, all ex- ploding out of their pods at once.

Winter brought not only Christmas, but also Harold's birthday on Christmas Eve. It was a busy time both at the church and at the house, but somehow his grandmother always arranged a celebration for him. "You have a special blessing to have been born on the Lord's own birthday," she would remind him.

Grandmother would serve a small feast at suppertime and invite Har- old's Jones relatives as well as Grandfather's relatives. For an hour or two, the house would be full and the table laden with treats. The oldest relatives sat around the dining table, and Harold helped to serve them. Grandmother made special small gifts to give his relatives in honor of his birthday; Harold would pass them out and received their solemn nods of thanks. At the church on Christmas Day, there was always a gift for everyone.

After Christmas, January, February, and March seemed endlessly long. Harold was prone to bad earaches from blasts of winter wind, but the pain had some compensation—the luxury of being at home, sitting in Grandmother's warm kitchen as the bread smells rose from her oven, or of lying upstairs and listening to the voices of women as they sat around her quilting frame. Grandmother spoke Santee as easily as she spoke English, and Harold strained to hear the conversations, which were often accompanied by bursts of laughter.

Through all the seasons, the Sunday school class of Our Most Merciful Saviour Church continued to meet regularly. New young members were admitted, older ones graduated, and, before they knew it, Harold and Kenny had become "the big boys" in class.

And everyone saved money in cans and jars. After Harold's walk down the aisle with his bank, other mothers had asked Grandmother about the project. Now all the pupils and even some adults were filling cans or jars for the school. Grandmother's dream endured.

2

NIOBRARA

❧✝❧

1919

The most exciting time of the year came in early summer when the annual Episcopal Convocation of the Niobrara was held. First convened in 1870, the convocation included Indian lay workers and clergy who ministered to the congregations on the reservations of the Cheyenne River, Crow Creek, Lower Brulé, Pine Ridge, and Corn Creek districts. All the tribes of the Lakotas, two bands of Yanktons, and three of Santees—sometimes as many as ten thousand people—gathered for days and nights of meetings, feasts, family reunions, campfires, singing, and praying. Harold once heard Grandfather say that Christian Indian people found inspiration, meaning, and strength in these gatherings that replaced the fellowship they had experienced from the now forbidden gathering at the Grove of Oaks. Whatever the participant's motivations might have been, Niobrara meant fun and excitement for Harold, Kenny, and their grandparents.

Grandmother would start preparing in earnest weeks ahead. The family's large tent was aired, and the tent pins counted. Clothes were laid out, along with moccasins and waterproof boots. Everyone wore long-sleeved shirts for protection against mosquitoes and jackets and caps for sudden cold winds—two elements that were a part of every Niobrara Convocation, it seemed. Blankets and quilts—at least two for each person—were folded in four piles. The large coffee pot and a big soup kettle, along with frying pans, tin plates, cups, and several boxes of food gradually filled the front hall until it was time to load them all into the wagon.

Grandfather seemed to grow younger as the preparations progressed. His steps were lighter, his eyes twinkled, and the prospect of long days of driving the horses and setting up camp each night didn't daunt him. Once the wagon was loaded and everybody and everything was safely on board, Grandmother relaxed too.

They never traveled alone. Others in the congregation accompanied their wagon from the beginning of the journey. Although two men and two women (later two young people also) were the official representatives of the congregation, almost the whole church would assemble for the journey. Only those who were too old or too ill to travel stayed at home and then unwillingly.

"We are like the people of Israel heading for the Promised Land!" Grandfather would exclaim gleefully, glancing behind him at the seemingly endless stream of wagons pulling out of town behind nodding horses' heads.

The closer they came to their destination, the more wagons appeared, converging into a long, meandering river of wagon wheels and horses' hooves, moving steadily in the same direction. Here and there, spurts of children on foot or horseback burst from the line, chasing one another or running off to explore. The plain stretched out before the travelers, an endless pale green lake immobilized in its troughs and swells with whitecaps of wild plum blossoms. As the wagons wound their way slowly through these stationary swells, they passed troughs filled with a more vivid green: the fresh leaves of cottonwood, Chinese elm, and willow. Pasque flowers bloomed beneath the trees and climbed into the greenness of the mounds, adding a sprinkling of lavender.

The procession skirted towns where white people lived but traveled close by the big ranches, with cattle dotting the landscape as far as one could see. At the sound of the rumbling wagon wheels, the cows would raise their heads, look long and unblinking at the travelers, and then nonchalantly turn to graze in another direction. The calves were more anxious. On unsure legs they wobbled to their mothers and nudged them, keeping the comforting expanse of their mothers' broad sides between themselves and the many moving wheels. The horses they passed provided a more exciting performance. Like Harold, the animals felt intoxicated by the fresh green grass, but to them the prairie was both banquet table and playing field. They buried their soft noses among the tender blades, nibbling and pulling, only raising their heads for a satisfying chew. Their coats were still patchy with winter's thick hair, but for the most part, they shone in the sun, sleek and beautiful. As the caravan passed, the mares sounded a warning whinny to the colts. Like a mechanical army wound by the same key, the horses would wheel and gallop toward the hills. The sound of many hooves was deeply exciting. Although softened by the new grass, it nonetheless spoke to the heart like the beat of Dakota drums.

Such moments reminded Harold of stories he had heard of his ancestors' lives. In earlier days, the young men had proven their skill and bravery by stealing horses from other tribes or from passing white men. In his mind's eye, Harold saw himself run after those fleet creatures, jump on the back of one, and then herd them all toward his grandparents' wagon.

But now horses belonged to white ranches, and life was different from the old days. Harold would catch himself sighing, the way he had heard some of the old men sigh when they talked about the past. Yet he was young; his melancholy would dissipate rapidly, replaced by the exhilaration of being alive on a sunny day, with the wind blowing and the smell of fresh, damp earth all around.

❧ + ❧

In 1919 the Holmeses and their grandsons made one of their longest journeys to the Niobrara Convocation, traveling 360 miles from Santee to St. Elizabeth, Wakpala. To Harold, who was eleven years old at the time, it seemed like half a world away. Estimating that it would take them at least two weeks by slow wagon travel, Grandfather decreed they would travel by train. They could climb on the Milwaukee Railroad in Springfield, he said, and it would take them right to Wakpala, all in one day. Many other Santees had the same thought.

When the great, steaming locomotive rumbled to a stop, Harold could see many white faces inside pressed to the windows. Some looked startled, some frightened, and some even scowled, but a few smiled and waved.

Fingers pointed at Grandmother and Grandfather, and eyes stared at Kenny and Harold. Ever since Grandfather had announced their plans for a train trip, the boys had been wildly excited. Even Niobrara paled in comparison with a train ride. The staring eyes and pointing fingers, however, took away that joy.

Once they were seated on board, Grandmother looked at her two boys reassuringly. Over the top of her stiff-brimmed hat, Harold caught a glimpse of a small pink face with bright blue eyes. The child's golden curls bobbed to the rhythm of the train wheels. Her small finger pointed at Harold, then another face appeared, and two arms reached out to pull the little girl down. He heard a scolding voice. "Those are Indians, dear. You can look, but you must not point."

"What's the matter with all those people?" Harold muttered. "What makes them stare so?"

Grandfather leaned over and explained. "You are learning a lesson, Grandson, that you were bound to learn some day. Your grandmother can explain better than I can the white man's rules of politeness. From your early childhood, we taught you not to stare. It is the Indian rule that you look away from strangers because to catch their eye might be an embarrassment to them. We forgot to teach you that all people don't live by this rule. Most white men and women feel it's rude if you don't look at them when they speak to you. These people are only trying to learn about us as they pass through our country. Don't let it bother you. Be your best self before them. Be friendly and courteous and don't stare back."

It was good advice. Harold turned away to look at the swiftly moving scenery outside and soon forgot the other passengers. When he did remember and furtively looked around, he discovered that interest in his family had waned, and people had returned to their books or their naps or were absorbed in the moving scene beyond the windows.

Later that afternoon, the train rumbled and screeched to a stop at the Wakpala station. A line of wagons, with both horses and drivers patiently battling flies, were waiting for the Santee travelers. Gratefully, Grandfather and Grandmother climbed into one, greeting the old friend who held the reins. Harold and Kenny trotted alongside the wagon, glad to stretch their legs. Grandfather pointed and called down to them, "Over there is Rattle-snake Butte. But that doesn't mean that all the snakes live there. Be careful when you explore the fields in the days ahead."

The fresh wind ruffled Harold's hair and made him squint against the tiny particles of sand that blew up from the road. The smell of wild plum and the clover that covered the hillsides was wonderfully sweet. Shadows from billowing white clouds glided in a continuous motion across the land, changing green to a deep purple as they passed. Along a nearby river were banks thick with berry bushes, willow, and marsh grass. Cormorants and geese stirred up in fright and flapped heavily away, but wrens and wild canaries continued their song unperturbed. As the wagon came to a curve in the road, the boys climbed on board. They could already hear that the great gathering was very near, even before it came into sight.

On a hilltop to the left of the road was a cemetery surrounded by a white picket fence. "Some fine people are lying there," Grandfather told the boys. "Sometime during the convocation you boys might like to come up here and see where Chief Gall is buried. His stone is marked 'Remember this upright man forever.' This was all his land once. He was the chief of the Hunkpapas, a strong and powerful man. When our good friend Tipi Sapa, Philip Deloria, was a very young priest, Chief Gall would come to the church at St. Elizabeth, wearing war paint and his ceremonial dress. He would sit outside the door and listen and watch, not showing whether he was pleased or displeased with what he observed. He held both his gun and a tomahawk on his lap, and Tipi Sapa had to preach facing him.

"One day the chief had a great feast and seated Tipi Sapa in the place of honor. They were of different tribes, so when he called Tipi Sapa *Misun* (younger brother), it was a time of great happiness for Tipi Sapa. On July 4, Chief Gall was baptized, and from his allotment he gave all this land that you see around us as a gift to the church."

The wagon rounded another curve, and a vivid panorama opened before them: a white frame church with tall steeple and other white buildings, which made up the school, strung along beside it on the hilltop. One of the smaller buildings was the home of the great Tipi Sapa, who still lived at St. Elizabeth. To one side of the buildings stood a great circle of tipis. Columns of smoke rose from hundreds of campfires, then flattened and spread on the wind to be carried as far as the valley they were traversing. The smoke carried the delicious, mingled scent of meat, beans, fish, coffee, and the crushed berries from which *wasna* (pemmican) is made.

Grandmother clasped Grandfather's arm, and her face shone. Grandfather began to sing. Loud and deep came the song, quickly taken up by other voices from wagons behind them. When the people in the camp heard the singing, they started coming out of tipis, and word spread quickly that the Nebraska Santees had arrived. Shouts, whistles, and hurrahs reached their ears in a joyful tumult of welcome.

Boys and girls on ponies were the first to reach them, dashing past the Holmeses' wagon, the animals' small hoofs sending up clouds of dust behind them. Grandmother was already waving her handkerchief over her head in answer to the welcoming voices. "Oh look, William! Herbert's whole family is here, and I do believe I can see Johnson Brown Eagle and his two little boys! And there are dear Martha and Betty!"

Grandfather laughed. "It looks like a fine time ahead for us all. How are we going to get any business done with so many friends to see?"

They were near enough now to see the bowery. Fresh green branches had been placed across latticed strips of wood to make a summer ceiling that offered protection from the sun. The constant rustling of the leaves, every day a little drier than the day before, was to become a sound forever linked in Harold's mind with the Niobrara Convocation. Beneath the latticework were rows of rough-hewn benches, enough to seat three hundred people. The rest of the attendees would stretch out on the grass nearby, on all sides of the bowery. Most of the business as well as some of the church services would be conducted there. The huge tent that the women always used for their meetings stood in the center of all the tipis.

Although each Niobrara Convocation had a unique setting, the spiritual power of the gathering was unchanging. The Holmeses' personal introduction to St. Elizabeth's Wakpala soon paled as the gathering transformed from a sociable meeting of friends and relatives into a spiritual experience that would support and strengthen all who participated through another year. Eleven-year-old Harold was not fully conscious of the profound effect of the convocation, but the coming together of so many Dakotas and Lakotas in the fellowship of the church gave him a sense of belonging to something much larger than himself. He lost himself in the volume of voices that rang out in song on that first night.

In the light of the setting sun, the clergy and lay leaders formed a large circle. Everyone else—perhaps two thousand people—gathered behind it. Tipi Sapa stood in the center of the circle. Though the wind was still brisk, his robe barely stirred, surrounded as he was by so many people. Tipi Sapa's deep voice welcomed those who had come from as far as Santee, Nebraska, and as near as Crow Creek, South Dakota. Harold felt rather than understood the musical flow of Lakota speech that then followed.

Tipi Sapa was old, but he still moved smoothly. Harold tried to picture him as he might have looked as a young man. Instead of gray sideburns and a white surplice, he would have worn a buckskin shirt with his hair in long black braids. Grandfather had told the boys stories of the handsome young man who loved colorful Indian dress and was proud of his shiny black hair. One time Tipi Sapa had gone to see Bishop Hare, who was in charge of the church's missions throughout all the Dakota Territory. He asked what it would take for him to become a member of the church. The answer was harder than he could bear. "Cut your hair, wear white man's clothes, and give up being a chief." Tipi Sapa had turned and ridden away. After more thought, however, he did those hard things. Grandfather believed that Tipi Sapa could have been as important a chief as Big Foot or Crazy Horse, but he gave up the old ways for Jesus Christ. He explained to his people that the old ways were good, but that Jesus had the best way and that he chose to follow him who had the greater strength.

Harold's eyes traveled around the circle of clergy, starting with his grandfather. Nobody, not even Tipi Sapa, was handsomer than William Holmes. The early summer sun had already tanned his face, and his cheeks shone red as they always did when he grew warm. Next to him stood Steven King, Father Luke Walker, Father Baptiste Lambert, Dr. Aaron Clark, and Archdeacon Edward Ashley. These last two clergymen were white men, but they were such close friends of their Native colleagues that the color of their skin was forgotten. Next in the circle were Father Henry Whipple and Uncle Amos Ross, who had grown a little stooped and looked tired. Beside him stood Father David Tatiyopa. Grandfather had told stories about Father Tatiyopa's exploits, and Harold regarded him with awe. The next face was that of Herbert Welsh. He was a tall man, straight and proud. His Dakota name was Bear Claw, and he came from Cannonball, across the border in North Dakota. As a young boy, he had been sent to school in Hampton, Virginia, where he was baptized and had chosen the name of his sponsor, Herbert Welsh. His sister, Mrs. American Horse, stood directly behind him. She wore a blanket around her shoulders, and her hair was plaited in two long braids. Beside her was a young soldier whose name Harold did not know. The soldier had only one leg and leaned on a crutch. The setting sun caught the silver Niobrara cross he was wearing around his neck and flashed its reflection onto Archdeacon Ashley's chin, but the archdeacon, who had closed his eyes, didn't notice. Next to Father Welsh was Bishop Remington, who had a kind expression. Compared to the man from North Dakota, he looked small, thin, and white.

After Tipi Sapa finished his greeting, the prayer service began, laced with hymn singing. "Guide Me, Oh Thou Great Jehovah" swelled into a strong and compelling chorus. According to one story, this hymn had been responsible for first arousing Chief Gall's curiosity about the church. As he rode by St. Elizabeth's one day, he had heard the congregation singing through the open church door. He reined his horse to listen, and that experience had led to his conversion. Now all were singing. The men's voices rolled across the hilltop, and the women's shriller, higher voices joined them with equal vigor. Finally came the hymn "Now The Day is Over," sounding both soothing and a little sad.

Suddenly Harold's legs felt very tired. Glancing to the west, he saw one bright star glittering in the blue above the sunset glow. With the benediction, the hush yielded to the hum of many voices as old friends found one another. The circle dissolved into groups, and the priests drifted away to hang their vestments in the church sacristy.

Grandmother had her hand on Kenny's shoulder and was already surrounded by ladies. Harold chased after Grandfather's retreating figure, and the two went into the church together. The interior seemed very dark. Then the altar cross caught the light from the opening of the door and glowed with sudden brilliance.

Grandfather stood still, looking at it. "Remember that cross, Harold," he said softly, "for the times that you will need it. The cross always glows for you in the dark of the world, wherever you are."

Puzzled, Harold looked again at the altar. His world was bright, full of good things to see, taste, smell, and do. Why did Grandfather call the world dark?

�֍ + ✖

Through all the days and nights of convocation, during the services, meetings, hymn sings, picnics, and private forays into the countryside, Harold remembered and watched for a hint of the darkness to which his grandfather had alluded. His first clue came in the flickering light of a large campfire, where the men and boys often gathered at the end of the day if meetings didn't run too late. The campfire gatherings were the best part of Niobrara for young people, who, around the fire, were accepted into the special fellowship of the men. It was a time of reminiscing and storytelling, and the young were expected to listen and to learn.

One evening at the campfire when Tipi Sapa had finished a tale related to his work at St. Elizabeth, a voice growled the accusation: "You are no more a true son of your people. You can talk with a smile and forget the past."

Harold looked quickly at Tipi Sapa. The priest showed no sign of surprise. His eyes searched out the speaker, a very old man, who was gripping the end of a willow cane so tightly that his knuckles shone white. His eyes were dark holes, boring across the firelight in Tipi Sapa's direction. So many lines and smallpox marks crisscrossed the old face, it would have been easy to miss the long scar running from cheek to chin.

After a long moment of silence, Tipi Sapa spoke, choosing his words carefully. "No, my uncle, I did not forget. And when I gave my life to Jesus Christ, I stopped living in the past. His power is stronger than all of the evil we have known."

The old man spat into the fire, not once but twice. In Lakota he poured out his scorn, "This Jesus talk came with the *wasicu* (white man). If you need a messiah, there is Wovoka. If he is the same, then call him Wovoka. The *wasicu* bring evil and death. They killed their messiah long ago, as they kill every good thing. They pass out blankets, pretending to bring help to us, but in the blankets is the smallpox disease, so that we can die and they can have our land. They make promises of food. When we starve and go to take it from where they store it, they shoot us or chain us in prison. If we complain, they hang us to a pole by the neck for all to see. You know, William Holmes, and you, Amos Ross. You passed under the feet of your relatives hanging in death when you were small children.

"Your aunts carried you on their backs from that prison to put you in another one, these reservations where you can be watched. White men have captured your souls with the talk of this Jesus. These white collars that you wear, the silver at your breast, the dark clothes that you choose instead of skins and feathers and blankets—these are the marks of slavery.

"These men who bring you their religion shot your parents, your brothers and sisters, wives and children as they ran. They dumped the bodies in a common ditch and covered them with earth. These things all happened in the time of your young manhood, and you are not yet old." The old man's voice grew hoarse as he spoke. He stopped, breathing heavily.

No one stirred. A twig popped in the fire, sending sparks upward with the flames. Hugging his knees, Harold waited what seemed an hour before anyone broke the silence.

"Few have suffered more through the coming of the *wasicu* than you, old man," Tipi Sapa replied respectfully, "but many have suffered equally. Many sitting around this camp fire carry deep wounds.

"Wovoka, like Jesus, spoke peace. But he prophesied that our place would come when the earth opened and swallowed up the white man. This prophecy has not come to pass, and it should not. We have found that there are good men among the whites. When they appeared among us, they brought both the very good and the very bad. The best that they brought was this Jesus Christ. His followers among the *wasicu* were those who suffer with us, who bind up the wounds that others inflict. They have introduced us to a power stronger than our own medicine. The magic of *yuwipi* is strong, but it cannot match the power of the God-man, Jesus.

"We let others pierce our flesh in the Sun Dance. This helped us to know the pain he bore when others put nails through his hands and feet and hung him on the tree. We made a sacrificial dance for our sins and to bring blessing to those we loved. Jesus made a willing sacrifice to death. The difference is that he sacrificed himself to save those who tortured him. There can be no greater test of strength.

"It takes the greatest strength to forgive. Even the *wasicu* are children of our grandfather, Wakan Tanka. Those who rob and murder have forgotten this truth. But the gift of eternal life that Jesus has promised us takes away the despair and brings us peace. For that reason we wear these crosses around our necks. The cross is his sign. With him we can conquer evil and come to truth. Our real foe is not the white man but evil itself. Jesus Christ does not belong to the white man. He belongs to all people. He was born into a race that has suffered as our people have suffered."

The old man raised his face to the sky and broke into a shrill lament in the ancient language of the chants. Harold could not understand the words, but the older men in the circle stirred uneasily and bowed their heads, remembering things that he had never heard.

It was Uncle Amos Ross who shattered the spell. "Do you remember that long, dusty walk from Minnesota, Cousin?" he asked Grandfather. "As I remember, your two aunts took turns carrying you on their backs, while I was walking my feet off."

Harold could hear, rather than see, the smile on Grandpa Holmes's face as he answered from the shadows. "My feet were saved from calluses but at the expense of my legs. Do you notice that they are still a bit bowed?" Then Grandfather grew serious. "My mother died in that prison at Fort Snelling after the uprising. My father never came back from the War between the States. My mother's sisters felt sorry for their orphaned nephew. They not only carried me, but they fed me their own rations." Harold pictured the gentle prod he must have given Uncle Amos. "I think I had some of your rations too."

"I have never before or after breathed in so much dust!" Uncle Amos reminisced. "We were a whole straggling, ill-fed army—Santees, Sissetons, Yanktonais, Tetons—going double-file, day after day under the burning sun. The hot wind blew up the dust our feet made. The patrols on their mounts would come by, kicking up even more. How we boys envied those soldiers their horses!"

A less uneasy silence settled over the campfire. Each person seemed to withdraw inside to give private thoughts free rein in the comforting closeness of the others.

❧ + ❧

The next evening, Grandfather took his turn at storytelling. This story was true, he said, and the children and grandchildren of the young men he would tell of were there in the circle with them. For them, it would be an old story but worth repeating for all to know.

"This is the story of how the 'fool soldiers' got their name. When several of us here tonight were young children, it was a time of much senseless suffering for both the Indian and the white man. One atrocity would set off another atrocity, and so it continued. At last, it looked as though both sides had had enough of war and were honoring the treaty made between them.

"But a band of Santees who were lawless and wanted only revenge set off on a spree of senseless killings. They tried to incite other bands to join them. Some did, thinking that everyone, whether innocent or guilty, would be punished anyway for the murders committed by these few. When the leader of the marauders came to the Teton Two Kettles band to tell of his exploits—the slaughter of women and children and the taking of some of them as captives—some young men of the Two Kettles band could scarcely believe the story. By then they had made good friends among the white settlers, and to be asked to help slaughter them was unthinkable. These eleven young men chose to do otherwise. They made a pact among themselves to rescue the captives and return them to their homes and families. The names of these men were Wanete, the leader, and Swiftbird, Kills and Comes, Four Bears, Mad Bear, Pretty Bear, One Rib, Strikes Fire, Red Dog, Charging Dog, and Sitting Bear."

Grandfather paused, giving his listeners a chance to absorb the names. Heads nodded solemnly around the circle. "Their relatives and friends laughed at them and gave them the name of 'fool soldiers' because they dreamed of this rescue in the face of impossible odds."

Grandfather had never told Harold or Kenny this story. Harold felt vaguely uneasy. Grandfather, his friends, relatives, and grandsons were all Santees. Why was he telling a tale that portrayed them as villains and the Tetons as heroes? The night before, Harold had burned with indignation at the wrongs perpetrated by whites. Tonight, however, white people were victims, and the brave Santees were villains. He rested his elbows on his knees and cupped his chin in his hands, listening and thinking as Grandfather continued.

"The first impossible thing was that the captives were well hidden. How would they know where to begin looking for them? In the second place, the eleven young men could scarcely take on a whole band in their attempt to free the whites, who were by now slaves of the band.

"Impossible it seemed, yet they overcame their first obstacle when they bought provisions for their journey at Primo's Trading House. Some white men had stopped at the trading house at the same time. The traders told the Tetons that on their way up the river, someone had shot at them from the shore as they pulled into Beaver Creek. As they had pushed away from shore in their boat, they had seen a white woman run to the edge of the water, calling for help.

"The young men set out immediately with their provisions and horses. On the second day of their journey to Beaver Creek, they came upon the Yankton camp of Bone Necklace. From him they learned that the Santee camp had moved farther down river—very near to where we are right now. They continued until they arrived at the Santee camp. The eleven young men invited the entire camp to a feast of coffee, sugar, and bread.

"Then the bargaining began. The Tetons announced, 'We are only young boys, and our people call us crazy, but we want to do something good. We have come to buy the white captives and to return them to their friends. We will give all of our horses for them.'

"The old Santee chief replied, 'We come from the east, where the sky is made red by the fires that burn the homes of the whites, and the ground is red with the blood of whites that we are killing. We will not again be friends with the whites. We have done a bad thing, and now we will keep on doing bad things. We will not give up the captives.'

"Several times the 'fool soldiers' tried to buy the captives, but the answer was always 'No!' At last Wanete said, 'You talk brave, but you kill white men who have no guns, and you steal women and children and run away when there are no soldiers. Three times we have offered our horses for the captives. Now we shall take the captives and place them on our horses and take them home. If you give us trouble, the soldiers with guns will come upon you from the east, and the Tetons will come upon you from the west, and we shall see if you are brave.'

"Then Black Hawk, the chief's son, spoke up in praise of the young men. He said that he knew some of them as friends. Their food had been good, and his people were hungry. 'I have one white child I will give up,' he said. 'Let the others do as I have done and give up the captives.' The child cost one horse and some other provisions. After that, each prisoner had to be bargained for separately. But the sad condition of the prisoners so touched the boys that they could not leave one behind. At last, all were paid for except one, who had been kept hidden from them. She belonged to the chief; he said he needed her to wait on him, and nothing could make him give her up. When Wanete persisted, the chief sprang at the huddled prisoners to kill them, but his own people held him back. He threatened the young men, who showed no fear.

"By now there were only four guns and one horse left to the 'fool soldiers.' The two sons of the chief offered to bring the last captive to them in exchange for the horse, and so it was arranged.

"Before anyone could change his mind, the young men set out on foot with their prisoners. It was November, and a blizzard was gathering. By this time, they had nothing left to eat, and some of the prisoners had no clothing. A hundred miles lay between them and home, and at any minute they might be attacked and taken back to camp as prisoners. One small tipi and a few blankets were all that protected them from the cold on the first night of their journey, but early in the morning two Yanktonai men came to them. Whether it was a gift or a trade I do not know, but the 'fool soldiers' and their prisoners obtained from them a precious horse. They quickly constructed a travois to carry the children and hitched it behind the horse. Not long after, they looked back to see the old chief coming after them. Wanete quickly took off his moccasins and gave them to the woman captive who had been the chief's slave. Then he thrust a lame captive onto the travois with the children and urged the horse to increase its speed. The young men and the two Yanktonai visitors lined up behind the travois. Walking backward facing the chief, they trained their guns on him. They retreated in this fashion for some time before the chief at last gave up the chase and returned to his camp.

"The weary band of 'fool soldiers' and captives arrived by dusk at the Yanktonai camp of Bone Necklace. You can imagine how they felt! A warm fire, shelter for the night, and enough food to satisfy their hunger and more to take with them for the journey ahead! Bone Necklace's kindness did not stop there. Seeing the pitiful condition of the captives, he offered a small cart to replace the makeshift travois.

"When morning came, the two helpful young Yanktonai friends offered to stay with them for the first part of the day's journey. The 'fool soldiers' accepted the offer, and when the time came at Swan Lake to say good-bye, their hearts were full of thankfulness.

"As they continued by themselves, they soon found that the small horse tired from pulling the cart with its heavy load. Bad weather threatened to break again at any time, and they desperately needed to get the ill-clad women and children—some already suffering from frostbite and weakness from their long captivity—to the journey's end as fast as possible. The eleven young men, plus Mrs. Wright, the last captive freed, divided themselves into three groups. While one group pushed the cart, the other two groups rested and walked. In this manner they made their way through rutted grasses, up and down hills, through thickets and brambles. They rested the first night, then pressed on through another day and night, across the prairie along the Oxbow, then back to the riverbank again as the light began to dawn. There, just across the river, they could see Primo's Trading Post and home!

"The first ice was forming on the river, posing one last danger to face. But Primo and his friends LaPlant and Dupre had seen them and soon brought a sturdy boat to carry them across the ice-flecked waves. At Primo's store, the captives were outfitted with proper clothing, and Dupre invited them to sleep in his home for two nights. Dupre and LaPlant accompanied the former captives to Fort Randall, where they were reunited with their relatives.

"Those eleven brave young men never sought the gratitude of the families of those they saved. They did a good thing because it was a good thing."

🌿 + 🌿

That night Harold pulled his blankets up under his chin and watched the bright stars for a long time. Who was good and who was bad? Sometimes the whites were evil, sometimes the Indians. Last night Tipi Sapa had said that the real enemy was the evil inside ourselves. It was too much to figure out.

Harold drew his hand out from under the blankets to touch the ground. The "fool soldiers" had passed over this very ground. These very stars had watched the happenings in Grandfather's and Grandmother's lifetime. If Grandmother had been in the wrong place, she might have even been one of the captives.

The darkness had been in the world for a long time. That night at Niobrara, it was difficult for Harold Jones to fall asleep under the cold, dim, lonely wash of the stars.

3

TESTS

※ + ※

1920–1928

During the meeting at St. Elizabeth's, Wakpala, the Most Merciful Saviour congregation had invited the Niobrara Convocation to the Santee Reservation in 1921. As soon as Grandmother stepped off the train on the return journey, she began planning for the event. The women of the congregation held extra sewing bees and bake sales. The boys' uncles laid out a garden twice as large as usual, and Harold and Kenny tended it through the summer months. But theirs was not the only oversize garden. Responding to the challenge of entertaining so great a gathering, the entire Santee community worked and planned methodically all through the year. Long, thin strips of meat hung on lines to dry in the hot summer sun. As the summer ended, berry pickers roamed riverbanks and thickets, and the smell of *wojapi,* Indian pudding made from crushed berries with sugar and flour, permeated the homes of the faithful.

The 1921 Niobrara Convocation came at last. Although Harold missed the excitement of traveling, the sight of wagons and horses, interspersed now with motor cars, streaming in from all directions was invigorating enough. Marvelous to behold were the unfolding of hundreds of tents and the constructing of more traditional tipis, which turned the fields beyond the church into a city. Before evening of the first day, campfires were producing an overpowering aroma of mingled supper smells that kept the boys' stomachs churning until Grandmother called them to their own feast. Glimpses of Grandmother were rare during those two weeks, but they knew where to find her. She was in the parish house kitchen cutting meat in chunks suitable for boiling in a hundred pots or slicing vegetables for the steaming caldrons of soup that were part of everyday fare. It was Harold and Kenny's job, along with their friends, to deliver some of the food to each family. Grandmother sent them often to the house for jars of stored *wojapi*, pickles, strips of dried meat, and *wasna*.

When the convocation was over, their exhausted grandmother praised both boys for their helpfulness. Grandfather as usual smiled but said nothing. By now Harold knew the difference between the way a white woman and a Santee man expressed thanks. Grandmother's words came from an outpouring of love; Grandfather's silence wordlessly conveyed his trust. Of course, the boys would help, he reasoned. It was their nature to be good boys, and they were true to their nature. They needed no praise for doing what needed to be done.

✖ + ✖

Two years later that trust tested Harold. Grandfather had worked hard to build a good choir at the Church of Our Most Merciful Saviour and was very proud of it. Harold was a member of the choir, and he loved to sing. Grandmother's eyes shone when Harold sang, and Grandfather told him that he must have swallowed a cello to have the sound of it in his throat.

In late spring of 1923, Grandfather received word that the bishop's visit, usually on the weekend, would take place in the middle of the following week because of unexpected scheduling pressures. Instead of the normally relaxed routine of such visits, the bishop would stay for two hours only to conduct confirmations and baptisms and then hurry off on the afternoon train. With the men at work and the boys in school, the choir would be small. In a community of Episcopalians, some of the men could take time off and come to sing. But Grandfather found it hard to understand why the boys' parents didn't insist that their sons be excused from a half-day at school. There was certainly no question that Harold would be in the choir that day, singing.

There was also certainly no question, however, that if Harold didn't appear in class that day for his final examination of the year, he wouldn't pass. Three times the teacher had warned the class that students who didn't take their tests would lose the whole year's work.

Harold sang, the notes coming fresh and clear from a dejected and despairing young soul. True to the teacher's word, he spent another year in the eighth grade.

❧ + ❧

One afternoon, several years after the Santees had hosted Niobrara, Grandfather issued an unusual summons to come into the kitchen for a family meeting. He lit his pipe, puffed out a pungent cloud of smoke, and smiled. He first asked Kenny and Harold how their day had gone at school, complimented Grandmother on the smell of something bubbling on the stove, and inquired whether the boys had tried out the new bridle. He then got to the point. "This morning, I got a letter from the bishop. He has done me the honor of asking me to join his brother John and Archdeacon Ashley in supervising the studies of the Indian divinity students at the new Ashley House across the river in Springfield, South Dakota. This is great work that they are doing, and I am proud to be chosen to serve with Archdeacon Ashley. He is the one, you know, who trained me for ordination. It would mean that we would have to move into town. My chief work would be translating and organizing lessons for the men seeking ordination. Our home will be close to Ashley House, and we would all be in close association with these two fine men."

He turned to Grandmother. "It would mean, my dear, that for the first time since our marriage, you'll have running water and electricity in the house! Do you realize that we have worked among our people on the Santee Reservation for thirty years? We will work with them still but from another vantage point.

"My grandsons, this will be a big change for you. We grow with change, and perhaps the time has come when you should become acquainted with the *wasicu* boys and girls, who have lived so near us all this time across the river off the reservation."

He stopped speaking and the only sound was the rhythmic tick-tock of the clock. Out of all that Grandfather had said, only two good things made immediate sense to Harold. "We're glad they appreciate you, Grandfather. And Grandmother, just think, nobody's going to have to carry heavy pails of water anymore. You'll have all you want right at the sink."

Both foreboding thoughts and excitement gripped the boys after they went to bed that night. They began to imagine new lives. All the animals except the cow and, of course, the dogs would have to stay behind. No more easy roaming of woods and fields in old, patched clothes. Happily, no permanent good-byes would be said, for after all, only a few city blocks and a river would separate them from old friends and relatives.

When Grandfather announced the move to the congregation of Our Most Merciful Saviour, he quickly assured them that he would be close by, seeing them every Sunday, and that he would be helping others to be priests. They nodded and said, "*Waste,* that is good."

The move went methodically. First to go were the dishes, pots, pans, sacks of sugar and flour, and all the jars of preserved food that Grandmother had put up during the summer days. Wagonload upon wagonload was carried on the ferryboat and taken to the new house. Before the last load was deposited, Harold and Kenny knew well the front steps of their new home, down to every squeak and crack.

On the first evening after the move, as the family sat among unpacked boxes, Grandfather rose and, with mock dignity, pulled the electric light cord dangling from the center of the room. Grandmother laughed, and the boys shouted as the evening shadows vanished in the sudden brightness. Archdeacon Ashley and Dr. Burleson stopped by that night to welcome them. In no time the three men forgot everything else, absorbed in planning the future.

The house was fine; the stores were fine. Trips back to Our Most Merciful Saviour on Sundays were reassuring.

🌿✝🌿

School in Springfield was another matter, however. For the first time, Harold was the only Indian in a classroom full of white students. They stared at him with unsmiling eyes. When he went to his assigned seat, the boy in front of him feigned fear by pulling his collar up around his ears and covering his head with his hands. Classmates whispered, "Stay away from me! I don't want to get scalped!" Harold was stunned. He lowered his eyes and wasn't aware of what the teacher was saying until a curious silence filled the room.

"Harold," the teacher said crisply, "we welcome you into this class. There are certain rules we all live by here. The first is that you look right at someone when you are spoken to. The second is that you answer 'yes ma'am' or 'no ma'am' when I address you." Harold nodded numbly.

"Say 'yes, ma'am,' Harold," the teacher requested, not unkindly. The class tittered.

"Yes, ma'am," Harold whispered.

For months school was a kind of nightmare, though none of the days that followed were quite as bad as the first one. Harold simply wasn't prepared for the thoroughness with which he was expected to learn lessons at Southern Normal High School in Springfield. For weeks the questions that the teacher asked seemed to have no right answers, and he couldn't understand her explanations of the lessons. Harold retreated deeper into himself, finding it easier to daydream than to find answers to this new problem of communication among the *wasicu*.

Harold felt much more at home in the big gym at the high school than in the classroom, for he was a natural athlete. Although unfamiliar with basketball, he learned quickly. It was his athletic ability that first won him acceptance in non-Indian society. He and Kenny discovered a hoop on the shed behind Ashley house, and, with a ball the archdeacon found for them, they practiced steadily every day after school, even when the snow fell. By mid-January Harold had mastered the new game and found himself playing on the first team—at least for a few weeks. Unfortunately, his poor performance on midterm examinations meant that until he learned to spell and do mathematics, the basketball team would have to do without him.

❧ + ❧

Of all of the turmoil during those first weeks of school, Harold had said nothing except to Kenny, who had fared little better. He knew what Grandmother and Grandfather would essentially say anyway; they had been through much worse things in their lives. In some ways the war between Indians and whites still was being waged. Deep wounds had been inflicted on both sides and were not forgotten. Yet on the reservation Harold had largely been protected from the currents of anger carried over from one generation into the next. He assumed that his grandparents were representative of all human beings. His wider world had consisted of the love and acceptance of Niobrara Convocations. Now the actions of his classmates and the lessons that he studied for history gave him an entirely different point of view.

No Indian heroes appeared in the history books. The same events Grandfather had recounted were there but changed and distorted. The soldiers who sacked and ruined Indian encampments were depicted as heroes. Those who discovered gold in the Black Hills and wrested the land from the Dakota and Lakota peoples in violation of the treaty were labeled "hardy pioneers." Pages he was assigned to read as history were painted in false colors, a protective patina covering the real truth. No wonder his classmates shunned him! History books portrayed him as their enemy. Yet Harold knew that Indians also had a proud past, one that in unacknowledged ways continued to influence mainstream white society.

Tipi Sapa had said that whites brought the worst and the best with them. The best was Jesus, and his message of love. That message sounded soft, but Harold found it harder than anything he had ever attempted. How could he love the boys who tripped him up and scorned him, who looked at him with hate? He was strong enough to beat them. He longed to hit them, flatten them, to blacken their eyes. In all of his life, he had never felt such a surge of anger. It threatened to undermine the control over his emotions that his grandparents had taught him since childhood; repressing the anger sometimes seemed to take away his strength.

Although Harold held his own in his inner battles, spelling and math proved to be formidable challenges. Every evening he went to Ashley House, where he always found four or five of Grandfather's students studying their lessons outside of his office. Harold was impressed by their earnestness. Reading was a new skill, and they worked hard to master it. The students accepted him, and soon he learned to join them in concentrated study.

To his amazement, this study strategy worked. His papers came back with fewer red marks, and when he was confident of an answer, he became less shy about raising his hand in class. The teacher's stern look gave way to an occasional smile. The heckling from his classmates, waiting for stupid answers or silence, finally stopped altogether. His grades improved. Harold was allowed to play the last few games of the season, and the cheers of spectators lifted his spirits.

✣ + ✣

Then Grandfather precipitated another family quake. After dinner one evening, he gravely announced, "Our dear friend Philip Deloria—Tipi Sapa—has had a second heart attack. The bishop wants him relieved of his responsibilities as superintending presbyter of the missions on Standing Rock Reservation as well as overseer of St. Elizabeth's School. He has asked me to take on that work."

Another move. What would make this one particularly difficult was that Standing Rock Reservation was not Santee. Most of the people on this reservation were of the tribes of the Yanktons, Oglalas, and Hunkpapas. Grandfather could speak in these dialects, but it would be a hardship for the rest of the family. Harold wondered if he would have to face more sly jokes and teasing from a new set of classmates who sounded their Ds and Ls differently from the way he did.

"Wakpala has a good basketball team," Grandfather smiled, "and you boys can make it better." He turned to Grandmother, the usual beckoning, teasing dance going on behind the gentle darkness of his eyes. "More hard work for you, my dear wife."

Grandmother smiled in return. "It will be all right as long as we can all be there together. The church could use you in so many places, there should be copies made of you."

✣ + ✣

With some awe, Harold explored the rooms of the old rectory that had been the home of the famous Tipi Sapa on Standing Rock Reservation. Suddenly it had become Harold's home, large enough and with room to spare for the four of them. The kitchen was full of unpacked boxes. Thirsty, Harold made his way around them to the pump outside the door. The water had a strange, sour smell, like old eggs or sauerkraut. The taste was even worse than he expected.

Beyond the yard the pounding of hooves sounded as two horses galloped side by side out toward the open prairie, manes and tails fanning in the wind, heads held high on arched necks. On the hill in front of the house, Harold shaded his eyes to look over miles of rolling prairie, a seemingly barren land in comparison to his reservation. Except for on the riverbanks and creases between buttes, few trees were to be seen. A train wove its way over the curving hills across the river, looking like a toy but whistling strongly as it came to a crossing. With the dogs Harold strolled behind the house to the barn, which was bigger than the one at Santee. He found their cow, Cowslip, contentedly munching her cud, gazing at him with wide, expressionless eyes. If she felt homesick, she certainly was not showing it.

In what was left of the long summer, Grandmother and the boys accompanied Grandfather on his visits as superintending presbyter of Standing Rock Reservation. Wherever they went—Bullhead, Little Eagle, Little Oak Creek, Fire Steel Creek, Wautaga, or Kenel—they were welcomed by friends whom they had come to know through Niobrara Convocations. They were even called across the state line sometimes to Fort Yates and Cannonball in North Dakota.

While their grandparents were busy in these places, Harold and Kenny would often make new friends in whose homes they sampled foods unfamiliar to them and listened to stories out of the past—tales of tribes once strangers to the Santee, now all living together within the bounds of one reservation. Harold's spirits began to rise. The immediate future promised some interesting new experiences in this new land.

✘ † ✘

By late August, the boys and girls began to assemble at St. Elizabeth's for another school year. The school had been established in 1883, when the young deacon, Philip Deloria, was sent to Standing Rock and took up residence on that high, wind-blown hill next to St. Elizabeth Church. Although called a school, St. Elizabeth's was also a home for students who came from all over the reservation and beyond to attend the public school in Wakpala. It was operated by the Episcopal Church, so here the students lived in a Christian community, attending church next to the dormitory and receiving religious instruction. In the dorm, kitchen, and dining hall, the girls learned homemaking skills while the boys learned ranching and agriculture in the stables and fields outside.

Although they were living in their own home and not in the dormitory, Harold and Kenny joined in the routine of the boarding students. Morning began with breakfast and then a half hour of wood chopping to help feed all the hungry stoves and furnaces during the winter months. Like clockwork, the two horse-drawn wagons appeared at the end of the half-hour to carry everybody into Wakpala. The girls sat in one wagon, the boys in the other, and there was always clowning along the way. The boys would pretend to ignore the girls who, in high spirits, would laugh and shake their heads in glee over secrets they saved to share on their journeys every day.

The Jones brothers did not need to worry as much about their schoolwork in the new school. With just twenty pupils and a small staff, the high school atmosphere was not burdened by the competitiveness so pervasive at Springfield High School. Harold was delighted that his fellow students were both white and Indian. The daughters and sons of the storekeepers and mail clerks fit into the Indian community with no friction. Friendship flourished, with little thought given to race or tribe. Because tribal differences could divide Indian peoples as much as culture and custom could separate them from whites, the Dakota Jones boys might have expected another time of isolation and heckling. It didn't happen, however. Grandfather interpreted the warm acceptance they received to the fact that they were all one in the faith.

In the midst of his new experiences, Harold was vaguely aware of the time and effort his grandparents took to learn the dialect of the people they now served. It was not too different from Santee, just enough to cause some bad or funny mistakes. An accent or an inflection could make a tremendous difference in meaning, and Grandfather had to be careful to say what he meant in his sermons. He recounted a popular story, retold in Wakpala, of an earnest young clergyman who arrived to preside at a funeral. When the clergyman thought he was saying, "ashes to ashes, dust to dust," he was actually solemnly saying, "ashes to ashes, skunk to skunk."

On New Year's Eve, the family was invited to Cannonball, North Dakota, where the whole community gathered in the mission house. It was a relaxed time at first, with the elders getting up to make speeches when they felt moved to do so and the children playing hide-and-seek among the chairs. When they grew too noisy, the grandparents would make a hushing sound. The Old Year wandered about the room, patting children on the head, nodding and bowing to their parents, and reminding them how good he had been. His clothes were stuffed with pillows, and he wore a gunnysack over his head, so nobody knew him. There were whispered guesses, however.

Excitement mounted as midnight drew near. Suddenly the door burst open from outside, and the New Year appeared! The children squealed, the women half laughed and half squealed too, and the men turned to smile broadly to face this strange new creature. He came springing in, club upraised, his head turning from side to side. The eyes behind his painted mask darted about the room until he found the Old Year and the chase began. He swung his bat with such seeming abandon that those around him ducked when it whistled over their heads. He struck the Old Year unmercifully on his padded back. Secretly Harold felt sorry for the Old Year as the New Year tossed him, complaining, out the door.

After that performance, they all stood up, and Grandfather led a single file procession around the big circle of chairs, with everyone shaking hands and wishing one another a happy New Year. Again came those inexplicable tears, but everyone was smiling or laughing as they cried. Harold and Kenny followed Grandmother when it came her turn to go around the circle. He felt the warmth of many glowing dark eyes and voices happy in their expression of fellowship. After completing the rounding of the circle, Grandfather led them all through the door into the church for a service. It was a quiet, reverent time that contrasted with the great hilarity that had just preceded it. Everyone knew without it being said that the first act in the New Year must be to offer worship and thanksgiving to God and to ask that he be with them through all the unknown days ahead. After the service came more feasting in the mission house until early morning.

That first January on the hilltop was bitterly cold. The winds that would come and go on the Santee Reservation never seemed to cease at Standing Rock. Grandmother's washing blew straight out, even as she wrestled with it along the new rope. The St. Elizabeth cattle huddled, heads together, tails out, their breath appearing to freeze in their nostrils. The cold sparked a tussle over blankets in the morning school wagons. Both boys and girls urgently pulled at flapping corners and ducked beneath the blankets to take refuge from the sting of snowflakes turned to needles by the force of the wind.

With so few boys at Wakpala High School, Harold and Kenny were welcomed onto the basketball team. At the approach of the season, they forsook the afternoon school wagon for an extra hour or two of practice in the gym after school. The boys would walk the two miles home along railroad tracks and then up the hill by the road, their way dimly lit by the waning sunset or early moon. Almost every evening the Milwaukee Limited passenger train thundered past with a shrill whistle of warning or greeting and a deafening roar of wheels; then as suddenly as it came, the train would leave them once more to a cold, lonely world of fading, gray light.

✵ + ✵

In the summer at St. Elizabeth's, there were many chores to do and much country to be explored on horseback. Grandfather enjoyed having one of his boys accompany him on his long trips. He bought a Model T Ford, which was nearly useless in winter ice and springtime mud but guaranteed faster and more pleasant journeys in the summertime. The engine was a mystery to Grandfather, but the speed with which he could cover the dusty roads and the brisk breeze created under the top, which shielded him from the intense, hot sun, were reasons enough for the purchase.

The earth and sky never remained the same on the summer car trips.

They might start out under a cloudless blue sky and in half an hour be engulfed in a hard rainstorm. Once, as they climbed the road into the bluffs, they confronted a wall of thick white fog that never quite moved across the road. It hung mysteriously over the bank to one side of them, while the remainder of the landscape was bathed in sunshine. Sometimes the wind sprang up with suddenness and vigor, rocking their fragile little Ford. At such times the boys and Grandfather would search the sky, and sure enough, off in the distance black clouds had boiled into a thin spiral, touching down on some far part of the earth. Whichever way they traveled, the plains seemed to have no boundaries. Roads turned and twisted among tall buttes, continuing onward across rolling green hillsides. Good farm country, Grandfather decided. He would also point out to Harold and Kenny nests of low buildings, each protected by surrounding hedges of berry bushes or by a thicket kept as a windbreak for the cold windy days.

The house of Joshua Iron Necklace in particular captured the boys' interest. He had been a bachelor, a lay reader, and a hardworking member of the congregation at St. Elizabeth's. Apparently, the churchwarden and the congregation had had a meeting, and all had voted that Joshua would be better off if he had a good wife. The following Sunday, Joshua agreed that if they could find him a good mate, he would honor that decision. The warden appointed a committee of three to search for a wife. At last, a widow in the town of Kenel agreed to give her daughter in marriage. The wedding was held soon after. In time, the marriage seemed to be a happy one, and the committee was well satisfied.

Harold looked closely at the Iron Necklaces' neat home as the Ford chugged by it, hoping for a glimpse of the girl who had been the hostage in that transaction. He wondered if she had submitted peacefully or if she had despaired—such as he had at one time when he had to repeat a year of school, like her caught between the church's demands and his own wishes. To most older people like Grandfather and Joshua Iron Necklace, nothing counted more than faithful obedience to those who held authority in the church and therefore represented the will of the Lord himself.

❧ + ❧

By the end of the second summer at St. Elizabeth's, Harold's grandparents decided that he and Kenny should return to Springfield for a year. The long, cold walks home after basketball practice had taken their toll, and Harold had contracted pneumonia. The boys would stay in Ashley House, under the kind and watchful supervision of old family friends. At school they would be joining acquaintances of two years ago. No doubt they would have to study harder to meet the standards of Southern Normal High School, but their grandparents believed that extra effort would be a good thing. To meet expenses, Harold would do farm chores at St. Mary's School for Indian Girls, just outside Springfield.

Happily, Springfield offered too many distractions to allow Harold to dwell on what he might be missing at home. The same boys who had once made his life miserable now welcomed him with shouts, remembering his prowess at basketball. Some weekends the brothers would steal off across the river to the Santee Reservation, where relatives and childhood chums accepted them as if they had never gone away.

When the boys returned to Wakpala at the end of May, Harold noted to his satisfaction that Grandmother had not changed at all during his year's absence and Grandfather was as energetic as ever. Away from the busy schedule of school, Harold occasionally had vague thoughts of the future. Although freedom from study was a tempting thought, he knew that Grandmother would not let his education stop with high school. When he dreamed, he pictured himself as a doctor.

Then one spring afternoon after school, Grandmother brought news that changed Harold's slowly fermenting plans. "My dear boys!" she exclaimed, eyes shining. "The bishop called us today to let us know that our school for Indian boys will be opening in the fall! They're naming it the Bishop Hare Industrial School. All of our hard work through these years has been worthwhile. Praise God! It will start small, but it will grow. It is going to be located at Mission, South Dakota. I told him that you two boys must share the honor of being in the first class!"

"But it's a whole year too late for me!" Harold blurted in dismay. His school years at Wakpala were drawing to a close.

Grandmother's chin was firm. She shook her head. "For you life has really just begun, Harold. All the preparation you can make for whatever lies ahead is for the good. An extra year spent in this new school that you've helped to build will bring you a better start in life. It is so right that you two boys should be there!"

If Harold had made firm plans for his life after Wakpala, he might have rebelled even against Grandmother. But he had not done so, and the habit of wanting to please her took precedence.

The opening class at the Bishop Hare Industrial School numbered twenty-nine students. Classroom work at an industrial and trade school gave place to the necessary tasks of building fences, carpentry work on new buildings, and feeding livestock. Harold was especially pleased that his experience tending horses and cows would guarantee a good grade in animal husbandry at least.

These many activities could be directly traced to Bishop Hare himself. On his last visit to Wakpala, Bishop Burleson had reminded Grandmother of what the first bishop of the Dakota Indians had said in the 1880s: "As the Indians are not accustomed to labor, the school's training should be such as would not only cultivate their intellect but also develop their physical functions, and teach them to do well with common acts of daily humble life." Of course, Bishop Hare did not mean that Indians were lazy or afraid of hard work, only that they were not used to the white man's pattern of scheduled work, eight or ten hours a day. As Harold had learned, the traditional Dakota way was to work extremely hard to meet the immediate need, as in a buffalo hunt, and then relax and enjoy the fruits of labor. But the world had changed dramatically for the Dakotas and Lakotas. Now here was Harold Jones, being trained in the industrial skills of mainstream white society advocated by Bishop Hare decades earlier.

Days and nights passed quickly. Harold and Kenny felt Grandmother's and Grandfather's presence most keenly in the daily chapel service, in which each student took turns reading the lessons or serving as an acolyte.

As winter turned inexorably into spring, Harold began making firmer plans for the future. Studying to become a doctor, with all of the cost and time involved, seemed now only a remote possibility, whereas becoming a reservation teacher was within his means and would allow him to practice a useful occupation. He had written to Southern State Teachers College in Springfield and had been accepted. Father Barbour, who had succeeded

Grandfather at Ashley House, had already written to invite him to live at the house again. Harold also occasionally pondered following in Grandfather's footsteps as an ordained minister, and Grandmother kept hoping he would do so.

Easter was over and only a few weeks of school remained. One day, Father Robert Frazier, the chaplain, stopped by study hall to speak with Harold. Something in the clergyman's expression brought Harold's attention into sharp focus.

"Harold," he said quietly, "your Grandmother has called with a message for you and your brother. Can you find Kenny and bring him to the office with you?"

Harold rose stiffly, fears making his heart pound. Grandmother called. What did she call about? Grandfather? He found Kenny among a knot of friends at the far end of the dining room and motioned to him. The two followed the long hallway wordlessly and entered the principal's office. Both Mr. Sacre, the principal, and Father Frazier were there, looking at the boys kindly and nodding a welcome.

"Sit down, boys," Mr. Sacre said. "Your grandmother has called to ask that you meet her in Santee. Mr. Whipple, your school advisor will drive you there."

"Did she say why, sir?" Harold hardly recognized the sound of his whispered voice. In the slight pause that followed, he managed, "Is it Grandfather?"

Mr. Sacre nodded. "He was taken ill suddenly. Your grandmother said to tell you that she wasn't worried and doesn't want you to worry."

It was true. Something had happened to Grandfather. And Grandmother would never call them to come if he were just ill.

Harold asked softly, "Is Grandfather alive?"

The simple question cut through Mr. Sacre's carefully phrased announcement. He blinked suddenly. "Mrs. Holmes said that your grandfather had a fatal heart attack while he was driving to Whitehorse." He hesitated for a moment. "Mr. Whipple will drive you down to Santee, where they've taken your grandfather's body and where your grandmother will be waiting for you."

Mr. Whipple's car was an old Model T Ford with no top. They traveled over gravel roads in a cold rain, stopping when it got dark and arriving in Santee by noon the next day. Wearily, Harold and Kenny climbed the back steps of their old home, now occupied by the George Lawrence family.

Grandmother was at the door, holding out her arms to gather a tall boy to each side of her. "Oh my dears, my dears, you are here!" Harold could not answer, but he drank her in so deeply that he would never forget that moment. Her face was drawn, and there were dark circles under her eyes. Grandmother hugged both grandsons again and pulled down their faces to kiss them. "You are so good to come this quickly! I thought it might be another day before I could see you!"

It was the first time Harold had heard Grandmother speak of herself alone. His face must have betrayed what he felt, for she hugged him again and then firmly but cheerfully continued, "You all need something hot to drink after your long ride. There is some soup ready and a big ham waiting to be sliced in the kitchen. Come with me."

Neither Harold nor Kenny was prepared for a kitchen filled with relatives and friends from Santee and Wakpala. Each visitor came solemnly in turn to shake hands with the boys and then drifted through the swinging door into the rooms beyond. The boys briefly caught sight of crowds of people. Grandmother almost forcibly sat them down and poured some soup into waiting bowls. "As you can see," she said, "we are well supplied with everything, thanks to relatives and friends. As soon as they heard what happened, they began coming and haven't left me for one minute. But now that you are here, they can go home again and get some rest."

She explained that Grandfather had left the house that particular morning to drive himself and Andrew Whiteface to Whitehorse, where they were to meet with Dr. Ashley. They took the Easter offerings from several congregations with them to deposit at the bank in Mobridge. Both were in good spirits, and Grandfather had kissed her and told her not to wait up for him because the meeting might be a long one. He must have had a sudden attack because the car had swerved off the road. When some minutes later another car passed that way, Grandfather was already dead at the wheel, and Andrew was trying to lift him out onto the roadside.

"Grandfather has entered into everlasting life quickly and easily," Grandmother reassured them. "This was a very good gift from the Lord.

He could never have been happy if he had grown too old or too ill to serve him. Out of a busy day, God has carried him into his kingdom."

Harold and Kenny slept through that night, exhausted by their sorrow, in the room where Grandfather lay in his casket. There just wasn't any other place for them to bed down. Waking the next morning, the loss hit them anew. Life would never be the same.

Our Merciful Saviour Church could not hold everyone who came to Grandfather's funeral. Friends and relatives from every place he had once lived or worked had traveled to pay their last respects: the very old who had been with him on the long walk from the Minnesota prison enclosure; people from Pine Ridge, where he and Grandpa Ross had taught school together, and from Rosebud, where Grandfather and Grandmother had lived after they married. Everyone on Santee Reservation seemed to be there, and almost as many people came from Standing Rock. Fellow clergy and Indians and white men from Nebraska and North and South Dakota walked in the procession behind the casket. In Harold's eyes, Grandmother looked for the first time small and defenseless, yet she graciously opened her arms to all and gently scolded those who let their grief overflow. As she had reminded the boys, she now reminded others that God had been gracious to William in life and now in death by sparing him the weakness of old age.

William Holmes's body was buried in the Most Merciful Saviour Churchyard, near the graves of Rebecca and William's children who had died in early life. Around Grandfather's grave, the soft new grass, still wet from melting snow, was trampled by many feet. While the casket was lowered into its sharply cut rectangle, hundreds of voices rang out in the hymn "Precious Name," a hymn that Grandfather himself had translated from the English hymnals into the Santee language. Shovels full of earth were tossed on top of the casket, soon covering it and finally rising in a smooth mound as the voices continued singing "Blest Be the Tie That Binds" and "Soldiers of the Cross Arise," other favorite hymns of his grandfather's.

For months afterwards, Grandmother's mail was full of letters from many parts of the country. Grandfather was respected in the wider world far beyond the reservations, especially in Washington DC, where he had been called to represent the Dakota people as an interceder and interpreter.

✄ + ✄

Bishop Burleson assured Grandmother that in a few weeks her widow's pension from the national church office in New York would begin. "The church provides one thousand dollars to all clergy wives who become widows," he told her. "You should receive a check in a few days. What your monthly payments will be I don't know. Those fellows have been setting up some kind of system based on years of service and amounts of salaries, but since your husband served the church he loved so devotedly for forty years as a priest, I should think you'd have no cause to worry."

When a check for one thousand dollars arrived a week or two later, Grandmother promptly turned it over to the bank account of the Indian missions on Standing Rock. She knew that their funds were almost gone and that the money Grandpa was carrying with him to deposit had mysteriously disappeared on that fateful journey. Nobody had ever found the bags stuffed with bills and coins from the Easter collections. Grandmother felt that the check was a godsend to replace that loss.

Back at Standing Rock Reservation, the people of St. Elizabeth's invited Mrs. Holmes and her family to stay in the rectory for as long as a year if need be, until she could make plans for the future. The bishop approved of this offer, although it was his duty to arrange for another priest to take over Grandfather's work at St. Elizabeth's and as superintending presbyter of Standing Rock.

To return to Hare School and leave Grandmother was unthinkable for both Harold and Kenny. The Milwaukee Railroad was advertising for workers. When the boys applied, they were set to work immediately as section hands just outside the small settlement of Stratman, a few miles down the tracks from Wakpala. Swinging a sledgehammer and hauling ties into place was hard work, but it brought each of them $.35 an hour, for a combined total of $5.60 a day. It was worth sore muscles and shoulders burned

black by the sun to see their grandmother's eyes full of love and pride because "her boys" were supporting her.

"It won't be long until my pension comes," Grandmother assured
them, "and then I can be self-supporting. By fall you must get on with your
education."

About a month later, the boys returned home hot and dusty one afternoon to discover that a letter from the Episcopal Church had come. What
value had the national church put on Grandfather's forty years of service?
Harold and Kenny skimmed the terse, typed paragraphs, looking for a dollar amount.

Only $33.33 a month. The annual total would be $339.96.

They reread the figure and then stared at each other. The letter explained that widows' pensions were based on a percentage of the amount
of salary received by the deceased over his years of service. The Reverend
Mr. Holmes's salary had been below the minimum on the wage scale used
by the office and so the pension could hardly be considered a living wage.
Although the pension would continue throughout her life, the national
church hoped that Mrs. Holmes had other resources that would supple-
ment this amount.

Did this letter really come from the church that Harold's grandparents
had devoted their lives to serve? Hot and sweaty as he was, Harold felt suddenly cold.

Money never had meant much to Grandfather. Money was a white
man's invention, he used to say. It was useful only in that it could be exchanged for food, clothing, or other necessities. Since Grandfather was
patterned in a more traditional Indian way of thinking, Harold had been
taught that the joy of possessions came from the opportunity they provided to share with others. And having money brought a special obligation. The Bible talked about a tithe, a tenth belonging to the Lord. Grandmother's budgeting was what had kept her family fed despite frequent
knocks on the door that had meant, invariably, other calls for help.

Now, Grandmother's total income would be less than the monthly
amount she and Grandfather had given to others. The only sign of the
letter's effect on Grandmother was some absentmindedness as she went
about her household tasks. She didn't mention it further. Anger boiled

within Harold, erupting at the sight of his little grandmother, who was now so vulnerable. At such times, he would slip out of the house, eyes streaming with tears, and run until his breath was gone.

At last his indignation grew too big to bear alone, and Harold confronted Grandmother with it. "What is the use of this church anyway," he blurted, "when the big people in the city office treat the little people on the reservation like dirt? I'd like to go back there and punch 'em out!"

In a flash Grandmother's eyes were on him, burning. He had never seen her this way before.

"Don't let me hear you say anything like that ever again!" she snapped. "This church of ours belongs to God. We do not stand in judgment over it because of the actions of a few within it who disagree with us. Neither are the people in the eastern office 'big people' and we on the reservation 'little people.' In God's sight we are equal, and his is the only clear sight. There are no cruel people back there. They are carrying out the orders that were made in good faith. This pension system may be hard on us, but, if it isn't just, then in the future it will be changed. We should be thankful for any help at all. Your grandfather and I lived as we wanted to live, and the Lord filled every day with blessings. No pension, no matter how large, could match the happiness of our years. If I could, I would pay the church for the privilege of serving it and through it our Lord."

She poured out words without pause, her tone becoming calmer as she spoke. "My grandson, we have had a wonderful life all together. This has been God's gift. Never turn away from him in times of trouble. He is the only one who can show us the way to go. We, who are part of his church, stumble along, sometimes hurting one another. But when we are hurt, we don't blame God. When we hurt others, as we will, he will forgive us, as we trust they will. He has the right answers for us if we turn to him for them."

4

DEPRESSION AND
DETERMINATION

❧ + ❧

1929–1933

September 1929 saw Harold and Kenny moving in different directions for the first time. Kenny went back to Hare School for his final year, and Harold boarded the train from Wakpala for Springfield and his first year at Southern State Teacher's College. Grandmother stayed on in the rectory at St. Elizabeth's, surrounded by staunch friends, who promised the boys they would watch over her. She promised that before long she would follow Harold back home to Santee country and Springfield.

Harold had more good friends on the Santee Reservation and in Springfield than he had left behind on Standing Rock, but his grandmother's new loneliness weighed heavily on his spirit. Still, he knew that she wanted above all else to give the boys the opportunities that education would open for them. Dr. Ashley and Dr. Paul Barbour had promised that Harold could live in Ashley House as long as needed and that there would always be room for Mrs. Holmes in the small house adjoining Ashley House. Thanks to government student loans, Harold could pay for tuition and books.

St. Mary's School was nearby. Bishop Hare had opened it as an industrial school for girls in 1874. Fire twice forced it to move, but it was now in Springfield. St. Mary's always needed handymen, and anyone related to the Reverend William Holmes would need no special introduction. Harold could work for his board even though the school had no extra money to pay a salary.

At Southern State, Harold found himself in classrooms predominantly filled by white students. He became self-conscious about his own skin color, which had darkened to deep red brown during the summer spent along the railroad tracks. His feelings of inadequacy, he ruefully acknowledged, were not caused as much by the white students' attitudes toward him as by his own distrust of *them*. Further complicating Harold's world were the increasingly admiring glances of Indian girls, who sometimes appeared during his early morning hours at St. Mary's, when he milked cows, or in the late afternoon hours, when he mopped floors, cut lawns, or shoveled walks as fall turned into winter. Several of the girls became good friends.

One of his jobs at St. Mary's School was to stand guard against party crashers of the monthly dances. Harold would flex his muscles, scowl, and block the door against unwelcome visitors, though it was often more difficult to deal with dates who came with liquor on their breath. If a gang of boys gathered around the door to rush Harold, Mrs. Elliot, the headmistress, would materialize at his side, her imperious finger pointing toward the darkness beyond the door. If one or two lingered, it was Harold's duty to march them down the steps, as far as St. Mary's gate if necessary.

One particular dance Harold never forgot. He stood as usual at his post, arms crossed, legs relaxed for the three-hour vigil. He watched the dancers, admiring the sleek, shining hair of his charges, feeling old and fatherly and rehearsing their names in his mind while looking around the room. On these Friday evenings, the girls were like young butterflies, spreading their wings for a brief life of freedom. Bright flowers and ribbons decked their heads, and if the dresses brought from home were dark in color, they would be trimmed with gay sashes and shawls. Perfume bottles, uncorked for the occasion, added a heady combination of fragrances to the atmosphere. For one reason or another, some of the girls refused invitations from boys and preferred to dance together. Most of them, however, never had a chance to pair off together or to take a restful interlude to sit and watch.

On this particular night Harold noted with surprise that one of the girls, Blossom Steele, refused a steady stream of boys and danced instead with her smaller and younger friend, Mugs. Blossom exuded an intriguing combination of daintiness and strength.

The progress of Blossom and Mugs around the rather small room was slow, swaying, and accompanied by a strong perfume scent. They didn't appear to be holding any kind of a conversation, and once, when Mugs stumbled over her partner's feet, Blossom frowned. She kept her eyes on Mugs, looking neither left nor right as the two passed Harold, but Mugs once lifted an enraptured gaze to his face. Mugs was humming the tune they danced to, and she smiled and giggled as Blossom swept her away. It was obvious that Mugs was tipsy—but how was that possible? And how would they keep the secret from Mrs. Elliot? Blossom adroitly danced on the side of the gymnasium farthest from Mrs. Elliot, who drifted about, smiling and nodding to the young guests. Blossom, her hand tightly clasped in Mugs's, eventually took an early leave of the dance, much to Harold's relief. She gave him a jaunty little salute as she left, and Mugs smiled soulfully.

Mrs. Elliot never found out, and only years later did Harold learn the whole story. To Blossom's and her sister Gladys's remorse, Mugs had been drunk on wine that the two sisters had made. The girls had been brought up not to waste food, and when Gladys discovered that a large bunch of grapes that she was saving as a special treat had turned soft, she was very unhappy. Deciding to make some wine, the girls borrowed a bowl from the kitchen, snitched a little yeast and sugar, found two bottles with good corks in the trash, and mashed the grapes. They corked the bottles tightly and hid them on the top shelves of their closet. One March night when they had forgotten their attempt at wine making, the bottles had popped, spewing the now fermented wine on the sisters' clothes and closet. Blossom and Gladys spent frantic early morning hours, rinsing out clothes and scrubbing the closet with strong-smelling cleaner.

The next evening while getting dressed for the dance, the girls let their friend Mugs in on the secret and produced the bottles. Mugs allowed the wine didn't taste that bad. By dance time she had emptied one bottle and was working on the other. The girls pondered what to do. If they stayed away from the party, Mrs. Elliott would come to find them, and they might be expelled. So to the dance they went, each dressed in her finest, and Blossom steered a woozy Mugs around the dance floor away from Mrs. Elliott's searching eyes.

The Mugs incident awakened Harold's interest in Blossom, who was four years younger than he. She was popular with the other girls, and he rarely saw her alone. If she passed him on her way to the dormitory or in the hall, she would nod but never stop to speak.

✼ + ✼

It was nearly spring when Harold received news that Grandmother would be arriving in Springfield soon, and for more than just a visit. The $33.33 a month that she received from the Church Pension Fund had not been sufficient, so Bishop Burleson suggested she supplement her income by supervising the laundry room at St. Mary's.

Harold again struggled to accept the events that had placed his gentle grandmother in such a position. Her years of church work in the Dakotas spanned a part of two centuries. As a young woman, she had moved away from her own culture to become a part of her beloved William's Santee people. Respect and honor surrounded the Holmeses, for they had been recognized as wise and selfless leaders in the church. Yet now she was not only widowed but also impoverished. Harold decided bitterly that God rewarded with hardships those who served him. When one ordeal ended, another, worse one would be waiting for you.

Grandfather's death had shattered the protective rim of warmth that the grandparents had placed around the boys. Harold wanted desperately to tell Grandmother not to worry, that he would care for her. He was strong, healthy, and had finished high school. But already he lived under a weight of debt, owing both the college for part of his tuition and the bookstore for textbooks.

Grandmother stepped off the train in Springfield, amidst a nondescript heap of boxes and suitcases tossed onto the platform as the train moved away. These pitiful bundles were all that she owned. Harold knew that Grandmother must have been forced to sell the furniture and livestock to keep herself warm and fed through the past winter months. None of the people looking out of the train windows knew or, Harold felt, cared to know that the small, erect figure with wisps of gray hair blowing in the raw wind of early spring was a special saint.

Maybe God didn't know or care either.

Harold hugged her so tightly that her stiff little hat slid back, and she looked up at him with twinkling eyes. "Oh, Grandson!" she exclaimed. "I'm here at last, and how happy I am to be with you!" She backed away, straightening her hat and scrutinizing him. "You look thin. I know you're working hard. I'm going to enjoy cooking for you again."

He drove them in the school car to the familiar Ashley House, where she could rest a bit among old friends. Grandmother's friends shook their heads warningly when they learned what she was planning to do, but no one offered a better solution.

With accustomed cheerfulness, Grandmother announced that the St. Mary's laundry would be a perfect place to get acquainted with the girls. "Tongues loosen better over work. While our hands are sharing a job at the scrub boards, it will be much easier to share ideas and feelings too." Scrub boards were indeed used for stubborn dirt, but most of the washing for the fifty girls at St. Mary's tumbled in large roller washers. Grandmother supervised the operation of the machines and instructed the girls in their careful use. As the weeks went by, though, all too often Harold would find her in the big, steamy room by herself, washing and ironing for fifty girls. The girls had other commitments—sports programs, choir rehearsals, exams to prepare for—or some simply "forgot" laundry duty. Harold's temper smoldered.

The situation grew steadily worse. Although they lived rent free in a cottage behind Ashley House, Grandmother's small pension plus the minimum wage she earned in the laundry barely saw the two of them through each month. No money was left to make even a token payment on college tuition or books. Harold saw no alternative: he must drop out of school. He knew Grandmother was disappointed, but there was no other solution to their dilemma.

Springfield, like the rest of the country, was experiencing the Depression. Harold now spent his days walking from store to store, dairy farm to warehouse, ice house to hotel, searching for any available work. Except for temporary jobs, lasting a half-day or less, he found nothing.

"Don't be discouraged, Grandson," his grandmother would console him. "Things will work out, maybe not as you envisioned, but God is watching over us. Trust him. He will not fail us."

How could she be so certain that God cared? Harold wondered, taking inventory again of their misery. Her own family had renounced her when she married Grandfather. She had outlived all but one of her five children, and now she was a widow. The church that she and Grandfather had served so faithfully for more than forty years awarded her a tiny monthly pension, while the church school paid an equal pittance for the menial job at the laundry. And her grandson, try as he might, could not find a paying job. Where was God in this picture? In despair, Harold considered throwing himself in the river and lightening Grandmother's burden, but he knew full well that she now lived for him and Kenny.

Harold tried to get a loan to reenter school, visiting in turn the bank, church, school, and the Indian Office. He wanted the loan so desperately that he stumbled over his explanations and stood clumsily before those who took time to listen to him. "What collateral have you to offer?" a bank manager had asked, his gaze cool, seeing him, Harold thought, only as an untrustworthy Indian. A clergyman was more sympathetic but had no funds. The federal government was broke too, and the college, already strained to meet its own expenses, had nothing to offer a poor Indian student.

When he was not doing his chores at St. Mary's, Harold now stayed in his room, reading. Books helped him not to think about his situation. He knew his depression was worrying Grandmother, but he couldn't help it. Harold also came to realize, with some irritation, that she was praying for him. Why?

❧ + ❧

In early May of 1932, the Reverend David Clark and his wife, good friends of the Holmes family for many years, traveled through Springfield on their way home to Fort Thompson. Grandmother's welcome was joyous. They were equally happy to see her but said they had come especially to see Harold.

He remembered Elizabeth and David Clark from the Niobrara Convocations. David was always friendly and talkative, filling all pauses with a running monologue, which his wife sometimes cut short or superseded with her own quick observations. Elizabeth had once been a professor at Columbia University, but, like his grandmother, she had become an accepted part of the Dakota scene. "She was wrapped up in it, even wrote papers about it," Grandfather had once said. Her love for Indian people was genuine. Harold warmed to her, though, at the same time, her learnedness made him feel uneasy.

Elizabeth Clark turned to him now, interrupting her husband's pleasantries about the weather. "We do hope you are free for the summer, Harold, and would be willing to help Sister Horner on Crow Creek. She is one of that wonderful group of lay workers in the Church Army. She has more than she can do right now but feels that a vacation Bible school is needed there. She's getting too old to play sports like baseball. Being English anyway, she'd probably end up teaching the children cricket. She needs your kind of help desperately."

Elizabeth paused and looked at Grandmother. "Your life should be easier in the summer, Rebecca, shouldn't it? I know you will miss Harold, but there is such a need! David cares for the Big Bend area, both for the white ranchers and the Indian people. He manages services twice a month, and Sister Horner does everything else. We're concerned about her health if she has to go through one of our broiling summers, trying to do everything herself. There would be no compensation, I'm afraid, except room and board and one dollar a week for spending."

She continued, smiling affectionately at Harold. "What do you say? You wouldn't need to come for another two weeks."

No money but Grandmother would be spared some expense. He could keep busy and be useful, and he would like to please the Clarks. Harold didn't know Sister Horner, but she had come all the way from England to help his people. The smile on Grandmother's face told him that she saw this opportunity as an answer to her prayers. He nodded his acceptance.

Later Harold was to think of this summer in the early 1930s on Crow Creek as a pivotal point in his life. The Clarks became a second set of parents to him. He hadn't realized how much he missed Grandfather until he found in David Clark the kind of sure wisdom that brought him the first peace he had known in many months. Equally important was the fact that Sister Annie Horner did need his help. On some days as many as forty children arrived for Bible study and on others as few as fifteen. Some of them came by horseback across the prairie from homes all along the river. The older boys and girls at the Bible school were growing restless from an overdose of biblical stories and mimeographed pictures to color. If Harold hadn't been there, he knew Sister Horner, dressed in Church Army uniform, black oxfords, and brimmed hat, would have willingly studied the baseball rulebook and plunged into the game, broiling sun and all.

When Harold wasn't busy with Sister Horner and the children, he went to the Clarks' house, part of which had been made into a small museum. David told him that in 1881, when white settlers were asking for legislation to do away with reservations so that they could buy the land, the Indians from Crow Creek had given many cherished keepsakes to the Reverend Mr. Burt for safekeeping. Even after the imminent danger had passed, thanks to a petition that the Crow Creek chiefs signed and Mr. Burt sent to President Arthur, the people left their cherished mementos with the Burts for safety's sake. When Mr. Burt died, the Clarks were asked to keep the collection intact so that local Indian children could come and learn about their history.

The time when Harold could be alone in the museum room was peaceful and instructive. The voices from the past spoke powerfully. Some of his own people, the Santees, had been placed in this area after the long trip from Minnesota. The Yanktonais and the Two-Kettles band of Teton Sioux came to settle here too. The camps of notable Indian leaders of the past, Medicine Crow and White Ghost, had not been far away. The small museum with its heirlooms seemed in some ways like a church. Harold exulted in the wisdom of his people, which he had learned from his grandfather and the elders he had met. For countless generations, they had worshipped the Holy One, Wakan Tanka, and communed with him through his creatures and the earth. Wakan Tanka was one God, Harold reasoned, like the God of the Bible. For that reason, his people could accept the message of the white missionaries.

Among the museum artifacts were some old crosses, prompting Harold to recall Tipi Sapa's words to an old man around a Niobrara campfire years ago: "He sacrificed himself for those who tortured him. It takes the greatest strength to forgive. The gift of eternal life that he has promised us takes away despair and brings us peace. That is why we wear these crosses around our necks." Old men and women still living were among the early converts baptized in the new faith. They believed that this faith, along with the actions of the missionaries who remained with them through the years of ordeal and change in the nineteenth century, had saved the Santees and other Sioux peoples from extinction. And Harold knew that some white people still would have preferred that all of the Indians had been exterminated. Yet, God loves *all* of us. Harold began to understand truly for the first time the power and responsibility of this Christian message.

Harold spent most mornings in the old mission house with the children, while they memorized prayers, listened to a Bible story, and colored pictures in an atmosphere of tidy discipline. Sandwiches, lemonade, and a brief rest divided the day into distinct halves, the second of which belonged to Harold and baseball. Spirits rose as soon as he grabbed their only glove and led them out the door to the field that served as their baseball diamond. Never mind that the sun blazed down fiercely on the little group leaving the shelter of the building. The heat was soon forgotten in the excitement of the game. Sister Horner would sit on an old tree stump at the edge of the field, while the youngest children stretched out at her feet or ran in circles, making the ubiquitous grasshoppers jump. The ever-hungry insects even managed to suspend the baseball games once, when Harold left the glove out over night. All he could find of it the next morning was a button, a few shreds of leather, and a small wad of stuffing. Fortunately, the Clarks had another to replace it.

The Clarks let Harold use a 1921 Ford Coupe as compensation for his work. In the late afternoon, after the children went home, Harold would give Sister Horner driving lessons. He was proud of his British pupil. She would sit grimly behind the wheel, clenching it with both hands, her forehead lined with concentration as she raised and lowered the foot pedals.

Harold felt needed and happy again. He loved the children. Sister Horner was a good companion, possessing a low, authoritative voice and cheerful willingness to tackle anything that needed to be done. She was fifty and he was twenty, but camaraderie grew between them. They were both poor. During that summer, the bank in Philadelphia where the sister had kept her savings went bankrupt, and she lost everything. One day Harold borrowed a dime from her to replace his broken comb. In queenly fashion, she took a quarter from her purse and handed it to him, ordering him in her brisk English accent to "keep the change." He did, knowing that in spite of her turning the gesture into a joke, it was a precious gift.

❧ + ❧

Harold returned to Springfield at the end of the summer, confident and buoyed by good memories. He discovered that Kenny, fresh out of the Bishop Hare School, had found a job and a wife. His good fortune was a comfort to Grandmother.

For Harold and Grandmother, however, the economic situation appeared little altered. The bills from Southern State were still unpaid; jobs were as scarce as ever. Yet they were surviving. St. Mary's School and the dairy remained sources for a few dollars, and Harold found other odd jobs to pick up. Grandmother's summer had given her a chance to rest, and she was ready for another year of laundry duty.

Autumn and winter arrived and departed swiftly. Harold managed to keep busy at odd jobs, supplementing Grandmother's checks with a few dollars each week.

The world may not have changed much, but something fundamentally important had changed inside of Harold. When he prayed, he now knew that he was being heard. With chagrin he remembered that only a few months before he had contemplated suicide. His predicament, still the same, felt pierced with rays of hope, although he couldn't yet tell why.

❧ + ❧

Harold was paying a small installment on his debts at Southern State Teacher's College one early summer day in 1933 when he ran into his friend Harold Shunk. Shunk was a student and the school's foremost athlete. He was planning to organize a baseball team in Springfield for the

coming summer and asked Harold if he would be one of the team's pitch-
ers. Nothing could have sounded better to Harold.

Early in the season, the team played the formidable Greenwood Indians
from Yankton Reservation, and Harold pitched. In the first inning, he got
them out three in a row. Wiping sweat from his forehead and walking
from the pitcher's mound to the bench, Harold almost didn't see the manager of the Greenwood team holding out his hand.

"What's your name, young fellow?"

Harold told him, and the man nodded.

"Have any plans for your life?" the manager asked casually.

"I want to go back to college as soon as I can."

"Then what?"

Harold gulped. "I don't really know, sir."

The Greenwood manager smiled and said, "My name's Holcomb. I've a
proposition to make. Anyone who plays for the Greenwood Indians gets
$2.50 a day as long as the season lasts, but you have to be good. Joe Cook
is our pitcher. He's a crackerjack and has a lot on the ball. If you can get a
hit off of Joe Cook, you're on. If not, you can forget our conversation."

Two dollars and fifty cents a day for playing ball! Harold was glad he had
a little time to study the pitcher's technique before batting. Even that preparation, however, did not help to quiet his nerves when the moment came.

The first pitch was a ball. A twist of Joe Cook's wrist delivered the next,
a slider. Harold swung and sent the ball clear over the bleachers, but it was
foul. With a two-strike count, his hands were clammy; wiping them on his
shirt gave him a better grip on the bat. Then came a fast ball, which he hit
squarely. Harold dashed around first base, not waiting to see what had
happened, and stretched towards second. He made it just as the throw arrived from the outfield and got away from the second baseman. Harold
sprinted for third and then home, with the ball reaching the catcher just an
instant too late.

Manager Holcomb met Harold after the game was over and invited him
to come to Greenwood as soon as possible. Once again Harold packed his
bags and left Springfield and Grandmother for the summer months, hoping this time to earn enough money to pay his debts and reenter college in
the fall. Niobrara Convocation had encamped at Greenwood on the Yank-

ton Reservation in 1925. Seeing the place where the Holmeses had pitched their tent brought Harold an unexpected twinge, a momentary finding and losing of Grandfather all over again.

The manager of the Greenwood Indians saw to it that the team had little free time. They played two and often three games each week; traveling and practice kept them busy when there were no games. Through June and July, they covered the western and central towns of South Dakota. The money in Harold's wallet grew, and he was very careful not to spend any more than necessary.

Harold's unaccustomed prosperity was short-lived, however. Mr. Holcomb called a special meeting of the team the last week of July and announced that there were no more funds to pay the players. The superintendent of the Yankton Reservation had been accused of embezzling funds. He was fired immediately, even though he accounted for all the money in question. The superintendent had diverted money from certain allocations to channels that he deemed more important, such as creating new jobs to help feed hungry Indian families. Unfortunately, the ball team's pay had been siphoned for this cause, and now their checks would be ending abruptly. The players held a council and decided that they would finish the season anyway, without pay.

The last game was held at Flandreau. The team was quartered in the Flandreau School dormitory, and Harold had his bags packed, ready to return home to Springfield. He felt very tired. It would be good to get some real rest after the season was over.

The sun had been blistering, and when the final game was over, he felt dizzy and his head throbbed. Harold's friend Bill Picotte drove him back to the dorm and helped him up the stairs. Dismissing Bill's offer to get a doctor, Harold closed the door and collapsed in a half stupor.

He remembered nothing more until morning, when the sun, shining through a crack in the shade, fell across his face. Harold raised his head gingerly. The headache was gone, though his back and stomach muscles felt stiff and sore. With the exception of being weak and hungry, he felt all right. Across the room, Bill was sleeping soundly. Harold pulled on his clothes and reached for his wallet, intending to extract one more precious dollar for a good breakfast.

The billfold wasn't there. He searched the room with no success. He woke Bill, and they combed the playing field for the wallet but found nothing. After hours of fruitless searching, Harold was forced to accept the realization that his summer savings had disappeared. He would return home as penniless as when he had left it.

A heavily tanned but downcast Harold opened the screen door of the Springfield cottage and walked into the welcoming arms of his grandmother. He just couldn't tell her about his loss right away. He was ashamed of his carelessness and furious with the faceless thief who had made off with his earnings.

After supper as they drank tea, he finally blurted out the news. Shock, then disappointment, and then something unidentifiable flashed across his grandmother's face. Her mouth twitched and her eyes crinkled at the corners. Was she going to cry? To his amazement, however, she began to shake with mirth, laughing so long that in the end he had to laugh too, although he didn't understand the joke.

Finally Grandmother wiped her eyes and reached over to pat his hand. "Well, Grandson, let's look at it this way. Except for that last miserable day, you've had a happy, healthy summer. You've come home safely. The lesson we can learn from this might be the reminder that true riches are the joys of living experiences, which no one can take from us. Our possessions are always vulnerable. It's good to learn this truth while you are young. And it's good, Harold, to learn to laugh at the jokes that fate plays on us. Life is full of the unexpected. Of one thing you can be sure, your life will not be humdrum."

The next morning the two of them talked with the bank president, who had been acquainted with the Holmeses over many years and had watched Harold grow up. This time they arranged a loan to pay off the debts to the college. When Southern State began its fall term, Harold was enrolled once more.

5

DECISIONS

❦ + ❦

1934

Harold plunged into study, stimulated by the classroom atmosphere of the college. He had managed to complete some basic courses during the first months of his interrupted college career. This year he concentrated on the sciences, with the vague hope that in the distant future he might become a doctor.

One basic course he still needed to take was English composition. Harold was surprised to see Blossom Steele in that class, sitting third row from the front. She was talking to the girl sitting on her left, but the seat on her right was vacant. Harold hurried to fill it and then waited quietly until her conversation was finished. As if by accident, he bumped Blossom's elbow off the desk and exclaimed with elaborate concern, "Oh, I beg your pardon!"

Blossom Steele was poised, beautiful, perhaps a little more restrained now, but her dark eyes held the same lively fire. Those eyes flashed a sudden, delighted welcome, though her answer was demure.

"Hello, Mr. Jones. Do all those pitcher's muscles of yours need more space? I'll keep my elbows out of the way."

Composition became Harold's favorite subject. He managed to keep the seat next to Blossom Steele, and, by the end of three weeks, she allowed her elbow to rest on the corner of the desk where his arm rested too. He managed, not by chance, to edge it over to hers and spent the hour blissfully aware of the gentle touch.

In the next few months, Harold learned how quickly time can pass when one is happy. On their first date, Harold and Blossom attended a college concert and hummed the tunes on the walk back to the dormitory. That fall they took walks around the campus, the yellow leaves of a Chinese elm whirling around their feet in the wind. Harold saw that Blossom loved the outdoors as much as he did, and her step kept easy pace with his. One time a sunset held them entranced with its red and gold rays shooting through slate-colored banks of clouds tinged with silver.

They had time on their fall walks to talk and learn more about each other. Blossom had grown up with three brothers and two sisters in a three-room house in Rockyford on Pine Ridge Reservation. Her father owned cattle, mostly red and white Herefords, and a few dairy cows. The children would spend long hours on horseback, watching the cattle and rounding them up in the evening, for cattle rustling was a persistent problem. When Blossom's mother was a young girl, she had gone to live with a white family in Pennsylvania and had attended school there. The women in the family had taught her embroidery and other useful domestic skills.

"We children were brought up far from any of the exciting cultural things mother told us about," Blossom reflected. "But she taught us what she had learned and kept our lives full and busy. She told us to remember one thing even if we forgot everything else. She said over and over that we were always to remember that we were as good as anyone else anywhere in the world. Just as good—but no better. When any of us came home crying to tell her about some unkind thing that was said about us or to us, she would ask, 'Is it true?' If we said, 'No,' she would say, 'Then forget it.' If it were true, she would say, 'Well, then, you deserved what they said.'"

Blossom's family lived near the reservation boundary, so she and her brothers and sisters became acquainted with both white and Indian children. As the girls grew older, they were sometimes even invited out by white boys. "We never felt strange or inferior to them," Blossom remarked, "and we used to joke about our two races." Blossom didn't share Harold's reticence as an Indian among a majority of white students. She felt at ease with all of the students, Indian and white.

All the Steeles, including her grandparents, lived in the Badlands in

Rockyford, north of the town of Pine Ridge. Years ago Blossom's grand-father began breeding local horses from stock stolen from neighboring tribes and from soldiers stationed in the area. Now he was much more se-lective in capturing wild horses that had strayed from the battlefields and had lived free lives for many years. Her grandfather also tended a garden and an orchard and opened one of the first general stores on Pine Ridge Reservation.

On one memorable day in late October, when the first snowfall sent lazy flakes through the air, Harold and Blossom abandoned their books and met under the bare branches of cottonwoods outside the gymnasium. From there they set off down the now familiar walking path that led to the open field beyond the buildings, raising their faces to feel the soft sting of flakes falling from the gray sky. More flakes began twirling and dancing in the wind. Without warning, Blossom flung a handful of snow in Harold's face and dashed away down the path. With Harold at her heels, Blossom suddenly turned and collided with him, sending him sprawling at her feet. Doubled over with laughter, he had no strength to get up again. She put a small boot on his chest, raised her voice to the sky, and shouted "See how the mighty have fallen!"

At that instant, Harold realized beyond a doubt that he had indeed fallen and that Blossom was the conqueror.

🌿 + 🌿

Harold had less success with his studies. After Christmas he earnestly tackled his schoolwork, spending every free moment in the laboratory when he wasn't studying assignments and cutting his sleeping time to four hours. This renewed dedication had little impact on his academic per-formance, however, and he continued to falter.

After the first quiz sessions were over, the dean called Harold to his of-fice and confronted him with the facts. If Harold planned to go to medical school, he would need a college degree rather than the teaching certificates awarded by Southern State. He would also need to improve his scholastic performance in science courses. Harold was presented with a decision: focus on a teaching career at Southern State or transfer next term to the larger campus of Northern State in Aberdeen and work towards a bachelor of science degree.

The dean was right. Despite the personal and social advantages of Southern State, it could not advance his career.

Blossom accepted the news calmly, a proper response for an Oglala Sioux but disconcerting nonetheless. "I'll come back every chance I get," Harold promised.

"Of course," she replied simply.

"I like to think that you're my girl," Harold blurted. "But I won't tie you down. We mustn't let our feelings for each other stand in the way of friendships with others. These months will be a trial to let us know how deeply we care for each other."

"That's the way it should be," Blossom answered demurely, betrayed by a twinkle in her eye.

❧ + ❧

It was very difficult to leave family and friends, but Harold was cheered to learn that his good friend Scott Whipple was also transferring from Southern State to Northern State. The boys agreed to room together. Two days before their departure, a dejected Scott announced that he lacked the train fare to Aberdeen. Harold's summer earnings, fortunately, were enough for both their fares to the Northern State campus.

The dean's secretary at Northern State gave Harold and Scott a list of names and addresses of Aberdeen citizens who rented rooms to students. The boys first tried a respectable looking two-story brick house on South Main Street. The screened door hinted at a wide hall within, cool and inviting. Harold pressed the bell lightly; the resulting jangle seemed to fill the entire house. A tall, middle-aged woman with eyes and hair as dark as their own came to the door, and Harold instinctively braced for rejection. She invited them in cordially, however, and introduced herself as Dr. Chalfant. She was a chiropractor and a widow, with a son in school. Harold and Scott liked her immediately. The room to be rented was large and airy, containing a double bed, two tables and chairs, two dressers, and a closet. The rent would be ten dollars a month, but Dr. Chalfant understood that fed-eral grants were often processed slowly, and she was willing to wait for payment.

The year at Northern State proved to be one of Harold's best. It was a busy time, but he was at peace and his studies seemed easier. When pres-sures mounted, he would telephone home or to Southern State. After these phone calls, he always felt bolstered and refreshed by Grand-mother's warm affection or Blossom's happy exuberance. His financial worries were also temporarily forgotten. The Bureau of Indian Affairs paid for his room and board, and a music scholarship covered the expense of books and lab fees. Beyond those school costs, he had little need of money. The BIA was erratic in making payments for rent, but Dr. Chalfant was flexible and understanding. When after two or three months a check ar-rived, she would celebrate the event by cooking a batch of pancakes and in-viting the boys to the kitchen to share them.

Experience in the laboratory soon convinced Harold that he lacked the scientific skill to become a doctor. He decided to prepare to teach science after graduation. To do so, he would need to carry twenty-one and one-half credit hours for the last semester to be eligible for a bachelor of science degree.

The winter term became very busy, packed with academic responsibili-ties and extracurricular activities. The night hours became as familiar as the day, with Harold often dividing his time between sleeping and waking in two-hour intervals. Working toward a degree in science meant more hours in the lab as well as in the classroom. There didn't seem to be time for sports, but it was impossible to let baseball season go by without join-ing the intramural team. And because part of his tuition was paid by a mu-sic scholarship, Harold also sang with the college quartet, the mixed cho-rus, and men's glee club. He had to be prepared to sing at a moment's notice, when the choral groups were called upon to substitute for speakers who failed to appear at a college event. Harold also bore the important re-sponsibility for performing the opening and closing song for a Saturday morning radio program that featured the college's president. Surprisingly, Harold found it easier to sing in front of a black microphone than before classmates, whose expressions often distracted him.

The school year raced to a close. The yearbook stated that Northern State's "ideal man" should have Harold Jones's voice, and Harold was chosen to sing for commencement night. He dedicated the song publicly to his grandmother, who had been saving money all year to attend the ceremony.

Commencement night was the culmination of dreams—mostly his grandmother's. Harold was more surprised than elated. He could scarcely believe that his long-held goal of college graduation, tattered from repeated discouragement, had been achieved.

After the ceremony, Harold grasped Scott's hand. "When a parting of the ways must be made," his grandfather used to say, "do not waste your spirit in mourning over the past. It is the way of the Dakotas to look forward, not back." Harold and Scott's year of shared good and bad experiences meant that their friendship would not end soon. Scott had accepted an offer from the BIA to teach on the Rosebud or Cheyenne River Reservation. Harold, however, had still not made a final decision about his next step.

At the age of twenty-six, no longer a poor Santee Sioux without a job and many debts, Harold Jones faced a pleasingly unfamiliar and perplexing situation. Three paths could be followed.

Become a teacher in a BIA reservation school like Scott? That sounded attractive and would yield some immediate financial benefits and the possibility of marrying Blossom in the near future.

Perhaps sing? A scholarship offer from the McPhail School of Music in Minneapolis had come in recent weeks. More than once he had been told that with more training his voice could lead to a well-paying career in entertainment. However, more schooling would mean further delay before earning anything.

Undertake a more spiritual journey? In recent weeks a letter had also arrived from Bishop Roberts, who spoke about Harold attending seminary and following in his grandfather's footsteps. The bishop seemed confident that a scholarship could be found to make seminary possible. Weighing against the bishop's wishes and family tradition were three more years of study, more debts, and a longer postponement of marriage.

An offer to teach junior high school science in Lac du Flambeau, Wisconsin, made Harold's decision easier. The position and location piqued his interest, and the pay sounded good. He was sorry he would not be closer to Scott, but surely they would meet often in the years ahead.

✦ + ✦

The future seemed set. Or was it? Back home in Springfield a few weeks later, Grandmother raised the subject of attending seminary as they sipped tea one morning. Bishop Roberts had apparently also mentioned his idea to her.

"If I go to seminary," Harold reflected, "that means that I can't get married for another three years. I'm twenty-six now. Blossom is twenty-one. I love her, and I believe she loves me." He looked at his grandmother. "I've been thinking that the best plan is to take the teaching job in Lac du Flambeau for at least two years, until I get the worst debts paid off. Then I'll marry Blossom, and we can go to Wisconsin together. And when we are settled, we will call you to come too." Harold hesitated and then asked shyly, "What do you think of my marrying Blossom?"

Grandmother smiled. "My dear, as your grandmother, trying to take your mother's place, I have often been too zealous in influencing you," she admitted. "You and Kenneth have been the joy of my life in these last years, and it is hard to let go. But the choice of a marriage partner is yours alone. Blossom is a fine young woman. All I ask is that you take your plans to the One who gave Blossom her charm and you your talents and ask his advice before you take it up with her."

She paused and added quickly, "Your decisions this summer are important ones. You would be a good teacher, but these times are quite different from your grandfather's early years. The Bureau of Indian Affairs can find teachers more easily than the church can find good men who meet the high standards set for priests in these days. Even more important is finding a priest who has the respect of his people and a good understanding of their background. Of course," she acknowledged, "going to seminary does mean more years of study, more debts, more partings, and unknown hardships."

Harold again confronted uncertainty and again wrestled with difficult decisions, yet this time it was different. He had worked hard, had grown up, and no longer needed to rely on someone else's judgment. He felt excitement and exhilaration at this opportunity to decide for himself—with God's guidance, of course. He folded his napkin and stretched luxuriously.

"Well, the first thing I must think about is a summer job and the next is where to find Fred Kane, so I can join his team for another season of baseball." He grinned at his grandmother. "My brain has got to rest a while after all I've been cramming into it. I promise to keep all these ideas in the back of my head, though, and I'll be listening for the Lord's advice."

Within a day of returning home, Harold was again working at St. Mary's, painting and doing other odd jobs. Blossom had delayed her own return home after Southern State classes ended so she could be with him for a few days. But time was growing short, and Harold soon had to propose if he were going to do it before they separated again. With Blossom on his mind, painting the school hall floors went quickly.

One summer morning, Mr. Hauck, the caretaker, clapped him on the shoulder and suggested painting the water tower next. The old tank was streaked with lines of rust, an ugly sight on an otherwise well-kept landscape. Harold estimated the distance from the top of the tower to the ground to be about sixty feet.

"It would take a lot of paint," he said flatly.

"We have it," Mr. Hauck assured him.

Armed with the heavy paint can and a brush, Harold ascended the water tower, becoming increasingly conscious of the height. Gritting his teeth, he managed to climb to the platform on which the tank rested, but there the steel ladder ended. Only spikes remained, providing precarious foot and hand holds. Harold froze. Going up was impossible, and now going down felt equally so.

"Something wrong up there?" Mr. Hauck's voice drifted up from far below.

Harold tried to laugh and clung to his perch, trembling.

"It's all right," the caretaker's distant voice continued. "You're okay. Keep your eyes on the tank. Don't look down."

Hauck's voice, strong and confident, coaxed and guided Harold back down to the ground. Knees buckling, he sat down on the grass and closed his eyes until his head stopped swimming. He felt empty and bleak, an Indian failure in front of a white audience.

When Harold finally did open his eyes, he looked up into the sympathetic face of the older man. "That's okay, Hal," the caretaker chuckled. "It's good for the soul to find things we can't shine at. We'll just let the water tank go until we can find a human being with bird blood in his veins. I wouldn't touch it, I know that, so that makes two of us."

Harold shared his traumatic adventure with Blossom later that evening after a baseball game, as they strolled through the long twilight back to her room. When she looked up to laugh with him, the glow from the setting sun reflected in her eyes.

Happiness welled inside him. He burst out, "I've been doing a lot of thinking and praying. God knows I want to marry you, and God's answer when I ask him is 'yes.' Will you marry me and go to Wisconsin with me?"

Blossom slipped her arm out of his and didn't answer. A small pucker lined her forehead, and she studied the ground ahead. When she finally looked at him, he was reassured by the love in her eyes.

Her words, however, were jarring. "Someday, Harold," she said, softly, "if you still want it and God wants it. I know I'll want it, but—it's too soon. I have a lot of living to do before I can settle down. I must use my teaching certificate now that I've earned it and pay off my college debts. You know I'm just twenty-one and you are twenty-six. Let me stretch my wings a little. In two or three more years, if you still want me—ask me again."

"Of course," Harold assured her, sounding sensible but collapsing inside like an old house in a tornado. Waiting for the tumult to quiet a little, he repeated, "Two or three years?"

She nodded and added firmly, "As long as it takes to get either of us settled in a career."

They strolled on in silence, taking the roundabout route that led at last to the dormitory where she had been living among boxes of books and a half-packed trunk. Before Harold could open the door for her, she turned impulsively and clung to him, head on his chest. "I do love you, Harold." The muffled words were barely audible. Blossom then abruptly released him and darted inside.

A few days after Blossom's departure, a letter from Bishop Roberts arrived. The bishop invited Harold to attend a five-day conference on ministry in Sioux Falls in early July. One of the speakers would be Dean Frederick Grant of Seabury Western Seminary in Evanston, Illinois. Grandmother tried hard not to show her excitement, but Harold knew that she wanted him to go to the conference, and there really was nothing to prevent him from doing so.

Harold's choice of a career had grown cloudy once more. He had received a second offer to teach, at the HeDog Day School, and before July was over he had to make a final decision. When he coldly considered the possibility of three more years of study versus an immediate teaching job, the scale tipped toward becoming a teacher. On the other hand, he owed his life to people who loved the church. Blossom's own choice had cleared the way for taking either path.

Harold attended the conference in Sioux Falls and learned a great deal about the ordained ministry. For the first time he considered the career with some real interest. Dean Grant invited him to come to Seabury Western Seminary on a scholarship, contingent on Harold writing an acceptable thesis on the Old Testament for the seminary faculty. Harold was familiar with the Old Testament, but he had no scholarly knowledge and little clear understanding of much of it. He struggled but managed to write the thesis.

July 15 was the deadline for deciding about teaching at the HeDog and Lac du Flambeau schools. He had received no word about the seminary's reception of his thesis. Grandmother knew a decision had to be reached that day, but she said nothing as she served breakfast.

Harold Jones made his way slowly to the telegraph office that July afternoon, praying while he walked. The young man raised by William and Rebecca Holmes was unsure what message he would send and what spiritual message he would receive. Years of testing, resolution, and faith trailed behind him on that walk. By the time the telegraph office came into view, Harold knew that he would refuse both teaching positions and wait for Dean Grant's answer.

In August of 1935, Harold learned that the Diocese of Minnesota had awarded him a scholarship to Seabury Western Seminary.

6

DAYS OF LEARNING

1935–1937

A husky young Indian, face and hands dark from a summer's work under the South Dakota sun, set down his battered suitcase in front of the gates of Seabury Western Seminary in Evanston, Illinois. Stone buildings rose before him in a quadrangle, set about with imposing elms and surrounded by lawns, clipped and very green. It was September 1935, and Harold Jones was suddenly conscious of the prairie dust on his trousers and new shoes. South Dakota still clung to him, and he felt wrinkled and uncomfortable.

Here he was, a twenty-six-year-old Dakota man and probably the only Indian in this place. How would he fare here? Harold recalled his first experience away from the reservation, attending the white school in Springfield and facing the bitter realities of discrimination. It had been better in the two South Dakota colleges, although there always lurked the shadow of condescension. Would it be different here in a Christian institution? His experience in white churches and among white church people in South Dakota unfortunately had not been altogether encouraging.

Only two other students had arrived at the seminary ahead of Harold. One was a senior, Alex Wood, the other, Vernon "Buck" Jones, a first-year man like himself. Buck's grin and warmth thawed Harold's reserve. He sensed that the other Jones was not yet accustomed to the seminary atmosphere either, and out of their shared uneasiness sprang camaraderie.

The next day the two Joneses set off to explore the Chicago Loop. The roar of traffic, subways, and trains were not new to Buck, but Harold was entranced. Tall buildings with many windows flashed in the sunlight. Cars spewing noxious fumes continuously streamed up and down the streets. Hardened black steel rails held the weight of massive train wheels rolling across them.

By the next afternoon, Seabury Western had come alive with seminarians returning or arriving for the first time. Alex Wood, the senior who had greeted him, became Harold's roommate. A heap of belongings on the third bed was the property of another roommate, Herbert Jerauld.

While Alex settled into the room, Harold sat outside on a bench under a tall elm, unobtrusively watching the coming and going of his future classmates. One student was from South America, another from Japan. Back slapping and hand shaking signaled seniors and middlers, third- and second-year students. As he watched and quietly listened, the sun filtering through the branches warmed and made him drowsy.

"Hey, Jones! I've been looking all over for you." Buck's sharp call from across the lawn startled Harold. Buck gestured to a young man with him. "Here's another junior, just arrived from the Dakotas. I thought you two should get together." The new seminarian, Chilton Powell, was from Devil's Lake, North Dakota. Harold was drawn to Chilton immediately. There was no need for wariness or unnatural pleasantries in the company of this man, and conversation came easily.

Before the afternoon was over, Chilton and Harold ventured to the shores of Lake Michigan, an easy walk from campus. They stood in the lakeside wind—except for the dampness, so much like the winds of home—shouting questions and answers to one another. On their way back to the dorm, Chilton spied a piano in the campus lounge. Harold listened as his new friend wandered from tune to tune until the dinner bell rang.

Seminary classes were smaller than college classes at Northern State. The entire junior (first-year) class numbered twelve, and a few of the class sessions became like family gatherings. Sometimes a professor would come down from his platform to join a circle with the three or four students in the class.

The students were not the mature, spiritual beings Harold had pictured seminarians to be nor were the sophisticated urban dwellers among them any more intelligent than he was. Yet he still felt wary of his classmates.

Since his high school days in Springfield, Harold had learned to respect the weapon of a white person: a warm smile but a sharp tongue that could wound carelessly and unintentionally. Harold felt he could never completely overcome his distrust of white groups. Even when the majority welcomed him, there were always one or two people whose words belied their friendly looks. It seemed easier to spend time with books rather than to mingle with classmates. In the meantime, his classmates were losing no time forging friendships. After the first week, they were greeting each other with easy warmth, stopping to talk as they waited for mail, stood outside the dining room at meal times, or passed on the dormitory stairs. Harold's stiffness made them uncomfortable, he suspected, and fellow seminarians would pass him with a nod or grunt or would not meet his eyes.

One Saturday evening in early September of 1935, Harold sat at his desk, idly thumbing through the pages of a new book on church history. The early fathers should have been good company, but bursts of laughter from a room three doors down the hall piqued his curiosity and added to his loneliness. Sighing, he got up abruptly, drawn to the commotion. The room down the hall was often bustling with students, but on this night it looked as if half the seminary had decided to visit. Harold approached the room tentatively. The host was nearing the punch line of a tale, his voice so soft that Harold moved quietly to stand at the edge of the doorframe. Before he could catch the gist, the story ended and another burst of laughter rang out.

To Harold's horror, all eyes suddenly turned toward him. "Hey, there, Harold Jones," someone suddenly called out. "Stop being a cigar-store Indian. Come on in!" Another burst of merriment—at his expense, but so good-natured that he had to join the laughter. Hands reached out to motion him inside. Harold became part of the crowd, surrounded by new friends.

❧ + ❧

The first-year seminarians were advised to attend churches of differing faiths on Sundays to acquaint themselves with a range of ministries and types of worship. When Harold complied, he was asked repeatedly to speak to different groups in Chicago who wanted to hear about his experiences as an Indian person. He was unprepared for such sympathy and interest. When he first told a white audience about growing up on the reservation, they listened respectfully, smiled or frowned appreciatively, and clapped loudly at the end of the simple recitation.

A Chicago Native organization called Indian Council Fire assisted him in his public presentations. Two members of the group came to the seminary soon after he arrived and invited him to attend their meetings. Membership was open to Indians of all tribes and to anyone who had a special interest in the welfare of Indian peoples.

One of the services offered by the Council Fire was supplying whatever Indian costumes feather headdress, beaded moccasins—a white audience would expect from Indian lecturers and performers. Harold questioned the need to wear such garb. Wearing "traditional" ceremonial Indian costumes for events designed to educate and entertain others clearly reinforced nostalgic, stereotypical views of Indians. Despite the Council Fire's good intentions, the garb threatened to separate Harold and other Native peoples from a sympathetic white audience. Yet despite these concerns, Harold needed the money desperately; his scholarship barely paid for tuition and books, so he accepted the speaking engagements when he could.

One Sunday morning in late fall, Harold set out to speak at a Methodist church. He took the El, then, with map in hand, walked a mile through city streets flanked by rows of wooden steps leading up to small porches and gray doors closed against the cold wind. He arrived half an hour early and took time to read the sign board in the churchyard. The clergyman's name and address were there as well as the date and times of the services. In large capital letters below was another announcement:

COME AND SEE A LIVE INDIAN

Harold read it again.

COME AND SEE A LIVE INDIAN

"I am it," he muttered. "The public is urged to come and stare at me." Rage flared, and he stood trembling until it turned into indignation.

COME AND SEE A LIVE INDIAN

After a third reading, a strong impulse to laugh seized Harold. "I'll bet they'd be disappointed to learn I have a white grandmother," he thought ruefully.

Harold pondered how to meet this challenge. The prepared talk by A LIVE INDIAN was surely going to disappoint his audience. It was based on a conventional, Biblical text, and he had polished it carefully, ensuring he would make no grammatical errors. Harold had arrived at the seminary with a hard-won conviction that the children of God are one. Now he was being asked to parade his differences.

He opened the church door and walked down the carpeted aisle to the chancel, where three ornate chairs upholstered in rust velvet stood in the center in full view of the congregation. It was quiet, the only voices distant beyond a door to the left of the steps.

Harold followed the sound and entered a hallway leading to what he guessed to be the Sunday school rooms. A young woman was busily tacking up pictures drawn by her primary class, while four of the children stood watching. All the pictures were of Indians wearing feathers, carrying tomahawks, riding horses, or advancing to meet armies of white soldiers.

Two men were sitting and conversing in a corner of the room. Both rose when they saw Harold. The older of the two, the minister, held out his hand in welcome. "You must be the young man from the seminary," he said. Giving Harold an appraising look, he continued, "You're a fine young fellow. I don't suppose you brought any moccasins or headdresses from home or bows and arrows for the children to see? They may find it hard to believe you're a Sioux Indian in that good-looking business suit."

A LIVE INDIAN. Harold shook his head and smiled. "Those things belong to our past, just as derby hats and hoop skirts belong to yours," he explained patiently. "My native costume these days is a pair of overalls and a work shirt, but for a city church I've put on my Sunday best."

The minister nodded, not completely understanding. Together they walked back to the hall, where Harold hung his coat and took notes from his pocket. "We will divide our offering three ways this morning," the minister explained. "You will have a third to send to your people, we will send another third to our missionaries in Africa, and a third will stay here for the support of the parish. We'd be obliged if you would say an Indian prayer over the plate offering. We are planning on hearing some words from you after the offering is received." He handed a bulletin to Harold and left to attend to final details before the service began. Harold stood as unobtrusively as possible beside the hall door and watched the congregation arrive.

The moment came to join the two others in the chancel. Once seated, Harold felt more relaxed; the many faces in front of him became friendly and interested. He recognized and could sing most of the hymns and listened to the sermon with interest. Apart from any lesson he learned, it was his seminary assignment to listen with a critical ear. The minister spoke with fervor, his voice alternately rising to a shout and dying to a whisper. He used the pulpit rail to pound out his points. The congregation did not quail but watched and listened respectfully. To Harold's surprise, amens occasionally erupted from one corner and then another.

When the sermon ended, the congregation quietly waited as the minister remained in the pulpit. "My dear friends," he said dramatically. "We have with us today a poor Indian from a reservation. He has come to our city to study in the seminary and take back the word of God to his people. His people suffer from dire poverty—deprived of the good things in life that you and I take for granted. Let us be generous today in our offerings to help the people of this, our poor Indian brother."

Harold was the center of attention, and he felt like an impostor. Poor some of his friends and family might be in comparison with many Chicagoans, but they were richer by far in so many ways that these people would not understand. His prepared speech now seemed irrelevant, and he crumpled the notes. While the offering was being taken, the organ played softly, then swelled triumphantly into the "Indian Love Call." When the clergyman turned to Harold for an "Indian prayer," Harold couldn't find his voice for the joyful song he had planned, the doxology sung in the Santee tongue. All he could do was to bow his head and say it in a voice that sounded gruff and unfamiliar.

He was thankful that the long sermon had left little time for his speech. What to say? Harold stood up and took a moment to collect his thoughts, aware that this action might be interpreted as a poor Indian trying to remember the right English words. Harold thanked the congregation for wanting to help his people, another branch of the human race. Then he recounted the coming of Bishop Whipple to the Minnesota prison camp at Fort Ridgely and of the hardships the young white clergyman, Samuel Hinman, had suffered with his Indian brothers. As politely as he could, he countered the minister's introductory remarks by explaining that Christianity had been received by his people almost a century ago and that he had come to the seminary to prepare to carry on the tradition of his own grandfather and other Indian priests. He thanked his white friends for sharing the gospel, the greatest gift they possessed, and invited them to visit his homeland, the reservation, on their next trip west.

Had they really heard what he said? He sensed they were deeply entrenched in their own ideas of cultural difference, but they did clap politely as he sat down.

No potluck was served after the service, and no one offered to take Harold home for Sunday dinner. The treasurer carefully divided the offering into three small piles and handed Harold $12.35 for "his people."

Harold dutifully sent the $12.35 to Bishop Roberts.

❧ + ❧

Seminary life soon fell into a comfortable, distinct pattern. The first-year seminarians were assigned unpaid jobs of varying kinds. Harold was given dining room and kitchen duty, bussing tables and helping to wash and put away dishes. The job was dignified by the wearing of a white coat. Thus Harold had to rise early to set tables for breakfast and to clear and wash dishes before the morning chapel services. Classes followed, then study in the library or at his desk. He recognized great minds among both faculty and students and welcomed the effort to meet the challenges they offered.

There was, however, an unsettling, troubling side to this world. Differences of personality, perspective, and ideas threatened to fracture the small and intimate group of men in the seminary and sometimes erupted in genuine fights. There were professors whose minds Harold admired but whose discipline and curtness outside the classroom seemed harsh and unnecessary. The firmness of his grandfather and the strong, gentle guidance of his grandmother had been difficult for Kenny and Harold at times, but the severity of the seminary's punishments for minor offenses (missing chapel services or being a day or two late in handing in a paper) seemed downright autocratic. Only once did Harold receive a tongue-lashing for missing chapel more than the three allowable times in one semester.

Diversions from study included sports and dances. Harold joined the "Wild Flowers," a team formed under the voluntary leadership of Dick Emery, an upper classman. Dick exercised his team mercilessly, until they were in condition to play baseball, football, and basketball against some of the intramural teams at nearby Northwestern University. Occasional dances given by sororities at Northwestern University seemed promising, though the juniors were warned that sorority women were not really interested in poor future ministers. Harold suspected, though, that age difference was also a factor. The Northwestern women were barely out of their teens, and he was nearly twenty-seven. Nurses and student nurses from Evanston Hospital, however, welcomed Seabury Western students with particular warmth. Harold and his friend, Chilton Powell, went together to test the sincerity of their invitation to the winter prom sponsored by the Nurse's Association. It was a happy evening, and his Native heritage didn't seem to matter to the white students.

After months of work, Harold was pleasantly surprised to discover that, if he studied hard and steadily, he could keep up with his class work. This success emboldened him. When he had first entered seminary, the dean had advised him against taking Greek. Bishop Roberts, the bishop of South Dakota, had felt it unnecessary for Harold to spend time learning a language that had once been required for all seminarians but from which he could now be excused for good cause. Harold discovered he was considered a "special circumstance." His native tongue had no relationship to Greek, and some faculty doubted that he would find it useful after graduation. Harold gratefully complied during the first semester, but by spring, when his grades were proving satisfactory, he decided to ask for Greek too.

The dean was doubtful. "If you take it and fail," he warned, "you realize this will bring down your average. It's legitimate to be excused from

Greek, you know. You probably will never be called on to be a seminary professor. Most other clergy, once they leave seminary, find they are too busy to keep up their practice of reading Greek, and they soon forget it."

Harold nodded in agreement but insisted. "I still want to fulfill that requirement. I don't want any exceptions made for me."

Harold added Greek to his courses in the spring semester. Greek was like nothing he had ever studied, and he found it very difficult. With no background in classical history and culture, he was unfamiliar with the concepts behind the words and the clues they might have provided to the new vocabulary. Harold refused to give up, however, and poured over the assignments with dogged and often draining determination.

❧ ✝ ❧

With surprising speed, the Illinois spring became summer, and the elms were in full leaf. During the journey home on the train, Harold sat quietly, looking out the window and thinking. The Harold Jones of nine months ago had been an inexperienced child in many ways. His grandmother and he had envisioned the seminary as a place of continual peace and sanctity. They had been wrong about almost everything.

It had taken determination to leave the security of the reservation and the company of his people. Happily, instead of rejection Harold had found—for the most part—warm acceptance. His decision to return to the seminary in the fall was his own.

❧ ✝ ❧

His second year at the seminary was energized and replete with surprises, not all of them pleasant. Only six of the original twelve who had entered Seabury Western Seminary in 1935 came back to begin the middler year. Both of Harold's roommates had graduated, and he now shared a room with Raymond Paulson from Iowa and Edward Harrison from Georgia. He missed his old friends but settled in comfortably with the new men.

Harold had even less time for study because the seminary appointed him to supervise the student work detail. This responsibility was always on his mind. He needed to be available at any hour to meet emergencies or to attend to the forgetfulness of those he assigned kitchen or housekeeping duties.

Harold continued to receive many requests from the Indian Council Fire of Chicago for various speaking and singing engagements, with the obligatory "traditional" Indian attire. Chilton Powell, likewise receptive to all job possibilities, was his accompanist. It became an adventure to start off with a suitcase full of feathers and musical scores, find the way to an unfamiliar address, and sing to an unknown audience. Sometimes their destination was a woman's club or a Kiwanis or Rotary gathering or, from time to time, a nightclub. Each occasion brought a small remuneration, which both seminarians needed. Chilton and Harold avoided Saturday evening performances, since they had agreed to serve as assistants and sing in the choir at Christ Church in Highland Park on Sundays.

Christ Church was large, with a wealthier than average congregation. The ushers wore morning coats, and the ladies and gentlemen were "well turned out," as the phrase had been in Springfield. Harold forgot these differences once the music began and the choir marched down the long aisle to the chancel. The choir director, Andrew Enshutes, worked his choir hard and with good results.

Since the seminary served no Sunday dinner or supper, the rector of Christ Church, Christoph Keller, and his wife often invited Chilton and Harold to join them for family dinner. The two Keller children soon overcame their shyness around the two strangers. Harold found it easy to accept the shy, admiring glances of the Kellers' teenage daughter and the boisterous enthusiasm of their young son, who would crawl on his lap after dinner and demand a war whoop or a song to the accompaniment of his toy drum. Sometimes there would be other guests at the Kellers' table—such as General Wood, President of Sears Roebuck and Company, and his wife and the Randolfs—who in turn would invite the seminarians to their homes.

Despite the wealth of their hosts and hostesses, Harold and Chilton found their company less formidable then the table settings. Poverty, as Harold had known for a long time, did not make saints of all who were poor. By the same token, he learned that great wealth did not make self-centered tycoons of all who were rich. Harold felt that the reaching out of wealthy families to poor seminarians (including one Indian) was not a patronizing act but one of genuine interest and friendship.

✖+✖

The seminary also emphasized the importance of knowing people from all parts of society. The professor of Social Relations gave his class an assignment: "In order to become a well-rounded clergyman, it is important to mingle with all segments of society. Make the slums your home; take a stroll along the wealthier sections of the town; go down to the waterfront, and don't ignore the back alleys—but be careful!" Harold saved the assignment for Saturdays. He would put on an old windbreaker and work pants with the paint marks from St. Mary's School, carefully placing a folded dollar bill in his shirt pocket with a button-down flap and taking along a few coins for fare money. Although it was more companionable and safer to go with another student, he enjoyed the greater freedom of exploration alone.

One afternoon in a poorer section of Chicago, Harold could feel the covert stares of young men and women as they sat on doorsteps or leaned against the storefronts. "They're trying to figure out my race," he told himself. But they didn't approach, and he continued to stroll down streets, stopping at last outside a restaurant advertising corn dogs to listen to the raucous sound of the jukebox and the shouts and laughter of the crowd inside.

Later that evening, as a chill wind brought the first patter of sleet to the Chicago backstreets, he stepped into the front hall of an old apartment building to get warm before returning to the elevated station. A wave of smells and sounds of many suppers, wet babies, and perspiring adults greeted him like an unexpected slap. The sound of a door slamming echoed down the hallway, followed by a sudden stillness. Harold stood quietly, absorbing warmth and odors until, gradually, sounds resumed behind the closed doors. A baby cried; a man cursed a woman, who answered him plaintively; someone turned up a radio, switching dials until a blues singer drowned out all other sounds.

The experience gave Harold a strange feeling of kinship with the apartment dwellers. Reservation people aren't the only ones who can act like prairie dogs, he thought. In the heart of the city, as in closely packed burrows, all activity stops at a suspicious sound.

❧ + ❧

One Friday evening Harold was studying at a library table with a Chinese student who was doing graduate work at the seminary. The two were drawn to each other, sharing the experience of being minorities among white students. Chin came from an ancient civilization whose customs were in some respects like those of Harold's people and in others very different.

The library was empty of students except for the two of them. Chin tapped the table gently and said, "Harold, you know downtown Chicago night spots. Before I go back to China, I would like to see some. Will you go with me?"

Harold was taken aback. His usual forays into Chicago were not the kind Chin meant, he felt sure. The evening was dull, however, so he agreed, albeit reluctantly.

Chin was in high spirits, but Harold was dubious. He had avoided the dizzying neon-lit section of downtown Chicago, crammed with bustling dance halls, bars with swinging doors, and nervous, blinking signs.

Harold chose an establishment with a seemingly discreet sign and soft light, advertising a floorshow. A bowing waiter seated them at a small round table on the edge of darkness, ringing a circle of white light within which danced heavily painted, scantily costumed women. Arms waved, hips swayed, and eager smiles fixed sightlessly on the darkness where the audience sat and watched.

Harold had never seen such a performance. He was repulsed at first— Dakota women were modest in their dress, preferring to melt in the hot sun rather than to expose themselves to weather or men. Next came scientific detachment. How did the dancing women manage to keep the shreds they wore from falling off entirely? How did all of them get their eyes to look so deep blue? They kicked precisely. He wondered if they practiced the same kind of exercises that he used in football. His mind next wandered to the Old Testament studies of Baal worship and temple prostitution and then to the story of Salome and John the Baptist. In comparison to the expert sensuousness of Salome, the dancing women, try as they might, could only mimic seductiveness. Harold chuckled at the incongruity, and Chin agreeably joined in, not knowing the reason. The circle of light then slid over to include their table, and the dancer on the end flashed a wider than required smile in their direction. Embarrassment swept Harold, and he studied his drink until a protective darkness closed over him again.

Chin seemed more at ease in this atmosphere but at last he motioned politely to Harold that he was ready to go. The evening, however, was not over. Chin held up his arm to see his watch in the night club's flashing lights. "Ah, my friend, shall we try some dance hall?"

When the two seminarians reached the foot of a set of long stairs to "Mazy's Dance Parlor," Chin suddenly grew thoughtful. "I would rather you look it over first for us" he demurred. "I will wait for you here." Puzzled—anybody who could enjoy a floorshow would hardly feel squeamish about a tame dance floor—Harold climbed to the top of the stairs, where the cheerful thump of a drum accented a lively fox trot.

The ticket seller nodded pleasantly. "How many tickets?"

Harold motioned downstairs and said "Just two to begin with, one for my friend Chin and one for me."

The man hesitated, then leaned around the corner for a view of Chin, standing in the light of the open door.

"Sorry, young man," he said, shaking his head, "We don't allow Chinamen in here. You can come. Indians are welcome, but we draw the line on Chinks."

"But," Harold stammered, "he's in seminary and is a graduate student."

"He's a Chink, isn't he?" the man retorted. "Come if you want, but he'll have to wait outside."

Harold turned and walked slowly down the stairs. "They don't want any more customers now," he explained to Chin, his voice husky and hollow sounding. "They'll be closing up after this dance."

"I see." Chin's smile was serene. "I have done enough for one night's spree."

I think he does see, thought Harold. Indians were not at the bottom of the social pile after all.

❧ + ❧

Harold was still shaken by this racist incident when two days later a student stormed into his room after dinner. "Hal," he thundered. "I hold you responsible for telling the kitchen help, especially that forward colored woman, that seminarians are not to be addressed by their first names! As director of student help, it's up to you!"

The student was normally a polite Southerner, who was also a friend. Harold felt the blood rushing to his face. "I don't know any forward colored woman in the kitchen," he said as calmly as he could.

"That's just the trouble," the student snapped, "Darkies come north, and you spoil them. I'll not be demeaned in this way. Either you speak to her or find me another job that keeps me away from her." He stalked past Harold and walked away stiffly.

Harold talked the incident over with Chilton that evening as they set off for choir practice. His friend shook his head. "Add that to your prayer list," he advised. "You can't change a Southerner's outlook in a year's time. Just keep him away from the woman for her sake. You can switch him over to my janitor's job," he added brightly. "I'll be glad to wash dishes with Lillian."

The problem continued to bother Harold, and he prayed about it. What was the use of education for ministry if it didn't alter an attitude that was unjust and racist? It seemed possible to be a top student in theology without humility and commitment, without involving one's heart or probing too deeply into one's motivation. Harold wondered how his grandfather would have dealt with this situation.

❧ + ❧

The days passed quickly, too quickly—days full of studies, football, basketball, baseball, swimming, or music. Harold benefited from compulsory singing soirees taught by Madam Normalli, the sole woman professor at Seabury Western. Madam was an American, but she had married a Swedish count. From her years spent in Sweden, absorbing her husband's culture, she had picked up not only a slight accent but also an animated, almost vehement manner, which some of Harold's classmates liked to mimic. Harold admired her enthusiasm for all things musical. Madam was convinced that everyone had some musical ability, and she worked long and hard to bring it forth.

Harold recalled the shock he felt the time when Madam reached for his hand and placed it just below her heart. She commanded him to "feel here while I breathe hard from my diaphragm." Flushed, Harold obligingly "felt" and became overwhelmingly aware of a warm roll of flesh, corseted firmly in place. He attempted to concentrate on the vibrations that accompanied the rich, deep tones of Madam Normalli's voice.

Madam Normalli's professional interest in voice showed Harold a new dimension to singing. Perfection in tone quality, pitch, and range could and should be given attention and improved. Harold worked with a kind of earnestness that not only pleased Madam Normalli but also stimulated his own interest.

Madam gave no examinations; instead, she held an annual concert attended by the neighboring faculty of Northwestern University and a goodly number of Chicago and Evanston dignitaries. She dangled the prospect of the concert before students during the first sessions of her classes. Some years for her were triumphal ones, when the seminarians boasted a number of melodious voices. But some years were lean, and it was her opinion that Harold's class was one of these meager years. Consequently, when the concert night arrived during Harold's middler year and the auditorium filled with formally dressed ladies and gentlemen, his name was on the program as a soloist. He did his best, and Madam Normalli was pleased.

The concert bore fruit in the form of invitations to the opera and the Chicago Symphony from members of the audience. The opera La Bohème disconcerted Harold—so many vehement voices "singing from the diaphragm" with such earnestness in an unknown tongue! And it was all about a ridiculous situation that could have been avoided. Hearing the Chicago Symphony was, however, a rapturous experience, transporting him from the first sharp violin strokes through the blending of drums, horns, and strings. Closing his eyes, Harold let the world fade around him as he was absorbed in the beauty of the sound.

❧ + ❧

A very busy school year spun out another spring, with its promises and challenges. The ice along the lakeshores melted into buttercups and cornflowers, yet the icy pallor of exams threatened to freeze students' hearts. For Harold, none of the exams would be easy—Christian Doctrine, Church History, Old Testament Studies, and especially Greek. He had little time to prepare for the oral exam in Homiletics, but thanks to kindly, retired Bishop McElwain, who was professor, he was allowed to preach a sermon in the Dakota language, using the Yankton dialect. Harold's experience with the Yankton dialect came only from years at St. Elizabeth's, so in the sermon he combined it with the Santee dialect, which he knew fluently.

When Harold entered the chapel to preach the Dakota sermon, Bishop McElwain was already sitting in a pew. Harold climbed into the pulpit and sent his impassioned message over the empty pews toward the small white face, barely visible among the shadows. A sudden flash of light from the bishop's spectacles acknowledged that he was listening. Enjoying the sounds of the Dakota language, Harold spoke eloquently. No sound came from the far shadows after he finished and made his way down the aisle. Harold felt good about the delivery, and in this case he obviously had no need to worry about content.

Yet Bishop McElwain was frowning down at a paper in his hand. For a few seconds he did not look up. When he did, he looked half amused, half exasperated. "That" he burst out, "was the worst Yanktonai sermon I have ever heard. It was half Santee. No bona fide Yankton could make any sense out of it!" At Harold's shocked expression, he chuckled. "I know your background, Jones. You're a Santee. But there's no telling where your bishop may send you. Better practice up on some of the other dialects." The bishop rose and nodded as he disappeared outside the church door. Stunned and chagrined, Harold sat down in a pew. He then remembered that the bishop had once been a missionary to the Dakota Indians.

Harold passed the other exams satisfactorily, though not brilliantly. Adding to the joy of completing examinations was the news that he had been elected class president for the senior year.

But dark clouds were gathering on the horizon. While Harold was packing to leave, a message came from the office that Dean Grant wanted to see him. The dean greeted Harold cordially, shook his hand, and congratulated him on the election. "You have made a commendable record over the past two years," he remarked, "and the fact that you were elected president demonstrates your ability to get along with your classmates." He then frowned. "Sit down, Harold, there is something unpleasant that I must show you."

He reached for an envelope on his desk, opened it, and handed him a letter and clipping. The clipping was a romanticized, overplayed article bearing the headline "First Indian to Enter Seabury Western Seminary Becomes Senior Class President." The story had been picked up by an AP reporter, and the clipping in his hand had been cut out of the *Sioux Falls Argus-Leader*.

The letter, addressed to Dean Grant, came from the Board of Examining Chaplains of South Dakota. The tone was unmistakably critical, as Harold would long remember. "We do not approve of the way the seminary has pampered Harold Jones. The publicity he has received is distasteful and can only have the affect of spoiling him. So much notoriety given to a young man from his poor, reservation background can do him no good. In order to satisfy ourselves that his time has not been wasted totally, we intend to give him the canonical examinations sometime this summer after he returns to South Dakota. We would appreciate your apprising him of this."

Harold turned to the dean in disbelief. "They haven't seen me nor written to me nor talked to me for two years. How can they say that I'm spoiled?"

"Only supposition," the dean admitted, "but I thought you had better be warned."

"Can they give me my final canonical exams before I finish seminary?"

"They can do anything they choose. Do the best you can. That is all you can do."

It took time and some mental and emotional readjustment for Harold Jones to come to terms with the latest turn of events. He was accustomed to racist attitudes and actions from some whites, but he had hoped those chosen to be examining chaplains in South Dakota would be above such things. How many more unpleasant surprises awaited him in this church he loved?

7

TRIALS

⚜ + ⚜
_____

1937–1938

The dry, swirling South Dakota wind was an invigorating shock. Cotton-woods were already sending out their gift of summer snow across the hot landscape. Hawks circled lazily in the pale blue sky, ready to pounce at any moment upon an unwary hare. Groups of people, some in rancher's hats and jeans, some in city dress, waited on the train station platform. Grand-mother was there—almost hidden by a party of girls clustered around her, eager and excited to be leaving St. Mary's for home and summer vacation. She waved, her small hand barely visible over their heads. With the first good laugh he'd had since reading the letter in the dean's office, Harold swept her off her feet in a hug to the glee of the girls, who squealed and spun around in a way he had almost forgotten.

It was good to be home. In another week Blossom arrived, fresh from her teaching year at Pine Ridge. She had done well, and the Bureau of Indian Affairs (BIA) had offered her a summer job at twice the fifty-dollar-a-month salary. She refused it regretfully in favor of returning for the summer session at Southern State in Springfield, nearer to Harold.

Duty soon called Harold, however, in the voice of Bishop Roberts. He asked Harold to spend the summer at Pine Ridge, again helping Sister An-nie Horner and Frank Thornburn, a new graduate of General Theological Seminary. Frank had grown up in Indian country and planned to devote his ministry to the Dakota people. Harold reluctantly consented.

Sister Horner proved to be the same loving, giving soul he had come to know during the summer at Fort Thompson, only a little more worn. The summer of 1937 passed quickly, this time more full of pastoral calling and preaching than of baseball tournaments and campfires. There was little time for serious study.

One Sunday afternoon after service, Harold set out on a long walk to Rockyford, where Blossom's family lived. He was lonely without her and wanted to meet the Steele family. It was a long, tiring journey. The sun poured down, and no relief could be found in shadows. The hot wind blew the perspiration off his face as soon as it formed, and Harold grew very thirsty. Hiking along the long, rutted road that hot afternoon, he began to feel foolish. What if no one was home? And what if he became too exhausted to even get to Rockyford, a scenario that seemed increasingly likely?

Two ounces of warm water remained in the canteen at his belt when Harold finally glimpsed the scattered rooftops of Rockyford. Remembering Blossom's description of her home, he sought and found "a house not far from the main road as you turn down the street into the village," with a large cottonwood in the backyard. A man was sitting on the front steps, enjoying the breeze.

"Mr. Steele?" Harold asked.

"That's right, young fellow, and who are you?"

"My name is Harold Jones."

A moment of silent reflection followed, and then the older man smiled broadly. "Harold Jones! Well, it's about time we met! I'm Blossom's father." He turned and called through the screen door. "Ma! Come on out and meet this young man here!" Before Mrs. Steele could respond, Blossom's sister Gladys, now a lovely young woman, rushed through the door and threw her arms around him. How long it had been since they had teased one another in the laundry room at St. Mary's! Blossom's mother and two of her brothers added their welcome, and by the time the evening ended, Harold felt a strong bond of affection for all of the Steeles.

The family wouldn't hear of his hiking back that night and made him a comfortable bed on the couch in the front room. He slept soundly until awakened by the sun in his eyes and the smell of coffee and fry bread. After breakfast, Blossom's mother filled his canteen with fresh water and his pockets with two large sandwiches wrapped in paper napkins for the long walk back to Pine Ridge. Twice more that summer Harold repeated the journey.

❦ + ❦

On August 15, Harold received the awaited summons to appear before the examining chaplains on August 20. At their convenience, he would be tested orally over the following days to determine his readiness for ordination as a deacon in the Episcopal Church. The exams would take place during the annual District Convocation meeting in Huron, South Dakota.

The summer had been busy enough to take the edge off the allegations of his being spoiled by the seminary. The summons reopened that wound, and the unfairness of the examining chaplains ate at Harold. He tried to reason with himself; he tried prayerful meditation; he even tried to open his books and concentrate on a bit of Greek. Nothing worked. The injustice of the situation threatened to consume him.

Harold had to marvel at his grandmother's equanimity. He wanted her, who had prayed so constantly that he be led into the ministry, to be angry, but she wasn't. Her only words on the matter were: "This is a testing. It is your hardest so far, but you will have many all through your ministry. I know you can take it."

He struggled to understand and to cope. Grandmother's words kept returning; old memories and bits of conversation with Grandfather also came to mind. Both grandparents had deep lines in their faces that spoke of hardships, even if their lips never mentioned them. The tale Grandmother told of her marriage had sounded exciting and adventurous to his ears as a little boy, but now he was beginning to really understand the hurt and injustice underlying her family disowning her. Her equanimity had been tested, proven, and forged by fire. Harold would certainly not err by following her example. If he could not directly deal with his frustration and anger, then he could choose to ignore both until the heat of the moment had passed.

The testing was academically and psychologically stressful and even harder than Harold expected. His examiners were busy attending the convention during the day; when one of them found a few minutes after lunch or in the evening, Harold would be summoned to meet with him in an unoccupied parlor, bedroom, or empty dining hall. He was not always told which subject he was to be tested on until his arrival at the appointed place. More than two months of summer had passed since his seminary classes. Specifics of Church History had faded from memory and Greek—hard at best to decipher during class—now appeared to be hopelessly forgotten. He believed he might fare better in Theology and Philosophy of Christian Thought, perhaps even in Liturgy. Harold hoped that these subjects and a compassionate examiner would enable him to pass.

On the second evening of the convention, Harold was tapped on the shoulder as he picked up a supper tray. It was Father Barbour, an old friend of his grandfather and grandmother. The priest looked almost austere, with a white collar shining against a black suit. "I'll meet you in the front parlor after supper, Jones." The voice was curt, speaking with the authority of the Reverend Dr. Paul Barbour, whose reputation as a historian had spread beyond South Dakota.

Reaching the parlor before his examiner, Harold stood with hands in pockets, his thoughts skipping and scattering across a jumble of dates and names.

"Sit down, Jones." The voice was crisp but not unfriendly. Harold sat in the chair near the window.

"No. Sit here!" barked a command, and Harold moved to a chair facing outward toward the light of the setting sun.

"Now, then," Father Barbour continued in a more relaxed voice. "My job is to find out what you've learned about Church History. Of course, everyone who seeks ordination must have a proper foundation in the history of the church; otherwise the rituals that are an important part of the services can have little meaning for the priest or his congregation. You, I, every baptized member becomes a part of history, and it behooves us to give every other part of it due consideration."

"Now, can you tell me when the first council of the church was held, and what were the issues that made it necessary?"

Harold was relieved. Those facts had been drilled into him during the first year of seminary, and he remembered them without trouble. His interrogator nodded.

At random the questions shot at him. Harold's answers were halting, and he finally confessed, "I'm sorry, sir, this summer at Pine Ridge there has been no time for study. Some of what you ask me will be included in the courses I will be taking this coming year."

"Very well, then surely you can have something to say about the Reformation."

Summer recollections flooded Harold's mind: a jumble of faces, old, young, impish, and sad; the sound of strong, hot winds blowing through the cottonwoods; the Dakota hymn sung slowly and reverently; a beer bottle flung carelessly against a rock on the side of the road, out of which surfaced at last a distant seminary classroom and the voice of Professor Tander. Harold could picture the face and hear the voice, but what was it saying about the Reformation?

"We'll try once more. Repeat for me as accurately as you can the Chalcedonian Creed and explain the circumstances that made the Council of Chalcedon necessary."

"About the year 400 A.D., there were several schools of thought about the Trinity," Harold replied. "One argued that God the Father was solely God and that Jesus was not eternally begotten but endowed with the Father's Spirit. And the Spirit—" Harold wavered. "The Spirit is the Eternal Action of the Father. On the other hand, there were some who argued that Father, Son, and Holy Ghost were coeternal. I'm sorry, sir, but I have not memorized that creed."

"The date," Father Barbour said crisply, "was 451. I'm afraid, Jones, I cannot pass you in your Church History examination. Perhaps your performance in the other examinations will be more profitable for you." He rose as the chapel bell announced the time of the evening service. Numbly, Harold followed him out the door and joined the jovial group of clergy moving toward the chapel. None gave him so much as a nod. There were no Indian faces among them.

That evening's prayers seemed distant, and beloved hymns caught in Harold's throat. The Old Testament lesson was from Isaiah, and that portion of the service alone spoke to him. At the end of the service, he went as far as the door with the rest of the men, then stopped, quietly closed the door behind them, and returned to kneel in a pew sheltered from the rays of the setting sun. Isaiah's words came back to him.

"The Spirit of the Lord God is upon me; because the Lord hath anointed me to preach good tidings unto the meek; he has sent me to bind up the broken-hearted, to proclaim liberty to the captives, and the opening of the prison to them that are bound; . . . to comfort all that mourn . . . ; to give unto them beauty for ashes, the oil of joy for mourning, the garment of praise for the spirit of heaviness." (Isaiah 61:1,3) This passage described Grandfather's vocation, and he had been instrumental in pointing Harold toward his. But Isaiah also advised, "Let the wicked forsake his way and the unrighteous man his thoughts; and let him return unto the Lord."

In the eyes of the examining chaplains, Harold abundantly needed pardoning—but why? He pressed his forehead against the pew in front of him. They were all committed men, white men who had chosen to come to the mission field, cutting off tempting possibilities to serve wealthy parishes.

It had been a shock when he had heard some of his classmates at the seminary, discussing their ambitions openly. Even the church seemed to have a pecking order—from poor to rich, from humble to powerful. But that was the opposite of what Jesus had taught.

A rush of tears filled his eyes and dropped on the wooden rail. "My God," Harold earnestly prayed, "open my eyes that I can see where I fail to please thee. Guide me into thy truth; not mine, not anybody else's, but thine."

Harold did not know how long he knelt there. Gradually, however, turbulent feelings faded away, thankfulness filled the vacuum, and once more his eyes overflowed with tears.

"For ye shall go out with joy, and be led forth with peace: the mountains and the hills shall break forth before you into singing, and all the trees of the field shall clap their hands. Instead of the thorn shall come up the fir tree, and instead of the brier shall come up the myrtle tree: and it shall be to the Lord for a name, for an everlasting sign that shall not be cut off." (Isaiah 55:12,13) The lesson that evening had ended that way, and it was a message to anyone who was hungry or thirsty. Never mind what lay ahead. God's gift, his assurance that he was with Harold, would see him through.

Harold's dismal failure of the Greek exam was not surprising. His examiner again was Father Barbour, noted among the other clergy as a gifted scholar in the Greek language. Harold did not resent him; Father Barbour explained that he was giving Harold the exact examination given to all the seminary graduates who applied for ordination to the priesthood in South Dakota.

Harold did little better at the last two confrontations. The examiners frowned at his failure, but he didn't need any special perception to sense the satisfaction that lurked just beneath the surface—the examining chaplains had justified their preconceived judgment that Harold Jones was not making use of his seminary opportunities. The scholarship aid from the neighboring Diocese of Minnesota appeared to be misspent.

He returned to the seminary the fall of 1937 with a grim warning from the examining chaplains to "study and forget the frills." A letter to Dean Grant chided the seminary again for spoiling Harold Jones.

❧ + ❧

With a will, Harold returned to the books, and the new classes went well. New duties came with the office of president of the student body; the seminary counted on him being present at parties and at social events that he had previously skipped. Fortunately, he was relieved of house chairman duties, and the assigned excursions into downtown Chicago had ended last spring.

Now that the completion of three years of seminary was imminent, Harold's yearning to see Blossom returned forcefully. Work absorbed their time and thoughts so completely that some months went by without even letter exchanges. Both of them set aside a few dollars each month—she from her small teaching salary, he from his speaking and singing engagements—so that she could come back to Chicago with him after Christmas for New Year's Eve and for two days of classes when the seminary resumed sessions. Before Harold left for home on Christmas break, he reserved a room for Blossom within easy walking distance of the campus and paid half his savings to secure it for four nights. The other half he put away for one big dinner in Chicago and the price of guest meal tickets at Seabury Western for the remainder of her visit. Blossom's visit to Chicago lived up to their expectations. They had a wonderful time, and Harold took pride and pleasure in introducing her to his fellow seminarians and professors.

After Blossom left, the weather became bleaker. A January thaw melted some of the snow, and the cold wind off Lake Michigan brought icy patches on the walks, bathed yellow-gray by the weak winter sun. It was a good time for studying, and Harold made use of every free moment to wrestle with Greek grammar and church history in preparation for the next round of testing by the examining chaplains of South Dakota.

From January through May the months passed like weeks. No day was long enough, yet it was a satisfying time. What had appeared just three years ago as a difficult goal for a poor Indian with inadequate education and no experience beyond his own environment was now almost within reach. Harold was walking the last quarter mile of his seminary journey. The professors, once energetically pushing, pulling, sometimes pummeling him along the path, now reached out to shake his hand cordially or to clap him on the shoulder. Although his own district was too poor to offer much help, the neighboring Diocese of Minnesota continued with its generous scholarship help and surprised him with what they called a "vestment award," in appreciation, they said, for his successful career in seminary. Vestments for all the church seasons arrived at Harold's room one afternoon, folded neatly in a large box. Deep red, violet, green, white, black—the stoles were all there, some of them even embroidered in gold. Underneath the stoles were a sparkling white surplice and a black cassock with small covered buttons down the front. "Like an English vicar's!" his friend Chilton Powell exclaimed enviously.

To Harold's delight, he was awarded first prize for singing and second prize for reading the service. The second prize gave him the most pleasure. Singing came naturally to him, but diction and the finer points of articulation he had worked hard to learn.

Graduation was two weeks away. After the grim experience of the previous summer, Harold felt no dread of the Seabury Western final examinations. First came the oral exam in Old Testament given by Dr. Albert. The tales once told by the Dakota peoples were startlingly like Old Testament stories; archaeological evidence and scholarly studies lent new and interesting points of view to them. The exam went well.

The exam in Homiletics, however, was interrupted by a knock on the door. Dean Grant opened the door and entered the room with a troubled expression on his face. "This is an inexcusable intrusion, but I'm afraid it's unavoidable," he said quietly. "Will you come to my office, Harold?"

They walked down the hall, neither speaking until the dean had closed the door behind them. When he reached for a letter on his desk, Harold recognized the letterhead. The dean agitatedly fanned the air with the letter as he spoke. "Harold, I owe you an apology. Unbeknown to you, I released a story to our local paper, giving a summary of your career here and listing the honors that had come to you, your election as president of the student body, the prizes you had earned. To me, it seemed a story worth sharing with the community. Once again an Associated Press reporter took it up, and it was reprinted in Minnesota and God knows where else. At any rate, your examining board in South Dakota read it, and they are upset again. They demand that you return to South Dakota to repeat their examinations before you take your seminary exams.

"Instead of a diploma, we can certainly give you a Licentiate Certificate. This certificate entitles you to preach and teach, to be ordained, and to administer the sacraments. In short, it serves just as well as an outright diploma, although it is not one. That fact should satisfy your board. Then come back, Harold, at your earliest opportunity to complete your exams, and we promise you a private ceremony if that would help. We will have that diploma waiting for you."

It had happened again. Harold thought for a moment, then shook his head. "No, sir," he said in a resigned but calm voice, "I don't think I'll ever have that diploma. When I get back to South Dakota, I'll have no money to bring me back here again, and I know what it'll be like. I'll be too busy to keep up my studies in order to pass the exams. I'm afraid, sir, that it's a closed door for me."

"I know you have studied hard," admitted the Dean, "and you could pass all your examinations without difficulty—but I have no alternative. I must comply with your board of examiners."

Though stunned and becoming irritated, Harold saw the pain in the dean's eyes. "I appreciate all you've done for me," he assured the dean. "Thanks for thinking my seminary career has been worth an article. What I came for was an education to fit me for ministry to my people. I have it now, and I will minister somehow, somewhere, in South Dakota."

After the meeting, the hallway seemed sepulchral and cold. Everyone else in the building was giving or taking exams, and Harold felt like a visitor or intruder. He stepped as quietly as possible to keep from hearing his own footsteps. Upstairs in the dorm, he didn't erupt, break down, or turn immediately to prayer. Harold Jones took down his suitcase from a shelf and began packing his belongings and books. Graduation exercises were still six days away, but for Harold the days of learning at the seminary had quietly drawn to a sad close.

❧ + ❧

Grandmother had been looking forward to the graduation exercises, and it was too late to cancel those plans. Harold spotted her among the hurrying, well-dressed figures on the station platform. She was wearing a new hat with the usual stiff little brim and black ribbon around the crown. The old, familiar suitcase that he had carried from time to time on his summer travels with the baseball team had been put to use again. It looked too heavy for Grandmother, and he ran past the advancing passengers to relieve her of it.

She dropped the suitcase and opened her arms. "Oh, Harold! How good of you to find me so quickly! I declare, I almost lost myself among all these tall people."

"Welcome, welcome, Grandmother!" His voice sounded uncommonly loud in his ears as he tried to keep it from trembling. How was he to tell her what had happened? He leaned down to tip back her hat and plant a warm kiss on her cheek.

Instead of immediately taking Grandmother to the Evanston home of old friends from Nebraska, Harold brought her to the campus to see where he had been living for the past three years and to meet his fellow seminarians.

As his friends bent to take his grandmother's hand, he was struck by the contrast between their youthful strength and freshness and her care-worn fragility. She had aged noticeably during the past year. Grandmother was thinner, and the shoulders that carried burdens over many years were stooped. Yet she charmed all of his friends, and her joy at meeting them was obvious. As she took their hands in greeting, his friends were capti-vated by the look in her eyes—forever young, full of love and wisdom.

Before they went into the dean's office, Grandmother laid a hand on Harold's sleeve. "Bishop Roberts called me, Harold," she said simply. "I know what the decision of the examining chaplains was, and I know what a hard blow it is for you. For that, I'm sorry. I want you to know that I am extremely proud of you. Our reservation world is a world unto itself. Since we love it so much, we put up with its hurts and trust in the faith that atti-tudes may change some day."

She looked directly at Harold and continued. "But we can be unend-ingly grateful for the gifts of those who have made your education possi-ble. You have what you came for; that is good."

Commencement day was warm and clear. The chapel filled to capacity with the families and friends of the small graduating class. Laughter from the groups outside the door reached even to the front pews, where the class sat together in caps and gowns. Inside was the sound of muted voices engaged in pleasant conversation, accompanied by the rustling of pro-grams being opened. Harold felt the quizzical looks of his classmates as they read and reread the names of those receiving diplomas. "Hey, Hal, they left your name off!" exploded George. All eyes turned on him, and he could only nod his head and say softly, "I know. It's all right." Chilton gave a muttered explanation to those nearest him, and shocked stillness fell over the line as they learned the news.

Madam Normalli had insisted that Harold sing a solo during the com-mencement exercises, making sure that the seminary would hear his voice one last time. Once again he dedicated the song to his grandmother. When Harold finished, to his delight the whole congregation stood sponta-neously to face Grandmother and salute her with deafening applause.

Before taking the train back to the reservation with Grandmother, Har-old made a point of calling on Madam Normalli. When she saw him standing in the doorway, Madam clasped Harold. She wept, then laughed at herself for weeping, as she told Harold how much she would miss him. "There's something I will tell you now, Harold, and perhaps I should have told you sooner, but I knew you were settled in your career as a clergyman." She wiped her eyes and went on. "Do you remember a Mr. Carlton who always likes to come to the seminary recitals? He has a dairy business and is a wealthy man. He told me he would pay for your voice lessons abroad if I thought there was any chance that you might become an opera singer."

Madam looked a bit more hesitant. "I told him that Harold has made up his mind to be a priest. Was I right, Harold?" She asked earnestly.

Without hesitation, he nodded.

The Rev. William and Rebecca Holmes, with their family. *Left to right:*
Ray, the Reverend William, Ida Edna (Harold Jones's mother),
Guy, Rebecca, May. *Courtesy of Harold Jones.*

Harold Jones (age 5) and his bank with the offering
for a new school. *Courtesy of Harold Jones.*

The clergy, catechists, and choir of the Church of Our Most Merciful Saviour, Santee NE, 1916. Rev. William Holmes stands on the far left. Harold Jones is in the choir, third from the right in the front row. *Courtesy of Harold Jones.*

The Ven. Edward Ashley, archdeacon of Niobrara, and the Rev. Philip Deloria (Tipi Sapa). *Courtesy of the Diocese of South Dakota.*

Indian Clergy in 1923. *Front (left to right):* Stephen King, Herbert Welsh, Philip Deloria, David Tatiyopa. *Back:* Luke Walker, Baptiste Lambert, William Holmes, Dallas Shaw. *Courtesy of the Diocese of South Dakota.*

St. Elizabeth's School and Church, Wakpala sd.
Courtesy of the Diocese of South Dakota.

St. Mary's School, Springfield SD, circa. 1930.
Courtesy of the Diocese of South Dakota.

Father Neville Joyner, 1930.
Courtesy of the Diocese of
South Dakota.

Harold Jones, just ordained deacon, with his first congregation at Christ Church, Red Shirt Table sd, 1938. *Courtesy of Harold Jones.*

Holy Cross Church, Pine Ridge SD, 1924.
Courtesy of the Diocese of South Dakota.

St. Peter's Church, Pine Ridge SD, 1944. Members of three denominations gathered in prayer for the ending of World War II. *Courtesy of Harold Jones.*

Father Paul Barbour,
circa 1945.
*Courtesy of the Diocese
of South Dakota.*

Kenneth and Harold
Jones, circa 1946.
Courtesy of Harold Jones.

Bishop Richard Emery (second from left) with Harold Jones
(second from right), Wahpeton ND, the late 1950s.
Courtesy of the Episcopal Church of North Dakota.

Blossom and Harold Jones's twenty-fifth wedding anniversary, December 14,
1963, at Trinity Church, Wahpeton ND. Their daughter, Norma Joy,
and Jerry Pederson, recently married, are standing with Harold
and Blossom. *Courtesy of Harold Jones.*

Harold and Blossom Jones, 1960s.
Courtesy of Harold Jones.

Harold and Blossom Jones at Good Shepherd
Mission, Navajoland. *Courtesy of Harold Jones.*

Bishop Harold Jones (*right*), with the Rev.
Creighton L. Robertson, 1993.
Courtesy of Harold Jones.

Jerry Pederson, Norma Joy Pederson, and Harold Jones, 1997.
Courtesy of Harold Jones.

8

NEW
BEGINNINGS

❧ + ❧

1938–1939

At home, dates and Greek verbs firmly in mind, Harold was prepared and ready to face the examining chaplains. But as the summer weeks passed, turning the prairies brown, his expectations and optimism deadened with them. He worked at a few odd jobs—cutting grass, picking up the paint brush again at St. Mary's, working in an ice house—always waiting for a letter or a telephone call that would set him on a path, some path, leading to service in the church.

Niobrara Convocation met at Holy Cross, Pine Ridge, in August of that year, 1938, and Harold attended with his grandmother. Once again a few of his examinations were given between sessions, but this time he passed them. The rest, he was informed, would be given at the convenience of an examiner during the coming months.

Two weeks later the call came. Father Joyner, the superintending presbyter of Pine Ridge Reservation, told Harold to be at Wounded Knee on the first of September. Harold was dumbstruck. He was not yet ordained and had not even finished the canonical exams, yet had just been assigned to Messiah Chapel at historic Wounded Knee. He assumed he was to be the lay minister or vicar, but exactly what he was supposed to do was still a mystery. Was he to serve as pastor, preacher, teacher, and leader of a congregation whose members he had not yet met?

Grandmother and her friends did not share his uncertainty. They began assembling supplies for his new position. Returning home at the end of a day of odd jobs, Harold might find a dishpan, dented with use but shining and filled with paring knives, scrapers, a rolling pin, and potato masher; or it might be a blanket, tea kettle, or frying pan. Over the next few weeks, the gifts grew until the entire space between his bed and window was filled with them.

Dawes Truckers would help move the large pile of possessions to Wounded Knee. Dawes and Son owned an ice-delivery business, and years earlier had once hired Harold as an ice cutter. When not delivering ice, they rented out their truck for other uses; this time they would be delivering watermelons to a market in the Black Hills. For twenty-five dollars, Harold bought a corner of the space among the melons for his mattress, dresser, two chairs, a large bundle of kitchenware, two blankets, and himself.

September 1, 1938, was a day of departure and elation, rain and melons, and a misplaced key. Harold propped his mattress against the cab of the truck, folded blankets under him, pulled his hat down, and watched as the scenery of home receded between the dark green curves of the melons.

Harold felt it was a momentous day. He had not yet faced all the exams, but with this assignment, the board obviously gave its consent to his services as a kind of apprentice-deacon.

The sun shone as they began the journey, but before they had left Springfield, rain started, gently at first, then turning into a drenching downpour that struck the roof of the cab and pounded the tarpaulin hastily pulled over the melons and Harold. The strong smell of the damp melons enveloped him as they traveled through that long day. When the heavily loaded old truck rounded curves, Harold watched warily in case the pile of melons loosely packed around him would suddenly break loose. By sundown they arrived in Martin. Stiff and damp, Harold jumped down from the back of the truck to join the two drivers for a bite of supper. They pressed on as the long dusk of the west began to fall.

Lights from the trading post at the junction of Wounded Knee were a welcome sight. Father Joyner had said that the key to the mission house would be left there. The storekeeper shook his head, however; no key had been dropped off.

Mr. Dawes motioned impatiently to Harold to climb into the truck. More rain was falling, and the way leading to the isolated community of

Wounded Knee was treacherous in wet weather. The narrow ribbon of road leading to Messiah Chapel, normally engulfed by clouds of choking dust, was now a thin line of yellow ooze. The truck's wheels sank deeply into it, making a new set of ruts as the vehicle toiled and slithered up to the small, dark mission house.

Drenched and still pelted by more rain, Harold rattled the door and then the windows of the mission house, but all were tightly locked. To his great relief, however, the adjacent church was unlocked. The two drivers quickly helped him unload his possessions and then drove away into the rain and darkness.

Somewhere in Harold's sack was a flashlight, but a small book of matches in his damp pocket proved easier to retrieve. One of the matches at last flared briefly, long enough for Harold to find room for the mattress. He gratefully stretched out and rolled himself up in blankets.

❧ ✝ ❧

A thin shaft of light coming through a crack in the door and the muffled shouts of children woke Harold the next morning. Scrambling to his feet, he flung open the door to let in the sunlight. The voices abruptly fell silent, and startled eyes turned toward the disheveled man standing in the church doorway. A small girl screamed and ran toward a nearby house, with the other children streaming after her, shouting that the new preacher had come. The children's grandparents came out of the house and walked over to him, smiling in greeting. Showing no surprise at his bedraggled appearance, they nodded soberly and shrugged when he explained about the missing mission house keys.

In the churchyard Harold built a bonfire just outside the parish house. The children watched as he brought out his pot and coffee can, found a pump beside the hall, and made a strong drink to take the edge off his appetite. As he settled on the steps of the mission house, two new neighbors approached, bringing a plate of eggs and two puffy portions of fry bread. Harold's spirits rose.

Wounded Knee! Here he was, on his first assignment and at a place that was sacred to all the Dakota people. Here the blood of hundreds of women, children, and men, slain during the massacre of Wounded Knee in 1890, mingled with the ground. It was a frightful mistake, that slaughter of the innocent, and the story is now well known not only to Dakotas and Lakotas but also to Native Americans everywhere. A few days after Christmas, the band of Indian men who had brought their sick chief, Big Foot, in to surrender were ordered out of their tents by soldiers, who lined them up and began to search for weapons. Accounts disagree regarding who fired the first shot—the soldiers or the Indians—but there can be no doubt that the ensuing slaughter was unjustified. Armed not only with rifles but also with cannon, the army unit mowed down Indian women and children fleeing from the tents along with men. Their bodies were found scattered for miles, testifying to the brutal manner in which they had been hunted down. On that day more than two hundred Indians died, along with seven soldiers. The few survivors were carried all the way to Pine Ridge and into Holy Cross Church, where they were cared for and a few, at least, saved. Nancy American Horse, a member of Harold's congregation-to-be, was eighteen at the time and had helped tend the wounded. In the face of such a devastating event, Harold wondered how he could worthily minister to this community. He prayed for God's empowering grace.

Later that morning he walked over a mile to the warden's house to pick up the elusive key. The afternoon and all the next day were spent sweeping out mud and clearing trash left on tables and floors from the last congregational gathering in the mission house. The locked door hadn't kept out flies, which swarmed over the piles of plates stacked in a sink in one corner. Two field mice cocked their big ears at him and scurried away from scraps of dried meat and bread crusts on the table. Sunlight filtered mistily through windowpanes streaked by dust and fingerprinted by many children. A half-filled water pail beside the sink had become a death trap for two more mice and a spider.

Harold had new reason to be grateful for the food, utensils, and cleaning supplies that his grandmother and her friends had assembled for him. Before the evening of the second night, the flies had departed, and he made up his bed in a well-scrubbed corner of the guildhall that was now his home. For supper that night, he lit kindling under a flaming sunset sky. As Dakota winds leisurely wrapped around the churchyard and sparked the fire, Harold heated the contents of two cans of spaghetti and meatballs that Grandmother had tucked into the bottom of the sack.

Much like the unhurried assembling of a jigsaw puzzle, the pleasant pattern of life at Wounded Knee began to fall into place. Near the hall Harold found a horseshoe pit with horseshoes stacked over a post. It took just one evening of pitching alone before other men from the village drifted by to watch and then join in. They were a friendly group, and the game provided an easy way to get to know them. Trips for groceries and mail resulted in a pleasant acquaintance with the Gildersleeve family, who kept the store. Before the end of a week, Harold called at the Milo Blower Day School to meet the teacher and pupils. They too greeted him warmly.

Harold was barely settled in his corner of the hall when his new congregation gave him a welcoming party. The congregation gave food and other small gifts. He would remember the occasion for years to come as the first of many acts of kindness demonstrated by the small communities of his various reservation homes.

The first welcoming party also stood out for another, more embarrassing reason. There were speeches, of course, all in the Lakota language of the Oglala Sioux. Harold listened very intently, knowing that he must reply. One of his new acquaintances from the horseshoe pit stood to face him across the room. He spoke deliberately and politely, but his first sentence stunned Harold. With no hint of a smile, he said he wanted to welcome, as he phrased it in Lakota, *"Wiciyela wan Wiyohiyuhpuluetonhun"* into their midst. Harold looked quickly at the others in the room, but no one smiled. He could feel himself blushing, but he continued to smile through the remainder of the speech. As he stood to reply, he shook his head slightly, smiling still, for he knew all Indian brothers hid their feelings behind imperturbable faces.

"Thank you, my brothers and sisters," Harold began. "To all of you, I am grateful for your kindness to me in this short time of my being here at Wounded Knee. I am still not ordained, but I hope that will be changed soon, and I am sure to make many mistakes in the days ahead. However, I am not a *wiciyena*, a girl, and you will soon see this when I marry and bring my bride back to Messiah Chapel."

The impenetrable masks suddenly crumpled, and a roar of laughter filled the hall, continuing so long that Harold finally sat down, completely baffled. An elder, sitting nearby on the bench, clapped him on the shoulder. Managing to become grave again, he explained to Harold that the word was *wiciyela*, not *wi-ci-ye-na*, and that it meant "a Dakota from the east," not "an eastern girl," as it did in the Santee language. Harold had followed the simple rule of switching consonants, but in this case replacing the *L* with an *N* had changed the Lakota word (for a Dakota or Yankton) to the Santee word for girl! Harold's own laughter was loudest of all, and Bishop McElwain's finger waggled at him from the not too distant past, warning him to improve his dialects.

After two weeks of cooking over an outdoor fire, Harold was offered an oil stove for four dollars, a happy addition to his living arrangement. When Blossom, who was teaching just thirty-five miles away in Rockyford, made her third visit in her Model A, he had the stovepipe attached and the stove top freshly blackened. They shared a joyful meal from the bag of groceries she brought, sitting within the small circle of warmth that the stove provided.

Having Blossom so near—and yet so far—was tantalizing. What sense was there in putting off marriage? The answer of course was always the same—no money, not enough even to support himself. Father Joyner had never mentioned what the salary would be or, for that matter, the mode of transportation to the other two missions that Harold was to serve in addition to Wounded Knee. St. Thomas, Manderson, was eight miles away, and Tuttle Station on the Nebraska Road was fifteen miles beyond that. September was almost over when Harold realized he had only a few cents over five dollars left. He spent twenty cents making a call to Father Joyner in the town of Pine Ridge to ask for an appointment. The next day he rode the fifteen miles to the priest's office on the mail truck.

Father Joyner was cordial in his greeting and pleased when Harold told him of his hope to marry Blossom. He nodded. "She's a fine girl from a good family. She will be a real help to you, son."

Harold hurried on to his next concern. "Can you tell me, Father Joyner, what my salary will be? And what arrangements are there for my travel to the other Pine Ridge missions?"

The smile vanished from the priest's face. "For a minister of the Gospel, money should be the least concern," he said reprovingly. "You are young, just starting out. You have led a sheltered life up to now. In fact, the last three years have in some ways been a corrupting influence on you. Transportation? How about your own feet? Or I am sure there is some way you can find a ride with another person in Wounded Knee. The district has no money to buy cars for young Indian deacons. And, as a matter of fact, you're not even a deacon."

Harold shrugged off the last comment and pressed on. "But I need to know what I am to be paid," he insisted. "I've not quite five dollars in my pocket, and if I'm to walk to my missions, I'll need food for strength to do it."

Was the young Indian deacon (but not a deacon) being impertinent? Father Joyner looked sharply at Harold, and his next words were brittle and blunt. "Your stipend will come to forty dollars a month. Your expenses at Wounded Knee should be slight. I can let you have twenty dollars in advance now, and the other twenty on the last day of the month if you feel it is absolutely necessary."

Despite his continuing financial problems, Harold's determination to marry Blossom remained strong. A few days after his tempestuous visit to Father Joyner's office, he was delighted to be offered a part-time job as an adult education instructor through the WPA in the Wounded Knee school system. The pay would be sixty dollars a month. Blossom was ecstatic; Father Joyner less so, but he made no outright objection.

A week later an urgent message arrived from Father Joyner, asking Harold to come to his office as soon as possible. Again Harold hopped the mail truck and fifteen miles later was at the priest's door. Father Joyner leafed through some papers, saying nothing for a few minutes. He then looked up and smiled. "Great news, son! I have chosen you to go to Christ Church, Red Shirt Table. There is some concern about a sect that has moved into the tableland and is preaching a kind of Christianity that is not of the true faith. You, with your background in theology, are thought to be the right one to take over the mission there and the other outlying stations."

Harold's tantalizing dreams of marriage and more money dissolved. The time at Wounded Knee had been brief, but already he was warmly attached to the people of Messiah Chapel. He knew Red Shirt Table only from occasional visits, and he'd heard from Grandfather about the place when it had been called Christ Station. More importantly, he also knew that Red Shirt Table was fifty-five miles north of Pine Ridge on the furthermost rim of the reservation. Without a car, his chances of seeing Blossom would be slim.

❧ + ❧

Ten days later, in November of 1938, Harold Jones stood at the door of his new home, a one-room cabin beside the small log Christ Church at Red Shirt Table. His bureau, table and two chairs, kerosene lamps and stove, water cans, and axe fit easily in the cabin.

Red Shirt Table was eleven miles long and four miles wide. It was named after Henry Red Shirt, who chose this mesa in the early twentieth century during the land allotments. Gradually, over the years, Henry's relatives and friends had joined him. Near Harold's cabin lived Grandmother Two Bulls, a widow with eight children. Their many children made up a large part of Harold's new congregation, along with James Comes Again and his wife and the Crow Family. Henry Red Shirt's daughter, Mary, and her husband and children, the Peter Crows, lived in a house whose windows faced north and east over the most spectacular landscape Harold had ever seen. Far in the distance, where the Badlands lay, sunsets brought the dead land to life. Its pale mineral-tinted shades of green, pink, and yellow danced and leaped like flames, joining the purples, oranges, and blues in the sunset sky. No less beautiful but perhaps even more awesome were the storms, the most violent coming from the south. The approach of slow, rolling black clouds laced with lightning could be seen for some time before the ominous sound of thunder reached the mesa.

The community was the most isolated place that Harold had lived. Mail came twice a week to a mailbox ten miles from the mesa. The day school teacher, who had a car, brought it to the schoolhouse that temporarily became the post office. Red Shirt Table had no store of any kind. When anyone made a trip to the nearest town thirty-five miles away, he or she would end up spending the day buying food, axes, bolts of materials, medicines, brooms, and garden tools for most of the Table's residents. In spite of Father Joyner's words about the virtues of walking, Harold knew he must have a car to do his work and to see Blossom. Through his new friends, he found a 1932 Chevrolet and pledged himself to a stricter diet to allow payments of ten dollars a month for it.

❧✚❧

Living at beautiful, rural Red Shirt Table also made clear another decision—Harold could continue to live as a poor bachelor, or if Blossom was willing, he could become a poor married man. Once he had made the decision, he could hardly contain himself through the Sunday morning service in late November before climbing into the Chevrolet and driving sixty-five miles to Rockyford. Years later, Blossom claimed Harold never did ask her to marry him. "He just took it for granted and set the date, and I went along with him," she recalled. Harold admittedly can't remember really asking her either. He does vividly recall the elation of that long-ago Sunday afternoon when he burst in on the Steele family in their living room. Blossom clasped her hands in delight over the car, and her mother and father came outside to pat a venerable fender and lift the hood to admire the engine. While taking Blossom for a test drive, Harold explained his idea about a wedding. They decided to get married on December 15, after his ordination to the diaconate, which had been set for December 9.

Once the momentous decision was made, everything moved quickly. Harold felt greater purpose now in chinking the cabin's cracks with moss and mud and in scrubbing the wooden floor that bore ground-in marks of many muddy footsteps. Harold and Blossom both agreed that Santee was the best place for the wedding. Sentimentality factored in the decision but so did tradition—marriages among the Sioux people usually meant giving quilts, blankets, and other gifts and hosting a large feast for many friends. Since this custom was financially impossible for Harold and Blossom, the best course of action seemed to slip into marriage with just the necessary witnesses, including of course Grandmother Holmes, Uncle Ray and Aunt Stella, and Blossom's youngest sister, Verna, who was in Springfield attending St. Mary's School.

While preparing for Blossom's arrival, Harold realized that his ordination, the goal toward which he had struggled for years, was becoming less a milestone and more a simple matter of fact. Yet it was still a sacred and solemn event, and although he knew the entire service almost by heart he rehearsed it every morning at breakfast. As he mentally retraced the steps that had led to this point, it seemed that his course had been directed not so much by his own decisions as by the leading of others: the example of Grandfather, the hopes of Grandmother, the counsel of his bishop. And where was God in his plans? They had talked a great deal in seminary about God's call, a spiritual summons that hadn't seemed very real for a long time. Now he did understand. God had been calling him, not through some inner voice or blinding flash of revelation but through the quiet leading of others and his growing experience of faith. Harold felt secure and content with his commitment.

The ordination took place on December 9. The examining board seemed unconcerned that Harold's examinations were still incomplete. He had passed two or three from time to time, but now that he lived in a remote area, far from the homes of the members of the Board of Examining Chaplains, the urgency or need for them seemed to have melted away.

Holy Cross Church was packed with family and friends. Indian clergy from Nebraska as well as from South Dakota attended. Grandmother and Uncle Ray were in the front pew, and Harold caught sight of Blossom's small red hat as he made his way down the aisle behind the choir. "Jesus Christ, *Wa-na-ni-ton, Pi Onoyate nipi kta,*" followed by the hymn, "Hail thou long expected Jesus," swelled through the church, expressing in two languages the shared Advent hope soon to be fulfilled. At the sight of the congregation gathered here on his account, Harold found it hard to sing over the lump in his throat.

For the first time he was wearing the gift vestments from the Diocese of Minnesota, until now kept carefully in a wrapped box. Bishop Roberts looped across Harold's shoulder and tied under his arm the Advent stole as a symbol of the yoke he chose on that day and forever to carry in the service of the Lord. The ancient words, repeated to new deacons through the centuries, were spoken now to Harold. "Take thou authority to execute the office of a Deacon in the Church of God committed unto thee, in the name of the Father and the Son and the Holy Ghost, Amen."

Almost immediately after that evening, Harold and Blossom plunged into frenzied activity—six days was not much time to plan a wedding. The old Chevy proved its worth on drives to the Steeles' home, on to Yankton to Uncle Ray's, and then to Center, Nebraska, for the marriage license, back to the Steeles' home to pick up Blossom, on to Springfield to pick up Grandmother, and then to fetch Verna at St. Mary's School.

They had planned on a very private wedding, with not more than four or five witnesses present and the Reverend Walter P. Reed, now priest in charge of the Church of Our Most Merciful Savior, to marry them. Instead, on their wedding day the church was surprisingly, wonderfully, filled with friends who had somehow learned of the event.

❧ + ❧

The Christmas holidays soon began, and Blossom joined Harold in the small cabin on Red Shirt Table. She quickly organized a special Christmas celebration at the mesa, in the form of a Christmas Eve pageant. On the morning of December 24, Blossom held the first dress rehearsal of the pageant. To Harold's surprise, she had persuaded seven people to take part in it, not counting the baby, who they hoped would sleep through his role as the Christ Child. In the cabin not much was left hanging on coat hangers and the bed looked bare without a cover, but in the mission house the missing articles were performing a notable duty as costumes for the pageant.

It was a Christmas pageant they wouldn't soon forget. Minutes before the Christmas Eve service began, Harold found Blossom busily pinning a tinsel halo over the bedspread, which now draped Mary's head. She looked distraught. "All my wise men have been drinking!" she whispered. "They can hardly get their costumes on. I don't know what's going to happen."

"How drunk are they?"

Blossom grimaced. "Very. But you have enough to worry about. Leave it to me."

There was no more time to talk; the church was filling rapidly. The children were barely able to sit still among their parents, uncles, aunts, and grandparents, all squeezed tightly along the benches. Almost everybody had a part in preparing for this celebration. Out of sight, hidden in three large bags, were carefully wrapped gifts, enough for every child. The smell of soup, boiled meat, *wojapi,* and fry bread hung in the air, brought in on the coats and persons of those who had left their stoves to come to the service. They would be hurrying home when the time came to bring back the banquet that followed every Christmas Eve service on Red Shirt Table. To one side of the chancel stood a freshly cut pine tree, made bright with mittens and socks, gifts from an off-reservation church.

Everyone was there for a joyful time: "*Chante ma waste.* My heart is happy." But so were the hearts of the wise men. Poor fellows, Harold thought. They didn't want to disappoint Blossom, but they took the all too common way of facing a hard task. Strengthen yourself with a bottle to the point where you don't worry about it anymore. But at least they did show up.

When the pump organ sounded the notes of the first carol, Mary, her flowing robe caught up under one arm and the baby nestled under the other, came up the aisle as inconspicuously as possible and then sat on the orange crate placed in front of the altar. An angel followed, the tinsel trimmings of her white sheet sparkling mysteriously as she assisted Mary with her robe and helped place a pillow under the wide-eyed, wondering child in Mary's lap. The angel then took her place protectively behind them. Joseph, his head swathed in a familiar scarf, strode down the aisle to join the little group. And there they stayed, as quietly as if they were made of stone, while the service began. Harold gestured for the lights to be turned off. Blossom's flashlight, bright with new batteries, focused on the figures in front of the altar, transforming them into a convincing Holy Family. A murmur of appreciation rose from the dark benches.

Harold needed no light to read the gospel. When he reached "the shepherds abiding in the fields by night," a lonely shepherd made his way down the aisle to kneel at one side of Mary. Small heads craned into the beam of light to watch while a voice softly sang, "While shepherds watched their flocks by night all seated on the ground," and the congregation hummed along in accompaniment. Then they paused.

From the dusky environs of the entryway came the sound of shuffling feet, some guffaws, and the clatter of a cover falling from a golden casket and spinning across the floor. "Whoops," called a jovial voice, shattering the reverent silence. Harold could feel, rather than see, the stiffening outlines of the congregation as children were whisked quickly away from their aisle seats to safer places on the laps of relatives further along the length of the benches.

"We three kings of Orient are," came the blithe tones of the wise men, who were beginning to enter into the spirit of the occasion. A shadowy figure emerged into the torchlight and made its way unsteadily down the aisle. He was wearing Harold's red bathrobe. "Gold I bring to offer have I," he sang earnestly. "Gold I bring to crown him king, king forever, ceasing never, here comes the gold for him." He moved with dignity but diagonally so that those sitting in his path ducked to protect themselves from the large gold-colored bowl he held out in front of him. The baby stared in wonderment, his eyes round and shining as he watched the first wise man approach and sink to his knees in obvious relief, still holding out his gift.

There followed a second voice, more earnest than the first and just a little off key. "Incense now to offer have I. Incense owns a deity nigh. Hmm hm ha hm ha hmmm hm on high." Where had Blossom found that old cassock? Harold wondered. It was impressive, with a large red sash tied around the waist and looped with tinsel. With nothing to secure it, the golden crown had slipped over to one side of the wise man's head, hiding a glazed eye.

"Sht sht," Harold heard along the darkened path. It was a familiar sound, the warning grandmothers gave to grandchildren who were carrying things too far. The admonition even worked on dogs and cats, but it seemed to have no affect on the second wise man, who occasionally brushed the shoulder of a grandmother with his elbow as he passed by before finally coming to rest in front of the happily gurgling baby. The child squirmed in his mother's arms to reach the familiar uncle kneeling before him.

The third wise man was the most drunk. From the short scuffle at the back of the church, Harold pictured Blossom giving him a determined shove to start him on his way. He bolted from the darkness into the shaft of light, slowing his pace and weaving from side to side until he finally tripped over his makeshift robe. He fell headlong in front of the Holy

Family but somehow managed to hold the frankincense aloft. A ripple passed through the congregation, and the baby shrieked with glee at the exploit of his other uncle.

By the time the gentle, soothing sound of "Silent Night" brought the pageant to its close, one of the wise men was fast asleep, lulled by the music and the heat of the nearby wood stove. When the lamps were lit once more, he awoke and with the help of his two good-natured friends was led outside into the brisk December air. Such was the equanimity of the people of Red Shirt Table that when it came time for Harold's abbreviated sermon, the congregation gave no sign that anything unusual had happened.

❧ ✝ ❧

As winter turned toward spring, Blossom transformed the fourteen-by-eighteen-foot cabin into a cozy home. Orange crates became kitchen cupboards. Two of them were turned into stools and another two into a dressing table. The windows sparkled anew, pleasantly disguised behind ruffled curtains. Harold's boots and Blossom's galoshes stood neatly side by side in another orange crate, just behind the door. Painted and sometimes padded, the crates no longer resembled themselves but became pieces of furniture. Visitors dubbed their home the "honeymoon cottage."

In the late afternoon of March 18, Harold was outside splitting wood when he suddenly straightened up in panic. It was Blossom's birthday. "Oh, God, what can I do?" It was a fervent prayer. Distractedly he gazed out across the tableland. The wind was bending the tufts of tall grass protruding out of the snow. But there was something else there too, a stealthy counter movement within the grass. It was a coyote, and to judge from the size of its bushy tail, a big one. There was a bounty on coyotes, and its fur coat would make a handsome gift for Blossom.

Blossom was peeling potatoes for supper. Harold burst through the door and tossed her coat to her. "Hurry! If you drive the car, I'll take my gun and we can get a coyote." She dropped her knife, dried her hands on her apron, and ran behind him outside. They recklessly drove across the

grassland after the coyote, which seemed unconcerned about their presence until it saw the gun barrel. Its first leap was its last one. It was a beautiful animal with a thick, sleek coat. Harold took the coyote to Grandmother Two Bulls for her to fashion into a rug for Blossom's perpetually
cold feet. The gift was beautiful, even though the tail was missing—Grandmother Two Bull's dog had chewed it off while it was hanging out on the
line.

Spring brought May, the end of the school year. Blossom was by now expecting a child, and the doctor warned her that she must take care not to
do heavy work or to travel rough roads. Neither could be avoided while
they lived at Red Shirt Table. Living there could be hard. Although they
were spared the complex problems that the rest of the world faced, nature
brought enough difficulties for them to contend with. On Red Shirt Table
nature was moody. Storms could bring havoc; droughts taxed the ingenu-
ity of the small community in bringing water to the tablelands; winter
winds made life impossible if woodpiles and oil tanks failed.

That summer of 1939, the sun burned the land, and the sky was cloudless weeks on end. Grasshoppers quickly finished off the small garden that
Harold and Blossom had planted. They worked hard in the beginning to
win the battle but finally gave up and drank evening tea to the sound of insects chewing, as stalk after fresh green stalk fell to the invading army. The
whole community suffered from the drought. The only plant that flourished was Russian thistle, too prickly even for the grasshoppers. Un-
daunted, the people of Red Shirt Table harvested the plants and chopped
and stored them for cattle fodder.

August 10—the date would be etched permanently in Harold's memory.
All day it was sizzling hot. He and Blossom spent most of it under the
shelter of the cabin roof. That evening Blossom was sitting at the window,
letting the hot breeze blow over her damp forehead, when she turned suddenly and doubled over with a cry of pain. Harold lifted and laid her on the
bed, and she brought up her knees convulsively. Nothing he tried eased
her pain. In panic he seized the car keys, brought the car as close to the
door as he could manage, and lifted her into the backseat.

Fifty-five miles of the roughest roads in the Badlands lay between them and Pine Ridge Hospital. Harold drove recklessly, speeding as fast as the old car and the ruts, curves, and dust permitted. He strained to see Blossom in the rearview mirror. Occasionally she managed a faint laugh to reassure him, but the laugh all too quickly turned into a moan. "Oh, God! Oh, God!" he prayed, his mind too numb to give words to his anguish. At the end of the nightmare, gentle, efficient hands lifted Blossom out of the car and into a bed and then administered a shot to ease her pain.

The couch in the visitors' room was Harold's bed that night and the next. He alternated between it and the chair beside Blossom's bed. Her face was more relaxed. A nurse had brushed her hair into a shining fan over the pillow, away from her forehead. "It's so hot in here," the nurse had explained, "and she has such lovely, heavy hair."

On August 12, their son was born prematurely, very small but beautiful in every way. Harold took him from Blossom's arms and held him awkwardly. He was so fragile! The feel of silky hair against Harold's bare arm, the movement of tiny feet against his elbow sent a rush of love welling up in him. Blossom's health had been his one concern. Now he desperately wanted their baby to live.

But it was not to be. "The baby won't last out the day," the doctor said as kindly as he could. Harold asked for a bowl of water, and there beside Blossom's bed, he baptized their child Lawrence William: Lawrence for a relative of Blossom's and William for Harold's grandfather. Lawrence William was received into God's kingdom before the sun set on the first day of his life. Two days later, Harold and a sad, frail Blossom took the small wooden box containing the child's body to the Steeles' burial plot in St. Mark's Cemetery in Rockyford. Harold's eyes stung from the whirling dust that the wind scooped up from the small heap of dirt beside the grave. But it was not the dust that made his voice choke as he said the words of the burial service while the box was lowered into the ground. He had known pain before but nothing like this. He felt Blossom press against him, giving him courage to complete the service.

They had each other; that was what mattered. The words of the twenty-third psalm, which he had read at the graveside, kept coming back to him as they made their sad journey back to Red Shirt Table: "Yea, though I walk through the valley of the shadow of death, I will fear no evil; for thou art with me. . . . Surely goodness and mercy shall follow me all the days of my life; and I will dwell in the house of the Lord forever." As he recited the psalm aloud, Blossom joined in the comforting words.

❧ + ❧

Another change, another goodbye was on the horizon. By the end of August, a message arrived from Father Joyner. Harold was ordered to relocate from Red Shirt Table to St. John's, Oglala, thirty miles away. He was to meet Father Joyner there on September 1.

"After only nine months at Red Shirt Table?" cried Blossom. "Must we leave all these new and kind friends so soon?" But Blossom, as always, accepted what the church demanded, even if she didn't always agree with what was being asked.

9

DEATH AND
GROWTH

☙ + ☙

1939–1947

Although still drained physically and emotionally from the death of their child, Blossom was anxious to see their future home and insisted on going with Harold to view the church. When they arrived, Father Joyner was standing in front of the neglected old building. The priest put his shoulder to the front door and pushed. It complained with a creak but opened slowly. They peered into the semidarkness. Three rough benches lined two walls, and at the far end was a bare altar. Cobwebs covered the windows. The smell of dust, long heated by the sun, made Harold cough.

It was hard to believe that this had once been historic Holy Cross Church in the town of Pine Ridge, where the wounded and dying from the Wounded Knee massacre had been brought. When a new Holy Cross Church was built, this old one had been moved to Oglala to become the house of worship for the people there, under the new name of St. John's.

"Windows need a good cleaning," was Father Joyner's terse comment.

They headed next for the building beside the church. Although not as old as St. John's, it nevertheless wore the same weather-beaten look. Once inside, they could see light slanting through cracked walls, brightening the musty interior. The two men tugged, then put all their strength into opening windows sealed by paint years before at the north and south ends of the building.

"If this is the meeting house, where will Blossom and I live?" Harold asked.

"Why, here of course," Father Joyner replied, looking somewhat puzzled by the question. "When you have church meetings, you can just move your possessions into a corner. There's plenty of room in here." He smiled at Blossom. "You could put three of your Red Shirt Table houses under this roof, eh, my dear?"

Harold knew that Father Joyner had spent his life living in places that most white men would shun. Austerity measured his life as well as the lives of the people he supervised. Pride he might have but not of possessions or of power. His pride, Harold sensed, derived from the hardships he could suffer, toughening his spirit through them. Father Joyner was a strong man, and his faith was unquestioned. Harold admired and feared him, but he worried about Blossom's welfare even more.

He confronted Father Joyner. "I can live here just the way it is, but I will not bring my wife here unless two changes are made. The first is to have windows cut on the east and west sides of this building; the other is to put a partition in the center to divide our living quarters from the rest of the hall. Unless these changes are made, Blossom must go live with her parents."

Father Joyner was silent for a few moments. To Harold's surprise, he agreed. "Good idea. We can arrange to have someone from the village saw you a new set of windows, and that partition can be arranged too." He went on matter-of-factly. "There's not much wood around here, as you can see. One of your future parishioners, Frank Bear Nose, has a grove of trees not far away. He will make a business arrangement with you so that you can cut your firewood there. Water is nonexistent. You can buy cream cans in the store at Oglala and bring your water back with you whenever you go into town for your groceries. I'm sorry there is no stove in this building for cooking or for heat. That is one of the first things you had better purchase before you move in."

The couple went outside and looked around at their new surroundings. It was indeed a barren, flat area, practically treeless. The village consisted of a dozen or so scattered houses, the store, and a community hall. At least it was bigger than Red Shirt Table and had a store. Harold and Blossom hoped that their new neighbors would be as friendly as the ones they were leaving behind.

They were later to learn that renegades from the town of Pine Ridge had settled the community. The priest who had been coming for occasional services, Andrew Whiteface, preferred to meet in peoples' homes rather than to open up the old church. St. John's had been neglected and unused for a long time.

And so they began again. Windows were washed, floors were scrubbed, holes in the walls were chinked, and more orange crates collected. Blossom framed the new windows with bright curtains, leaving unobstructed the view of the prairie. The new partition marking one side of their living quarters made a good wall for pictures and reflected a golden glow from lamp light in the evening. They scrubbed the church and cleaned cobwebs from the windows. By the first Sunday morning, a faint smell of yellow soap mingled with that of new wax candles on the altar.

Harold was nervous, particularly because his Lakota vocabulary was still limited. At Red Shirt Table the people were kind when he made mistakes, taking his meaning from the words he misused, but this was an unknown congregation. He carefully prepared two sermons, one in Lakota and one in English, and took both prayer books with him on that first October Sunday.

He needn't have bothered. Blossom was his only congregation. Harold nonetheless read through the whole service of morning prayer and delivered his English sermon as she sat meekly on one of the benches.

At the second Sunday service, there were two in the congregation, Blossom and a visiting Presbyterian.

Just three hundred yards from their new home stood the large Oglala Community Hall. The reason no one attended services on Sunday morning was easy to see and hear—on Saturday nights practically the whole community turned out for Indian dancing, which lasted well beyond midnight.

Harold prayed for guidance. It came through an invitation to hold a service in the community hall on Saturday afternoon before the dancing began. He took his vestments and set up a makeshift altar in the space that the drums would soon occupy. This sermon came more easily. He preached on the Ten Commandments. "When God gave them to us, he did not mean them as suggestions but as rules to live by." Harold recited the commandments, lingering longest on the fourth: "Remember that thou keep holy the Sabbath day." Those who came to dance listened to his halting speech and agreed that they would stop dancing by midnight.

At the third Sunday service, eight people came to church.

A pattern was set, and before two years passed, the little church was full every Sunday—full of good people, fine people, soon dear to his and Blossom's hearts. Austin Goodvoice Flute, Shotanka O'Waste, Henry Kills Warrior, Toka Pte, Frank Bear Nose and his family, Major Poor Elk, the Red Bows, Ross and Edna Red Paint, and Hobart Bissonet, the lay reader for St. John's and St. Jude's, were among the people who came.

Although the Joneses lived at St. John's, they continued to serve Christ Church, Red Shirt Table, and St. Jude's, White River. Sometimes only two or three families comprised the latter congregation, which met in the Ten Fingers' home. These gatherings were happy times for Harold and Blossom. They continued to meet with young people at Red Shirt Table for occasional sprees, ending with a supper or breakfast of pancakes served by the youths' parents in the Joneses' former "honeymoon cottage."

During the winter after these trips, they would drive home to Oglala through swirling snow to a bitterly cold house. Harold piled wood into the small stove, and they warmed themselves, first front then back, before burrowing into bed beneath five blankets. By morning the fire had turned to ashes, and while Harold rekindled it, Blossom chopped ice out of the water pail to melt for a cup of coffee. One morning Blossom discovered that the milk she had warmed on the stove to pour on their cereal had turned to ice again before they used it.

❧ + ❧

Three events made those two years they lived at Oglala noteworthy. The first was the birth of a girl, Norma, on August 6, 1941. Like her brother, she was born prematurely, but she lived and from the moment of her birth brought her parents joy (which became her middle name).

The second event was Harold's ordination to the priesthood on September 18, 1941, at Holy Cross Church in Pine Ridge. Blossom knew how significant the occasion was for him, and she worked hard over his vestments, scrubbing them clean and ironing out every wrinkle, heating her irons on top of the wood stove and then cooling them just enough so they wouldn't leave scorch marks. And then in the rush of getting everyone ready for the trip to Pine Ridge, the vestments were forgotten. Luckily, Father Frank Thorburn, Harold's friend from an earlier summer, had been appointed the new superintending presbyter upon Father Joyner's retirement two weeks before. Father Thorburn was a tall man like Harold, so it was in his vestments that Harold was at last ordained to the priesthood.

Father Joyner traveled from Nebraska to preach the ordination sermon. Relieved of the burden of his former duties, he seemed relaxed and friendly. When at the close of his sermon he called upon Harold to rise, the warmth of his voice was genuine as he addressed him as "my brother."

The third noteworthy event grew out of the second one. Nothing, of course, could keep Grandmother away from the ordination. But the sight of her stepping out of Uncle Jim Ross's car in front of the church wrung Harold's heart. In the intervening months since he had last seen her, Grandmother had become a fragile wisp of an old lady. Even the effort of walking into the church tired her. Later, from his seat in the chancel, his eyes sought her out. She was sitting in a front pew next to Blossom, who had linked arms with her. When Harold caught Blossom's eye, her look told him that she shared his thought—Grandmother must not live alone any longer.

That night after their return to Oglala, they made her bed on the couch. By the end of two weeks, Grandmother's small supply of possessions were moved in; some were stowed under the couch, while the rest were placed in more orange crates that had become cupboards. Her rocking chair—the same one in which she had rocked away Harold's earaches long ago—was close beside the couch.

"Not another piece of laundry will you touch!" Blossom exclaimed firmly.

Grandmother rested a great deal. When she woke, she would raise her arms eagerly to share in the care of Norma Joy. As the weeks went by, she regained enough strength to stand with Blossom at the sink to peel the vegetables for stew or to help with the supper dishes. When Norma grew old enough, Harold watched his grandmother strain small amounts of potato, squash, and apple to feed her, just as he remembered her doing for baby Kenny thirty years ago.

Norma's home was a laundry basket perched on top of the orange crate desk beside the bed. It was swathed in mosquito netting to keep out the spiders, flies, ants, mosquitoes, and beetles that shared their home.

One day Grandmother called to Blossom, who was in the kitchen. The autumn air had a chill in it, the kind that sent creatures in search of shelter before the coming winter. Blossom approached Grandmother with a cup of steaming tea. She could warm those hands, always so cold, on the cup as she drank, Blossom thought. But that was not why Grandmother had called this time.

"Please, dear, there is something or somebody at the door, I think."

The door had been left open to let in the sunshine, and on that late October day, the wind blew from the north. But curiously, the old screen door was closing and opening on its own, chattering nervously against the sill. Blossom went for a closer look.

Then she saw it. A large rattler was coiled inside the room; the snake was pushing its head against the screen in an attempt to get outside. Quietly Blossom reached for the broom and opened the screen door with the handle. The snake uncoiled and glided outside. Where had the rattler been hiding in the house? Netting could keep Norma free of bugs, but could it protect her from snakes?

Harold never heard Blossom complain about the many-legged or winged creatures in the house. It was, after all, the Jones family who was the invader. Once Harold brought Frank Thorburn, the new superintending presbyter, home unexpectedly. Blossom was cleaning the stovepipe when a spider swung out on an invisible thread and landed on her hand. Before she had time to shake it off, the spider had spun a web around her fingers. The two men arrived just as she managed to scrape her fingers free. Instead of a welcoming smile, she burst into tears, sobbing in a way that Harold had never heard before. Frank Thorburn stood admiring Norma behind her netting until the crying stopped, then turned, and asked gently how Blossom would like to move into St. Peter's vicarage, a house that was closer to town and with a good wood floor and an oil stove.

Leaving the log meeting house of St. John's wasn't a sad event because

St. Peter's was just forty miles away, and weekly trips back and forth for service would keep them in touch with people. Wooden floors, a well of their own, and a kitchen sink with a drainpipe would be luxuries for the Jones family. The oil stove was a thirsty necessity since there were no trees to be cut for firewood, but the warmth that spread throughout the small house was worth the price.

With this move, Harold was now serving five missions.

Grandmother's strength continued to wane. One of several small strokes sent her to the Pine Ridge Hospital. Happily, she returned home again. Her pleasure in the baby's company warmed Harold's heart. She never mentioned her own weakness, and although she couldn't help Blossom with housework anymore, she watched Norma, held her, soothed her to sleep, and loved her with the same love that had nourished Kenny and Harold.

December 1941 brought traumatic changes to Blossom and Harold as well as to the larger world. On December 8, the U.S. declared war on Japan and so joined the conflict of World War II. Young men on the reservations, like their counterparts elsewhere across America, began enlisting in the armed forces or were drafted. Both Harold's and Blossom's younger brothers answered the call to duty, although in the end they were not accepted. Harold, as a priest, was exempt from the draft, but he wrestled with the thought of becoming a military chaplain. Finally, with Blossom's reluctant agreement he applied to become a navy chaplain. He was scheduled to report to a base in the Twin Cities when Bishop Roberts, who felt that Harold would be of greater service on the home front, vetoed his plans.

Harold organized a monthly day of prayer at St. Peter's Church, which Presbyterians and Roman Catholics shared. This service gave the local community an opportunity to raise its prayers, hopes, and grief to God as more and more relatives and friends were called to serve. As reports of casualties came in, the need for a pastoral ministry to the anxious and bereaved increased in all of the congregations that Harold served. And when the war was finally over, St. Peter's hosted a community celebration of thanksgiving.

❧ + ❧

The second traumatic event of that December came on the twelfth. Harold was conducting a service in the Ten Fingers' home when a knock on the door brought news that his grandmother had suffered a serious stroke. By the time he reached home, she was dead. Compared to the national tragedy of war, the death of a sick old woman might seem unimportant, but in Harold's mind the two would always be linked. He was thankful that her heart would not be torn by the horrors of war that were bound to come. A fanciful thought struck Harold. Grandmother was never one to shrink from hard things. Perhaps God called her to be with him as thousands of souls swarmed into paradise from the battlefields. On earth she was skilled in pointing out God's truth to confused souls. God might well use her now to help the war dead adjust to the wonders of their new life.

Grandmother's body was buried a few days later next to Grandfather's in the churchyard in Santee, Nebraska. Kenny and his wife were present as well as some old friends who had heard the news of her death. One by one they came forward to take the spade and shovel earth over the modest coffin. Harold watched and at the last took his turn. Such a simple service with family and a few friends would be what Grandmother would have wanted.

Just a day before Grandmother's death, a check had arrived in the mail for $150 from a parishioner in the congregation of Harold's former roommate at seminary, Ray Paulson. With the check was a note from the unknown donor: "Please use this for your family in any way you wish." The donor could never have guessed that the gift would cover the cost of an entire funeral.

❧ + ❧

The next four years were busy ones for Blossom and Harold. They had welcomed the salary increase from fifty to seventy-five dollars that accompanied the latest move but soon discovered that the oil stove drank up more than its share of the budget. The automobile, needed to cover the miles to five mission stations, was another thirsty machine. Supplying the stove and auto left little money to buy milk for a hungry child.

When Norma was six months old, Blossom applied for a teaching job at

No. 5 Day School, two miles down the road from St. Peter's. Each morning, she left Norma in the care of a young mother who lived near by. Harold also was pressed into service by George Jones, the local school principal, who needed a coach for the girls' and boys' basketball teams. Harold took the job after warning Mr. Jones that there would be some days that the teams would have to do without him.

In no time at all, Norma was walking, to the delight and exhaustion of her busy mother. During the summer when Norma turned one, Harold took his family for a change of scenery to a small camp in the Black Hills. It was a place of magical beauty, where water glided in shining streams and even the stones sparkled under pine branches. This area is holy ground to the Dakota and Lakota peoples. Through an arrangement with the park manager, Blossom's help with the cleaning, laundry, and office work paid for a portion of their rent. The railroad tracks passed through the Hills, and Harold secured a temporary job loading and unloading freight cars. When he saw the tired lines smoothing out of Blossom's face and watched Norma's delight as she trotted on her small legs after squirrels, he decided to repeat the same schedule the next summer and again the next.

In 1944 Blossom ended her teaching at No. 5 Day School. At the invitation of Frank Thorburn, Harold moved his family to Pine Ridge to occupy a temporarily vacant house owned by Holy Cross Church. Blossom was expecting another child, and haunted by past experience it seemed wise to be near Pine Ridge Hospital.

On June 16, 1944, Harold Robert Jones was born prematurely. This time the baby lived for three days. Harold asked Frank Thorburn to baptize him.

Doubts and regrets plagued Harold. If only Blossom hadn't been teaching school and could have stayed home to rest more often. If only they could have found some other way to meet the mounting debts added to the old ones. But even with her teaching and his odd jobs, there was never quite enough money to pay the fuel and grocery bills. What kept them afloat, he realized, was the generosity of the parishioners, who were poor yet always generous with what they had.

With gratitude he thought of the storekeeper at the Oglala grocery store.

On December 20, Harold paid his last dollar for extra fuel to warm the cabin in the midst of a particularly cold spell. His grocery bill was already twice the size of his monthly paycheck, but the cupboard was bare again. At the store he filled a modest-sized bag with necessities and approached the cash register, mustering his courage to "charge it" again. Mr. Linehan motioned him to wait until he finished with another customer.

When the door closed behind him and they were alone, the storekeeper asked Harold, "Have you gotten any Christmas presents yet, Harold?"

Harold shook his head. "No, not yet." He watched while the grocer thumbed through a pile of papers in a corner of a drawer. Harold recognized the papers—his bills covering the past three months. Taking a pencil from behind his ear, the grocer quickly marked each one "paid" and then handed them to Harold.

"There's your first Christmas present," he said.

Such unexpected acts of kindness kept them going. They were rich in friendships, in their family life, and in that special joy that came from accepting whatever service the Lord called them to do. But the one big worry continually plaguing them was debt. How good it would be to owe no one! Long ago when Grandmother's pension of $33.33 a month was supposed to cover the expense of caring for two hungry boys and one aging woman, Harold learned that the economic side of life affects the body, mind, and soul. Grandmother's soul and mind remained unaffected by such matters, but her body suffered. And the two beautiful sons they had lost—would they have lived if Blossom had not had to work so hard?

✼✝✼

Returning to Oglala from a summer holiday in the Black Hills in 1945, the family was caught in a sudden downpour. The sky had been blue when they started out, but halfway home the black clouds massed over them, pouring rain so steadily that in no time the dusty, rutted road became a sea of mud. From long experience they knew that if they stopped, their tires would sink deep into the fresh mire, but keeping a straight path was impossible. Twice they slipped so close to the ditch that Harold called to Blossom to steer while he jumped out of the car to put his weight against it.

Sinking deep in the mud, he pushed against the side of the car until, like an unwilling horse, it turned back into the ruts, its spinning wheels churning still deeper.

The rain finally stopped and the sun came out, but the mud continued for miles. The car inched along toward Harold's goal: the crossroads leading into the town of Pine Ridge. They reached the crossroads with thankful hearts and a coating of thick mud covering the car and Harold. The house belonging to Holy Cross Church became their haven again.

Before they resumed their journey the next day, Frank Thorburn asked Harold to become his assistant at Pine Ridge and to move permanently into the house of refuge. While they were happy to have a more comfortable home, the move added to Harold's burdens. His ministry would now cover the whole western side of the Pine Ridge Reservation; he would have to travel to all the congregations he had served throughout his ministry: Red Shirt Table, St. John's, St. Peter's, St. Jude's Oglala, and now another one, St. James', between Pine Ridge and Oglala. Within the Pine Ridge Mission were two more congregations, Advent Church and St. Matthew's. In addition there was Holy Cross Church in the town of Pine Ridge, where he served as Father Thorburn's assistant. Two days each week, the two priests traveled among the village schools, teaching released-time classes of religious instruction, since none of the missions had Sunday schools.

The two years living next to Holy Cross Church were busy ones. Harold was away from home much of the time. Norma had her fifth birthday and began school. The house was never empty of visitors, for the town of Pine Ridge contained the tribal headquarters and the public health hospital, attracting a constant stream of people from every part of the reservation.

From this pressure cooker of activity, Harold and Blossom escaped briefly to fly to Denver for the first week of the pre-Christmas season of Advent. St. John's Cathedral had named Harold its missionary to Pine Ridge Reservation, replacing Vine Deloria Sr., who was now retired and living in Iowa. The dean of St. John's, Paul Roberts, was a brother of the bishop of South Dakota, Blair Roberts. Through this connection the cathedral congregation had chosen Pine Ridge to be a focus for its missionary concern, and they were glad to continue the relationship under Harold's ministry.

That experience buoyed Harold's spirits as he drove the many miles between missions and returned home after dark. The South Dakota darkness was always so very black. When the sky was overcast and no ranch lights or cheery glow from a distant farmhouse could be seen, only the small, intense beam of his car's headlights penetrated the gloom. As Harold drove through the darkness, the prayers and good will of the cathedral congregation stayed with him.

✴ + ✴

At Niobrara Convocation the following summer, Messiah Church, Wounded Knee, was chosen to host the 1947 convocation and Harold was elected its treasurer. While he felt honored to be given such an important role, he knew it would involve a great deal of hard work to plan and carry out the next meeting of these historic gatherings. He would also be subject to criticism. He knew he would have to be absolutely fair and scrupulous in handling the financial arrangements.

Back home he and Blossom began planning for all of the things that would have to be done. He recalled memories of the convocation years ago in Santee and of how hard his grandparents and the people of Most Merciful Saviour had worked to put it all together. A year was none too long to organize a fund-raising program, to find willing builders of a bowery and booths, a reception committee, a cooking crew, and attend to myriad other concerns that, when put together, made a good convocation. The Zephier family at No. 9 Day School volunteered to run a restaurant inside the school. With areas provided for outdoor cooking scattered around the site, the convocation would be well fed. Posts were raised to tether the horses, and a parking lot was cleared of brush and stone.

All was in order when the day arrived, bringing people—and rain. It was the wettest Niobrara Convocation Harold could remember. The prayer services and the meetings went on, and people were fed. What he remembered most vividly, however, were the muddy pants of the young men who joined with him to pull and push cars back onto the road after they had slid into ditches. By the time the cars were all safely parked, it was almost time for them to be moved out again. When the meetings were over, a tow truck driven by a Hare School student pulled the cars out of the parking area mud and set them on a slippery state road. All day and into the night, the truck worked until the last car drove out of sight.

By the time it was over, an exhausted Harold had learned two things. First, being a responsible leader at a convocation was very different and much more demanding than merely being a participant, enjoying the wonderful occasion. Second, another move was imminent. Bishop Roberts announced at the closing service that he was appointing Harold Jones to be the superintending presbyter of the Cheyenne River Mission.

Again, Blossom, Norma, and Harold packed their belongings and climbed into the car, leaving behind loved ones and bound this time for unfamiliar territory.

10

SUCCESS

⚜ + ⚜
―――――――
1947–1952

The old car was crammed with suitcases and boxes as the family climbed into it. With a few shudders and groans, the car lurched forward. Two hours later the groans were joined by grinding sounds, and Harold decided that an overnight stop in Pierre was necessary for both car and passengers.

By afternoon of the next day, September 1, they arrived at Eagle Butte, the site of the Cheyenne River Agency. Their new house was a famous one. One winter day many years ago, it had been moved across the iced-over Missouri River from Fort Bennett in the Oahe area so that it could be used as the home of the Reverend Edward Ashley. Ashley lived in it for most of the thirty-seven years he spent on the reservation, acting as peacemaker between the army and the Indians and preaching the gospel to many. It was said that Father Ashley and Buffalo Bill Cody had been good friends and had spent evenings together in front of the house's marble fireplace.

The Reverend Edward Ashley was the person whom Bishop Hare primarily depended upon for the training of Indian clergy as well as for leadership in his Niobrara jurisdiction in general. He was reputed to know Indian people and their language and culture far better than any other white man. Father Ashley had encouraged Grandfather, still a young man teaching in Moreau River Day School, to become a clergyman. At that time, the Episcopal Church prided itself on a highly educated clergy with college and seminary preparation for ordination. But Ashley and Hare realized that character and commitment in Native people were more important than academic training in furthering the gospel among Indian people. They took the bold step of preparing and ordaining men with little academic background. When Hare and later Ashley died, the number of new Indian candidates for ordination declined precipitously. Harold, in fact, became the first Native to be called forth in many years. Ashley House, where Harold, Kenny, and Grandmother had lived in Springfield, was, of course, named after this great man, and the training program he had initiated continued there.

Harold and Blossom were surprised and appreciative as they inspected the large living room. Tall Victorian windows reached almost from the floor to the high ceiling. A large bookcase, already partially filled, stood along one side of a fireplace. A handsome staircase rose from the hall beyond the living room, and to the right of it opened a smaller room with a dining room table and chairs already in place. Upstairs they found two bedrooms and a large storeroom. In the basement was an old coal furnace equipped with pipes to heat water. (A fine arrangement for the winter, they were to find, but it meant a summer with no hot water.) Equally important were electricity and a real indoor bathroom.

On two sides of the house was a long porch that overlooked a spacious lawn with a big maple tree in the center. At the edge of the lawn stood a small building that had been used as a guesthouse. The spacious church was just a short walk across the lawn. Their first glimpse of the church's interior was illuminated by the setting sun, falling across rows of polished pews and onto the altar. The family was grateful for the chance to quietly absorb the atmosphere of their new church before the congregation discovered their arrival.

"Do you think there are enough people around to fill this whole place?" Blossom wondered aloud.

Harold nodded. "Two fine preachers lived here—Dr. Ashley, and then Stewart Frazier, who has just left after many years. This time," Harold grinned, "You won't have to be the whole congregation on my first day of preaching."

The first Sunday turned out to be surprising in several ways. While Blossom was combing Norma's hair, Harold burst in, breathless from running across the lawn to the house.

"Blossom!" He exclaimed. "It's a whole ten minutes before the service begins and the church is full. The children from Cheyenne River Boarding School have come in together, and there's no more room! What do you think? They tell me that the minister's wife has always taught the Sunday school. When there are no overnight guests they hold it in that little building across the lawn . . . " He paused expectantly.

Blossom gave a final tug to Norma's hair ribbon. "I suppose I can, all right," she said nonchalantly. "I've had plenty of experience. How many are there?"

"About forty!" Harold called as he dashed back to the church.

To encourage, comfort, urge, and struggle—in company with faithful congregations of small missions—by now was a familiar way of life for Harold and Blossom. To shepherd a flock that billowed and grew beyond the physical limits of the church buildings and to find ways of sharing ministry among those who already wanted to serve would be an entirely new state of affairs.

Another new experience was serving a racially mixed congregation. The people of St. John's included several nationalities and races drawn to this center of Cheyenne River Agency by the hospital, government offices, and Indian school.

Blossom shared with Harold Clayton High Wolf's observations as they had stood watching the stream of people coming out of church to pick up their children from her class. "We're a rainbow church," Clayton had declared. "We have people of all colors and races and of many nationalities. If one of those colors should drop out of our rainbow, we wouldn't be complete." Harold felt that Clayton was right. God had promised to spare mankind from destruction by flood so long as the rainbow appeared in the sky, and that rainbow continues to be a parable for those on earth. Harold and Blossom were blessed to be in a place where their new friends understood and practiced this message.

Three days after their arrival, the Jones family was invited to a potluck supper in the parish house. At one time the small building had been a restaurant catering to the Bureau of Indian Affairs employees; eventually, the bureau had outgrown it and sold it to the church. Now the building was filling quickly, the combined fragrances of fried chicken, spaghetti, and fish wafting out the door to greet arrivals. As the Jones family entered, they noticed a large barrel near the door, rapidly filling with bundles.

They made their way through the crowded room to the farthest corner where there were still some empty chairs. A smiling committee member soon spotted the Jones family and brought them to the center table, where they were surrounded by the happy roar of voices, bursts of laughter, and the clatter of forks. The barrel full of bundles turned out to be gifts for them—bags of potatoes, canned vegetables and fruits, enough to fill a whole shelf, a ham, dishes, pots, a tea kettle, home-canned *wojapi*, dried meat strips, a quilt—everything they might need for months to come. Blossom stood to express her gratitude for this welcome.

Harold stood next. His attempt to voice his appreciation in two languages, Santee and English, brought louder shouts and clapping. "You have already done so much for us," he said. "Now we want to know how we can possibly be of help to you. I invite you all to our new home for a meeting so we can begin to think about things together. Will you come a week from tonight?"

The parishioners readily agreed, and that meeting proved to be a seed-bed in which new ideas rapidly germinated. Those who came represented a cross section of the Cheyenne River Mission. Some of the BIA employees mingled with the larger group of Indian people. The local high school principal was present, as were some personnel from the hospital, the storekeeper, and the post office clerk. Officers of the Women's Guild, the Brotherhood of St. Andrew, and the church committee attended. All sat around a long table, and Blossom continually filled coffee cups throughout the evening.

"What do we want St. John's, Cheyenne River, to be?" Harold asked first. In the few days they had been there, they had seen many positive things: enthusiasm, large numbers of people participating in the church, and a hopefulness that had been largely lacking in his previous congregations. But things could always be better. He hoped he could nudge these people along to a greater vision of themselves and their church.

It took some time, but people began to respond. "We're already too big for our buildings," someone remarked. "Then how can we build bigger ones?" another person asked. It was agreed that the church itself was fine, but the parish hall was far too small.

"There's no place in town where our youngsters can meet and have activities," someone else commented. "The boarding school children have their place, but what about the kids who live at home?"

"Maybe the bishop can give us some help for a new building," someone volunteered. "Let's ask him. He might even be pleased to know we want to expand. He'll probably say, 'I'll help you halfway if you can help yourselves."

What could the congregation do to raise money? Quilting bees were suggested but then ruled out because the parish hall wasn't large enough to accommodate them.

As the discussion continued, the parishioners agreed that a committee was needed to work on these ideas. Before the evening ended, they had selected a Bishop's Committee, the official title for a committee charged with running a mission church.

To Harold's immense delight, optimism was high, and expectations had been raised by the end of the meeting.

✄ + ✄

Days passed too quickly for Harold. St. John's was only one out of eleven missions under his care. His copriest, Harry Renville, who lived in White Horse, served three missions and Harold the rest. They included Emmanuel at White Horse; St. Mary's at Promise; St. Thomas-on-the-Tree; St. Paul's, LaPlante; St. James's, Bear Creek; St. Peter's, Thunder Butte; St. Andrew's, Cherry Creek; St. Stephen's, Red Scaffold; Ascension Church, Moreau River; plus two white congregations, a small mission called St. Stephen's, north of the Reservation, and Christ Church in Gettysburg.

Every Monday Harold taught released-time religious education classes at the Cheyenne River Agency Boarding School, first to the primary school classes and then to the high school in the afternoon. By 4 P.M. when the last bell rang, he felt wearier than he had after a full day of baseball pitching.

"Those kids would much rather talk to each other than to me," he complained to Blossom. "How can anything I say stick with them?"

Blossom teased, "Have you forgotten that we have two ears? We Indian people are very clever. We can wiggle and whisper and listen to somebody else, and at the same time listen with the other ear. Or at least we think we can. Never mind," she added more seriously. "There are bound to be some who are getting your message."

The rest of the week was spent traveling from one mission church to another. After an early breakfast, Harold would kiss his family good-bye before covering as many as three hundred miles in a day, visiting scattered congregations for midweek services and home visits. He tried to see the two white congregations outside the agency each week when he could work in the time, and he held two evening services a month for them. Wherever he went, Harold found old friends, and new ones became dear as they welcomed him—sometimes covered with dust, sometimes with mud, sometimes perspiring, sometimes bitterly cold.

Excitement mounted as the bishop's scheduled visit to Cheyenne River Agency approached. Bishop Roberts had written to tell them that since he would be traveling through another part of the district at that time, he was sending his coadjutor, Bishop Gesner.

Blossom scrubbed the floors, polished the old furniture until it shone, worked until late at night to hem up new curtains for the guestroom, and instructed Norma to be quiet and respectful while their guest was in the house. The house was as perfect as it could be—perfect until an hour before the bishop arrived. A water pipe broke upstairs in the bathroom, and the shining stairway became a gurgling waterfall. Luckily, Harold was home, so the pipe was replaced and the halls mopped up with only the mist from it covering the insides of the windows by the time Bishop Gesner stepped out of his car. He stretched after the long drive and took Harold's and Blossom's hands in his.

"How good it is to see you two!" he exclaimed heartily. "You both look well, but Blossom, my dear, I think you are working yourself too hard. She looks tired, Harold. Take care of this pretty wife of yours." Of course, the bishop wanted to see every corner of the house, and Blossom watched his face as she gave a tour. He said nothing, only nodding and smiling, but when they were finished, he turned to her with animation.

"My dear girl! You have kept this place as clean as Betty Frazier left it. And the floors! How did you get this long stairway so spotlessly clean?"

The visit was a great success. The congregation overflowed the church. That afternoon the Bishop's Committee arrived at the house to meet Bishop Gesner. The formation of such a committee was an excellent idea, he told them, and their welcome to the Jones family was praiseworthy. He was sure they would all find the choice of their new clergyman and his wife a fine one.

It seemed a good moment to broach the subject of future plans for St. John's. Bishop Gesner listened with head bowed. Did he know the Indian way of averting his eyes from the speaker out of politeness, or was he deep in thought? The thin crack in the table in front of him seemed to absorb his entire attention.

At last he sighed and raised his head. "Your plans are ambitious," he said. "I admire them. But they are not practical. Buildings require a great deal of money, which neither you nor the District of South Dakota has. We need our dreams, but we must recognize the difference between them and reality."

"We think we can raise half of the cost of the project, sir, if the district could help us to the extent of the other half?" The respectful tone of the committee chairman carried a hint of pleading. The other committee members assembled around the table turned quickly to study Bishop Gesner's face, then looked away again, knowing his answer before he gave it.

"I'm sorry. No. We are, as you know, a very poor district, and our congregations in the Indian field are many and a great deal needier than your St. John's. It would not be either politic or possible for us to squeeze out a penny for such a project."

Harold wondered if the bishop could sense how much his words shocked the group around the table. Certainly he could not have read it in the politely passive expressions of his Indian brothers, but the white members did not hide their disappointment. A smoldering storm gathered behind the eyes of the schoolteacher. Before it could burst into thunder, Harold quickly interposed, "Well, Bishop Gesner, it has been a long day for all of us. We thank you for the service this morning and for lis-tening to us this evening. Perhaps we'd better say good night."

The week after Bishop Gesner's visit was a gloomy one for many, but not for all. Most parishioners had not really expected a change. Others through the years had talked of changes that might be made for the better, but after all, times were hard and they were doing pretty well as it was. But the new committee members, appointed because of their special zeal for the church and the community, were especially disappointed.

"What good is our committee, anyway?" one of the members blurted out. "If our own district won't help us, why should we bother?"

"Sorry you were disappointed, Father." Donald Has Enemies met Har-old in front of the post office three days after the meeting. "But how are you going to change the thinking of the white powers in the church and everywhere else? They don't think we know how to succeed. I'll wager they don't really want us to either. They like it the way it is."

"Our strength here is that we work and think together, Donald," Harold spoke carefully. He didn't want to seem to agree with Donald, but he couldn't help feeling that way too. "There's that rainbow that Clayton High Wolf talks about. Not all the white men are prejudiced against us."

Donald Has Enemies looked across the street toward the offices of the Bureau of Indian Affairs and nodded. "You're right about that in this place, Father, but as I see it, we are a small, peaceful island in hostile waters."

Fleetingly, Harold felt an old despair grip him as he listened. He was a young boy in school, being observed by many pairs of disdainful eyes. He was a seminarian, facing an unsympathetic examining committee. He quickly brushed away the images. "It's time for us to have another meet-ing, I think. Will you come to our home again this Sunday afternoon so we can decide where we can go from here?"

This meeting was held in late March, and it began in character with the weather. Spring thaws had turned streets into muddy troughs, and the skies intermittently let loose flurries of snow and then deluges of rain. Like the weather, the meeting included thunder, a torrent of pent-up emo-tion, and some memories of the past—of the long, cold winter of past rela-tions, Indian to white man and vice versa, manifested in the moods of the committee members gathered around the table.

"Let's just drop it," was Donald Has Enemies's terse opinion. Many heads nodded in unison around the circle—but not quite all.

"Is that the way we all feel?" Henry Le Beau asked. "Are we going to let a forward-looking project drop without giving it a chance?"

"We say we are church people. Let's ask God to guide us. Maybe he will help us put up our own building," remarked one of the usually silent members.

Slowly the bleak mood changed, but still a consensus on the project could not be reached.

"We need to think things through a little longer," Harold observed. He sensed that the tide would turn in favor of action. "We need to pray and to talk with the rest of our congregation. Let's give ourselves until the second week in April, and then we can call a meeting of the entire church. Who knows what new ideas may turn up? I do believe it is God's will that we make it possible to grow. If it is, he will show us how."

Nobody waited until the second week in April. The women of St. John's Guild—a group made up of members of the church and also of townspeople who enjoyed the fellowship but were not church-goers—offered to give Harold six hundred dollars in war bonds, which they had been saving to dig a basement for the church. A parish house sounded even more promising. Encouraged, the Bishop's Committee drove to Gettysburg to a lumberyard owned by a Roman Catholic whom Harold knew through weekly trips to that town. The owner agreed to loan them three hundred dollars worth of rough lumber, some bags of cement, and a few tools needed to make forms for the foundation.

The true test of the congregation's enthusiasm came after the foundation was dug. The ground was still soft from freshly melted snow. Over twenty men volunteered to help, working under the supervision of experienced builders Weber Bill House and Nelson Le Beau. Each man was responsible for one section of the space, and every wheelbarrow in Eagle Butte was conscripted to carry soil. The workers hauled eleven truckloads of sand from the banks of the Missouri River at a place called Sand Pit, where sand was plentiful and free from pebbles and clay.

Shoveling, lifting, pushing, pulling, more shoveling—first into the back of an old truck. Once at the church, then more shoveling, lifting, pushing, and pulling as the precious burden poured into the small cement mixer that had been purchased with the guild's money. The sand, now turned into a heavy gray stream, gurgled from the turning mixer and was rushed by wheelbarrow to fill the man-made cavity before it thickened.

The men began work in the early morning before the sun shone down on their bare backs. By noon, however, it had turned their skin a deep red-brown and sent streams of perspiration flowing into their eyes, forcing them to wind kerchiefs around their foreheads. When the workers took a break and flopped down under the trees on the rectory lawn, Blossom and the other wives brought out tea, fry bread, *wojapi,* and thick slices of meat. A half-hour elapsed, and then they returned to work.

Since arriving at Cheyenne River Agency, Harold's muscles had lost some of their tone. Digging and carting sand gave him the satisfaction of responding to hard, physical work, which he had missed driving across the endless miles from one mission to another. Better yet was the comradeship that developed among the men as they strained and toiled together and watched the results of their labor taking shape.

The skeptical ones in the congregation watched and were impressed. As the new cement dried, they offered their services. The women, with La Dean as organizer, initiated daily picnics on the front lawn of the rectory. "Bring your supper, and let's eat together," she announced. "And bring a tool to help with the building. That's the admission price. No tool, no picnic."

News of the daily gatherings spread, and as many as one hundred people at a time visited the front lawn, bringing tools and later paintbrushes. The weather cooperated too, with many days of soft winds and clear skies. Under the watchful eyes of the two engineers-in-charge, the framework appeared over the foundation and the floor was laid.

Rummage sales took on a new approach. Blossom discovered boxes of secondhand clothing stowed in a corner of the rectory storage room. The boxes had been there for two or three years. New supplies arrived once a year from a church in the east and were always useful for money-raising projects. But what to do with musty clothes long stored in a dark corner?

Blossom brought the clothes out to the living room one day as the guild

gathered for a meeting. When Harold came into the house late that afternoon, he heard shrieks of laughter. Cautiously poking his head around the
corner of the living room door to investigate, he spied two of the women sitting on the floor, their arms buried in the old boxes. Around them were
strewn stockings, winter coats with fur collars, and a satin evening dress.
Blossom was standing up, holding a size forty-four corset—or so it looked
—in front of her slim self. On her head was an unkempt golden wig.

"We can sell tickets to come to our fashion show," she was chuckling.
"Or better yet, we can wrap things in bundles and charge ten cents a bag,
and everyone who buys one must put on the contents and keep it on during the picnic supper. We can have everybody vote on the 'best dressed person of the year' and have a funny prize as the reward. What do you say?"

Harold withdrew his head quickly as another peal of laughter erupted.

The project proved to be a great success. Both men and women bought
bags and ended up eating their suppers wearing wrinkled hunting caps,
floppy straw hats, pink curlers, or frayed scarves. Bill Picotte drew the gir-
dle and with a solemn face pulled its strings around his waist and sat with
garters dangling. He also managed to squeeze one foot into a large satin
slipper and wore an ancient fur piece around his neck. Bill sat eating his
supper, seemingly oblivious to the pointing fingers and laughter all
around him. Besides the fun it brought, the sale added sixty dollars to the
building fund. More money came from the annual bazaar held in November, and the guild worked hard to produce enough quilts and other
kinds of handiwork to hold another bazaar in May. As the money accumu-
lated, Maudie Grinnell, a newly confirmed member of St. John's, was appointed treasurer. Her position as an accountant for the BIA suited her for
the job.

The children from the boarding school returned to their homes for
summer vacation at the end of May. They had witnessed the first stages of
construction and had joined in a supper or two on the lawn, so they were
brimming with tales of the activities at St. John's, Cheyenne River Agency.
Word of the project spread across hundreds of miles, awaiting Harold as
he traveled from town to town to the mission churches.

Many people outside of Eagle Butte offered their services. One day after the service at Cherry Creek, Mrs. Running Bear, the mother-in-law of Red Fox, approached Harold. The old lady was bent from years of hard work, her face seamed from the strong winds and hot sun of many seasons, but her bright eyes shone with the trusting look of a child.

"*Tako-ja* [Grandson]," she said, "I hear that you're putting up a building and that everyone is helping with their own hands or with their money. I can't do either, but I have a dog. She's just had puppies. If I sell these eight puppies for fifty cents a piece and give the money to the project, will that be the kind of help you need?"

"Bless you, *Unks* [Grandmother]," Harold replied, thinking this was the kind of response that can move mountains. "You understand very well. With your kind of help, we can't fail in our plans."

The first boards for the base of the building were measured in May. By the end of September, the new parish house was completed, the last nail hammered, and the last door hung. How small the old meeting hall looked, now connected to the new one by a passageway and fitted out as the new kitchen! The shelves built inside were already outfitted with dishes bought at small cost from the government surplus store. Benches and chairs for the hall were bought there too. A large gas stove on loan from the BIA was put in the kitchen. A little over half the cost of the project was already paid for, and the rest would be easier now that the building was completed and could provide space for many activities. The Bishop's Committee agreed it was time to invite the bishop to visit.

Wednesday, September 19, was a golden day. The cottonwoods rustled gently in the wind that carried the ephemeral "summer snow" from branches and drifted it across the lawn. The afternoon sun beat down on the new roof as its builders strolled beneath, inspecting it critically. The windows, now sparkling clean, caught the sunlight. Sawdust and unused ends of board were piled neatly out of sight behind the building. From the small annexed building, now the kitchen, wafted the aroma of fry bread.

Everyone was dressed up for the occasion. The town store was closed for the afternoon, and children from the boarding school, already with a month of the fall term behind them, were excused early to witness the bishop's surprise and the dedication of the parish hall.

A group of little boys stationed themselves on the rectory porch, where they could see far down the road leading into town. When they saw a puff of dust in the distance from an approaching car, they ran back to their friends, exclaiming and waving with excitement.

When Bishop Roberts arrived, he stepped out to a line of smiling faces. Behind the assembled congregation stood a large, solid structure that had not existed even six months ago.

The bishop stared.

Harold and Blossom, coming forward to meet him, could see his genuine surprise.

"How in the world did this happen?"

"These people did it all." Harold's voice choked with pride. "Every bit of it."

Bishop Roberts turned from the building to the congregation, now crowding around him. "Do you mean to say you people did all of this with no financial aid from the district at all?" He sounded incredulous.

"Yes, sir!" said Maudie Grinnell exultantly, "and we want you to know, Bishop, that every bit of it is paid for except three thousand dollars, and with all our projects starting up for fall in our new building, that's practically in the bag!"

Over mounds of chicken, fry bread, corn, bounteous salads, pies, cakes, and coffee, Harold and the Bishop's Committee discussed their future plans with Bishop Roberts. Now that they had a proper-sized building, they could expand the Sunday school, provide meeting space for town gatherings, and proceed with plans for a riding club and a summer camp for boys. The women could hold their quilting bees, and the men would have ample space now for the Brotherhood of St. Andrew meetings. And now the youth would have a meeting place. Harold listened to the excited voices and saw the shining eyes of those who, just a few months ago, had sounded and looked so bleak. He wondered if the bishop felt the same thankfulness that filled Harold's heart.

It all came true. The Sunday school grew to 254 pupils with fourteen teachers and one superintendent. It had the largest Sunday school enrollment in the entire missionary district, including the white churches. The riding club flourished. Ranch boys and girls, who were already skilled riders, became experts under the disciplined eye of Wilbur BearsHeart. They performed for the state fair the following fall and were such a success that there was talk of a trip to Madison Square Garden. All winter long and into the spring, the youth group held meetings and organized dances. By the following summer, enough money had been raised from the dances to pay for basic equipment for a summer camp program for boys.

As Harold traveled each week around the reservation, he found that news of the activities at St. John's had spread even into the remote settlements. After a scheduled service, the congregation often lingered to ask him questions. The more they learned of those activities, the more eager they became to do something similar.

"Our boys need a camp like that too." The words were almost reproachful.

"Our church is falling apart. How can we get going on repairing it?"

"Our young ones get lazy when there's nothing to do while school is out. That's when the drinking begins."

The larger problems especially concerned Harold. Throughout his life, he had watched as poverty and isolation, a seemingly inherent part of reservation life for Indian people, led good men and women to lose hope and turn to alcohol. Most of them, however, still clung to the church. It was a part of their heritage, woven through the fabric of family life. But when alcohol took over after hopes failed, even the church had difficulty restoring normal lives to such people. What could offer solace, hope, and assurance that when they put away the bottle, something better would give purpose to life?

The success at St. John's kindled hope. Harold listened and prayed. Leaders were in every place, and some faithful folk always greeted him with a kindled fire in the winter and a cool glass of tea in the summer. There were willing workers and faithful followers who swept away the dead wasps, trapped in the church when the door was closed to the outside world for another week; who laid open the big Bible for him at the proper place for the lessons; who kept a mental list of the sick or troubled for him to call on; who took the time to go to lay reader's classes when they were held now and then; who kept faithful attendance at the Brotherhood of St. Andrew meetings.

❧ + ❧

It was time for another meeting, this time reservation wide. The burst of energy and now bustling church life at Eagle Butte had attracted attention, and so the new parish house became the meeting place for all eleven missions. The missions decided to organize as the Cheyenne River Mission Council, which would keep records and operate according to a charter.

Among those who came were the old and wise who, like Harold's grandfather, had lived through the bitter days of war and resettlement programs, when tribal ties were broken and land belonging to the tribe for generations became forbidden to them. Their faces were lined, the eyes of some milky blue from cataracts, but they still looked out upon the world and listened with the peculiar serenity belonging to the old who have endured despite adversity. In contrast to them were young ranchers, who drove pickups and wore the wide brimmed hats of cowboys. They were schooled to take advantage of the information and opportunities that the BIA offered from time to time to improve their allotted land. They were the luckier ones whose land lay near irrigation projects or fell within fertile stretches of prairie for feeding cattle and horses. Storekeepers, postal workers, and BIA employees came from towns, and others arrived from ranches and small farms that were not farms at all but land surrounded by sandy prairie. They came to sit patiently, led by hope that this time something practical might emerge from talking. Women also participated. Some were content to observe, listen, watch, and form their own opinions to be shared at home with their husbands in preparation for the next meeting. The women's guilds were there in force too, interested in the plans that were made to benefit children and youth.

By the end of the first meeting, the little children were all asleep, curled peacefully at their parents' feet, heads resting on folded jackets. Even after so many hours of sitting and listening, of pondering and discussing, the adults seemed in no hurry to leave. Some daring thoughts had been artic-ulated. At the end of the gathering, the future held a promise that had not been there at the beginning.

"That allotted land our missions were given fifty years ago," someone said during the meeting. "We don't have resident priests who need it for farming anymore. It's just forty acres of wasted space; a few have twice as much. The ranging horses find it alright, and some of us take our cattle to eat it down so the mission won't stand as much chance of catching fire some day in a storm. But really it's wasted space. The cemeteries take only an acre or two of the allotments. In a thousand years we'll never fill up the whole of the forty acres, no matter how tall we grow!"

Ideas flourished. "Are you thinking what I'm thinking?" someone asked. "Maybe we could trade some of the acreage to the tribe for a piece of land that we could do something with. We know it takes about forty acres to feed one horse for a year. And what can any of us do with one horse, ex-cept to let our kids ride it? If we could get five hundred acres of good grass-land all in one area, then we'd have something."

"We could get an expert cowhand among us to teach our boys how to care for cattle," someone suggested.

"We could have a real summer camp, where the boys could learn and at the same time be the cowboys to tend the herd and rake the hay and curry the horses."

"Those of us who have two or three cows or more could donate a calf to build up a herd."

"We can invent our own brand," another person speculated. "It will rep-resent the Cheyenne River Mission Council."

"We can have the initials CRM. We can get that done in Pierre. I know a good iron smith."

"Here we go again with extra bazaars and dinners!" The women smiled and nodded their heads.

"If you need a caretaker of that land when we get it, I'd like to be it," Henry Le Beau spoke up, and the others, knowing his reputation as a rancher and a good man, gave a cheer.

Afterward, as the attendees stood about drinking a last cup of coffee be-fore the long ride home, discussion turned to names.

"If all this really amounts to something, I think we should change the name of our organization. Cheyenne River Mission Council doesn't really say much. It's too broad."

"That's what we are, though, and have been for a long time. Maybe we'd better keep that title but introduce a new committee inside it."

"We could be a Council of Advice."

"Yes, but we want to do more than give advice."

Over the next few weeks, the name was debated. All eventually agreed to the Reconstruction and Advance Program of the Cheyenne River Reservation.

It was a proud name that befitted the elated group. The new parish house at St. John's became busier than ever. Church conferences began to meet there, bringing in a small income from the ladies' lunches and suppers served. Other clubs that used the ample meeting space were charged a modest fee. Hardly an evening passed when some group was not meeting there: quilters and cooks, bazaar workers, the riding school. Harold found he had to put in ahead of time his request to use the parish house for the Bible study group, the confirmation classes that were growing too large to meet in his home, the acolytes' training groups, and Sunday school teacher's meetings.

The first experimental camp for boys opened the following summer at the BearsHearts' ranch. Each boy brought his own tent or constructed a tipi modeled after that of his great-grandfather. Before the ten days came to an end, the plain was peppered with small, and some not so small, lodgings, brave with splashes, circles, triangles, and rectangles of color. Reds, blues, blacks, greens all carried individual messages on the sides and door flaps of the tipis, announcing in symbols the identity of the owners. The boys came from all the reservations in South Dakota and some even from North Dakota and Nebraska. John Artichoker, a well-known educator, became director of the camp. Evenings, after the sun sank slowly out of the sky, everyone gathered around a campfire to hear stories of the old days and to pray.

Harold's daughter, Norma, would often perch on a fence post and watch the riding class enviously. Her father began searching for a pony as he made his weekly rounds each week. He found a plump half-Shetland with flowing tail and long white lashes that gave her eyes a demure look, a look which, as they soon discovered, was quite deceiving. To Norma, she was the most wonderful pony in the world, and she named her Champ.

Never had the Jones family been busier or happier. Harold took his four services each Sunday and traveled miles across the prairies to reach the ten other mission churches during the week. Busy and happy they were, but they were also poor. Harold's salary of $150 a month didn't go far, even with the extra $90 that the district furnished for car maintenance. When the Gettysburg church learned that his travel expenses exceeded that amount, they added from $15 to $50 more each month, depending on how often Harold was summoned for special events like weddings, funerals, or sick calls. The garden lessened food bills in the summer months, but even so grocery bills amounted to more than the salary. Blossom resumed teaching.

One fall a violent blizzard foiled Harold's plans to attend a meeting of the missionary district's board of directors in Sioux Falls. His car got stuck in a massive drift on a lonely road near Dupree. He was lucky that the mishap occurred close to the home of a white rancher, who hospitably took him in for the two nights before the car could be dug out. Although dressed in his clericals and business suit, Harold attempted to repay the kindness by pitching in with the milking and chores. He was deeply disappointed to miss the Sioux Falls meeting, where he had been scheduled to present the plans of the Cheyenne Reconstruction and Advance Program. He had been confident they would be received favorably.

How could it be otherwise? It would be a welcome reversal of expectations. It was hard for whites to understand what they considered Indian laziness and incompetence. Even when such sentiments were not actually voiced, Harold could feel them in the manner some greeted him as he came into meetings, see them in the glances exchanged when an elderly Indian churchman took too long to make a response to a question posed to him, or hear them in the barely audible but unmistakably amused murmur that greeted comments by Hawkfeather, who wore a braid down his back.

This new stirring of enthusiasm for a plan to be self-sufficient would surely be met with pleasure. Harold could see the raised eyebrows and heads nodding in agreement. He could almost feel the handshakes of those who had spoken to him of the need to "stir up some action," to "raise a little capital," and to "show an interest in self-sufficiency" inside the reservations.

This was a people movement, he would tell them, generated by the congregation itself, not passed down from above. It had begun with a small circle of concerned parents and grandparents, thinking ahead to the time when their children would become adults. The old ones spoke of the past that had been better, not filled with the temptations of drink and idleness, with dependence on the government for life itself. The young ones saw a vision of how it could be and laid out a practical plan to make it happen. Like a pebble dropped in a pond, the small circle of initiative widened until the whole of Cheyenne River Reservation was caught up in the motion.

The plan had been carefully worked out. First would come the exchange of unused allotted lands to the tribe for land that would encompass at least five hundred acres in one place. It should be a place where grass grew well and the soil was suitable for gardens; where there would be water for the cattle and irrigation; and enough space, in addition to the land for grazing and gardening, for a summer camp. Here boys could come to learn ranching and farming. They would, in time, build a meeting place for church convocations or retreats. It would be a center for the training of catechists, helpers, and lay readers, who could come together from all over the reservation. Since every mission would have exchanged some land for this larger piece, all would have a personal interest in it.

The land that the tribe had allotted over fifty years ago for the use of each mission congregation was indeed Indian land. But it was also property of the missionary district, as was all church land throughout the state. But this unused land, now for the most part gone to weeds and brambles around the white church buildings, would be converted into property that could benefit the whole district. Once the land exchange was made, they could move the heifers and the young calves—already being branded with the new letters CRM for Church Reconstruction Movement and set aside within individual small herds—to the large area. It was a sound plan, and Harold was confident he could sell it to the district authorities.

Even in the planning of the project, Harold watched a new spirit of cooperation growing among people for whom distance had been a real barrier. A central committee now united them into one family. If St. Mary's,

Promise, had a carpenter in its congregation, then St. Luke's, Iron Lightning, might call on him to help with a rotting step. If St. Philip's, Dupree, or St. James, Bear Creek, had a flourishing Brotherhood of St. Andrew, then its members might visit one of the other missions that was weak in that organization. Ascension Church, Moreau, might establish a Sunday school teacher-training meeting for the other missions, while St. John's might offer training in the handling of finances as the budding ranch began to prosper.

This project was too large and important to be kept secret as the building of the St. John's parish hall had been. The whole Cheyenne River Mission Council was involved. News spread and other reservations became curious. When the bishops made annual visits to the Cheyenne River Reservation, their sharp questions betrayed their own interest.

❧ + ❧

In late spring of 1952, just five years after the Jones family had arrived at Cheyenne River Reservation, Harold and Blossom received a request from Bishop Roberts to meet him at Yankton College "for a conference."

Something was wrong. The summons sparked that nearly forgotten, foreboding sensation that Harold had wrestled with many times before in his life.

Bishop Roberts greeted them cordially.

He thought, he said, that they would be pleased to hear that the district had such confidence in Harold's leadership abilities that they were asking him to return to Pine Ridge as superintending presbyter with twenty missions under his care. Frank Thorburn, who the bishop knew was a good friend of Harold's, was leaving Pine Ridge after years of service there. It was an important position and one that required a good man to follow the able example of Father Thorburn.

Harold wondered if his face showed the consternation that transformed Blossom's at this news. "I appreciate your confidence in me, Bishop," he blurted, "but we're just on the verge of our big project on the Cheyenne. The people there are depending on us to lead them in it. We feel it's tremendously important that we stay with them for at least another year or two."

"Oh, please!" It was almost an involuntary gasp from Blossom.

Bishop Roberts reached out a large hand and patted her shoulder. "I thought you might like the prospect of going back to your home territory. The people will certainly be happy to see you again," he said kindly but firmly. It was settled.

When the congregations across the Cheyenne River Reservation heard about the bishop's decision, they sent letters and delegations urging that Harold be allowed to stay for another five years. The two non-Indian congregations in Dupree and Gettysburg joined in the petitions to keep the Jones family for awhile longer, but nothing changed the bishop's mind.

"I've done it again," Harold thought bitterly. "I've tried to go beyond the limits white society has set for Indians. They're not happy with innovations of our making. This is a terrible disappointment. But what can I do?" Duty struggled with frustration. "Never mind. The seed is planted; there are good people to water and tend it. I must go where I am sent."

Harold never found a satisfying reason for his sudden transfer from Cheyenne River back to Pine Ridge. Both bishops knew of their reconstruction and advance plans, and Bishop Roberts had pointed to the Cheyenne River Reservation as an example of people working together. While both bishops were complimentary, they obviously felt the Cheyenne efforts should be stopped. A number of reasons came to Harold's mind: fear of a new project, of entanglement with government taxes resulting from the ranching business, or perhaps of the complexity of the proposed exchange of church lands with the tribe.

The Reconstruction and Advance Program did continue, at least in part. When one of the missions needed money for a project or for other kinds of help, the program was there to lend assistance. But sadly the rest of the project faded away. The young priest who took Harold's place wasn't interested in the ranch business, and those momentous plans were simply dropped.

11

CHALLENGE
AND CHANGE

☙ + ❧

1952–1956

Pine Ridge Reservation, with its twenty missions scattered across a spectacular land of deserts, buttes, caverns, black forest, and windswept prairies, was not one that could be guided easily into cooperative action. Like the land, many of its people were recognized for their individuality and proud of it, seeing little reason to change or bend. And even if they would consider working together, the bitter winds of winter and dry heat of summer created barriers against frequent meetings.

Hard, long-standing poverty also deadened incentive. It took so much energy and fortitude to buck the dust storms, droughts, and long snows that little was left to fight for better schools, medical help, or farming opportunities. Even replacing a broken front step on a mission porch or a broken pew inside a church often seemed beyond the will of its members. When the elements so quickly undid what man accomplished, why bother? And anyway, who had a spare board long enough and strong enough for a new front step? It meant driving ninety miles into town to pick one up, a trip that would require car repairs first to ensure the trip could even be accomplished. And then who could furnish money for gas? It appeared to Harold that most people felt it better to leave things alone, hop across the first step, and find a good solid pew to sit on.

The first sermon Harold preached on his return to Pine Ridge in the late summer of 1952 was for the ordination service of Paul Clark. Paul lived with his wife, Lois, in the house the Jones family had occupied while assisting Father Thorburn. The young white priest alternated with Harold in the care of sixteen of the missions and the services at Holy Cross Church in the town of Pine Ridge. Father Andrew Weston, who lived in Porcupine, had the care of the other three missions in his area.

"I think the way to begin our work is to concentrate on one place first," Harold mused aloud to Blossom. "That should be our home mission church. We can find out what the needs are here and try to meet them. If we succeed, others around the reservation will see and perhaps take heart. What we have to fight here that we didn't have to face at Cheyenne River is a sense of despair. It's so deep seated that hardly anyone recognizes it anymore. When you grow up in a particular kind of atmosphere, you think of it as the normal one for everyone."

"*I* grew up here," Blossom bridled.

Harold looked at her quizzically. "So you did, and a good thing you made of it too and so did all the Steeles. But your family, Blossom, could make an oasis out of a desert island. I was thinking more of St. Mark's Church at Rockyford. Sure, they're a devout people and look to heaven, but what about *right now?* Do you know, Blossom, I think that the massacre at Wounded Knee still holds us in its shadow. The slaughter of one's grandparents, and in the case of the older folk, of one's parents, isn't quickly forgotten."

"Everybody knows we can't dwell on those things," replied Blossom, "but there are other things to keep people in a state of depression." She went on, her voice rising. "What about scarcity of water and the complete dependence on weather for the health of our crops and cattle? What about *poverty* with no possible way to escape? What about a government whose laws and treaty makers change every few years so laws and promises stop meaning much of anything? Harold Jones, what about a church that insists its priests be educated and then sets up impossible barriers for most to receive an education, and when one comes along who surmounts those barriers, it puts him into such deep debt he may never get out of it? And what's more, his superiors keep him so busy he rarely sees his family!"

"Enough!" Harold interrupted. "We may know these things, but they are all the more reason why the church should be strong in every place. The real church—God's own people. The church belongs to God. That's the prime fact.

"If people remember this, nothing is too hard for them. Life may be very hard, very sad, very hungry, very poor, but not enough to overwhelm them. It's our job, Blossom, to remind the people of this.

"Never mind if a priest comes for services less than six times a year. The church is *you,* and you can gather together to worship him and pray for the world and yourselves and give thanks for life, and he is right there with you. But," Harold added with a sigh, "the place to gather is sometimes hard to find. The old meeting houses are fast tumbling down. Broken windows, sagging steps, oil tanks stolen . . ."

"Be careful!" Blossom put her finger to his lips. "You're beginning to sound like me."

Harold smiled. "As soon as we get back from General Convention, we'll get together with the Holy Cross committee and see what they think."

❧ + ❧

General Convention, the triennial meeting of the Episcopal Church that brought together all of the bishops and an equal number of priests and lay members as deputies from each diocese, met in legislative session in Boston in September 1952. Harold was selected to be deputy from South Dakota, an honor and a responsibility. He arranged to have Blossom and Norma accompany him. It would do them all good to get a break from the daily challenges of reservation life.

The Jones family was invited to stay with a family in an elegant house in Brookline, a wealthy suburb of Boston. Norma's chief memory of the visit was watching from her bedroom window as maids gathered across the street to walk their employers' dogs. While Harold attended the meeting downtown, Blossom and Norma did some sightseeing in the historic city.

Taking a few days off from the convention, they visited New York City. Strolling down the streets around the hotel, they absorbed the strange new sights and smells of the big city. "On the brightest day the street seems overcast," noted Norma. "You walk in what you think is twilight, and suddenly a beam of light shines on you and you realize it's the shadows of the tall buildings that make a bright noon seem like evening."

"Everyone is in such a hurry!" Blossom added. "When someone blows a horn, it sounds so strange. It bounces off buildings, echoing all the way up to the top of the skyscrapers."

The second evening in New York, the family joined the audience of a radio quiz show. They entered quietly and took seats at the back of the studio, but it was not long before the roving eye of the quiz master spotted them. He walked back, chatting into his microphone until he reached them.

"We seem to have a man of the cloth in our audience today. And may we ask what branch of the Christian church you belong to, sir?"

"Ah, yes, the Episcopal!" he repeated after Harold. "You are just the one to answer some questions for us in the religion category. Will you please follow me to the platform, sir?"

Harold followed obediently. The quiz master continued his affable chatter until they were facing one another on the platform.

"First question," he began crisply.

Harold shook his head. "I would like to choose sports," he said.

"I beg your pardon?"

"Sports. Baseball."

The announcer stepped back, eyebrows raised. An audible titter ran through the audience. "Well, I'll be! A pretty sporty parson. Are you sure?"

Harold nodded. He put his head back and laughed, and the audience joined him, laughing and clapping. After each answer, correct and quickly given, the applause continued, and when Harold stepped from the platform with fifty dollars in prize money, shouts and whistles accompanied him back to his seat between Blossom and Norma. That evening they celebrated by having dinner in the Waldorf Astoria dining room.

❧ + ❧

It was a wonderful visit, the new experiences standing in sharp contrast to life on the reservation. Even so, it was good to get back home again and pick up some of the plans they had temporarily put aside.

"We'll call a meeting of the Holy Cross Church Committee first thing next week," Harold announced resolutely. "We will find out from them what they think is needed to reach people right here, and I'll ask for their thoughts about forming a reservation-wide Bishop's Committee like the one we had at Cheyenne River."

The meeting was a struggle and poorly attended. But out of it came a consensus of opinion that Holy Cross Church needed a new organ. It was a big church, and the small pump organ wheezed and gasped, sometimes fainting away in midhymn. Even when it behaved properly, the sound barely reached the back of the church. Most, though, believed that a new organ was out of reach. A new coat of paint inside the church and new materials for the church school could be managed but certainly no organ.

A good music store in Rapid City allowed the church to try out a new Hammond console organ. If the congregation liked it, the payments could be carried over a few years. By the end of six months, the organist, Evelyn Bergen, stated flatly that she "would not go back to playing the old wheeze box." The congregation was pleased with the new sound and responded to the committee's suggestion that it be paid for by memorial gifts in the name of departed souls. A plaque with those names engraved on it was placed on the wall beside the console. Holy Cross had its new organ.

✲ + ✲

Next came the formation of an areawide Bishop's Committee, with the smaller congregations following the lead of Holy Cross. The first piece of business presented to the new committee was the condition of the nineteen missions on the reservation. One by one, representatives from each of them listed sagging floorboards, broken windowpanes, missing hinges, peeling paint, and other signs of deterioration. When they had finished, everyone agreed that St. Julia's, Porcupine, stood in the greatest need. Apparently, no one dared to ring the bell at St. Julia's for fear the bell tower would topple. Also the steps of that church were ready to give way, and the pews were coming apart.

After the meeting Harold had an idea. Pine Ridge had been of special interest of the Cathedral of St. John in Denver for several years now. Harold decided that if the cathedral was gracious enough to take an interest in Pine Ridge, the people of the reservation shouldn't disappoint it.

Dean Roberts greeted Harold's call warmly. He was very pleased, he said, that the Joneses were back at Pine Ridge again, a place that the cathedral had adopted whole-heartedly.

"What do you mean by 'adopted' ?" Harold asked him forthrightly. "Exactly how interested are you in us?"

The dean seemed taken aback. He was quiet for a minute. "What are you getting at?"

Harold told him about the condition of the mission in Porcupine and of his hopes to restore it not only for its own sake but also as a ray of hope for other missions on the Pine Ridge Reservation. He concluded, "I should like to bring a delegation of people from St. Julia's to speak for themselves. Let them tell you what they want to do. If your congregation feels that it can become financially involved, we will be grateful for what help you can give us."

The dean agreed. The next task for Harold was to talk with Father Weston and his congregation at St. Julia's. It took several meetings to persuade people to take the matter seriously and agree to send a delegation to the cathedral. When the cathedral was notified, St. Julia's received an invitation to the morning service on the second Sunday in April 1953 to sing some Indian hymns and to be the guests at a coffee hour following the service. A half-dozen could scarcely be heard singing in such a tremendous place, so it was determined that nine must go. These included Clarence Three Stars and his wife, Evelyn Bergen, Bill Young Bear, Eddie Iron Cloud, the Westons, and Harold and Blossom.

Plans were laid for the long trip in two cars from Pine Ridge into Colorado. Norma would spend the weekend with Blossom's parents on their farm, so she would not be going to Denver. The old car was given a fresh tune up, and the Westons' livelier model was designated to carry the other five.

Blossom was packing the picnic basket for an early morning start when a knock on the door interrupted her. Bill Young Bear, looking very sober, asked to see "Father Jones."

After Harold visited with him a proper length of time, a short silence elapsed before Bill blurted out, "I'm sorry to disappoint you, but I can't go with you tomorrow."

"Is one of the children sick?" Harold asked anxiously.

"No, it's nothing like that, but I find I'm unable to go."

"Is there something I can do?"

Bill's eyes traveled over Harold, appraising him. "No, I'm afraid you are not fat enough and a little too tall."

Harold's laugh was so hearty that it brought Blossom out of the kitchen to share the joke. "If it's just clothes that's the problem, we can fix you up in fine style," she heard him say. "Come on over to the rummage closet. You can make quite a choice. We need you, Bill, even if you have to come in an old gunnysack!"

Harold watched proudly the next morning as Bill stepped between the imposing doors of St. John's Cathedral, looking as if he were accustomed to the grandeur of stained glass, velvet pew cushions, and a deep red carpet that stretched from the entrance right up to the altar. In his cream-colored suit, he was a splendid figure, straight and composed, turning neither left nor right as he was ushered to chairs set for the visitors at the foot of the chancel steps. Harold's eyes fell next on Blossom, standing beside him. He tried to see her as if for the first time. How would he describe her? Lovely, gracious, poised, her small chin tilted upwards just a little, and enough of a spark veiled behind that gentle gaze to keep one looking, wondering, and wanting to look some more. Evelyn Bergen was a lady at home in any place—a natural lady, full of spunk and keen understanding. She was a teacher and a musician and proud of her Indian heritage in a way Harold secretly envied. She took it for granted that everybody would naturally recognize that heritage as a special gift. As she took her long walk down the carpeted aisle, her head turned from one side to the other, nodding and smiling to those who were staring at the guests. For the Three Stars and Iron Clouds, Harold sensed this stretch of red carpet brought some pain. But they, like the others, were pictures of composure.

Harold was happy and proud to sit with the group. What a relief it was to be able to listen to a sermon instead of preaching one for a change! Bishop Gesner was guest preacher at the service. His voice rolled across the large expanse of the nave, describing the immensity of the task of attempting to bring the Christian message to one hundred Indian missions as well as to the white congregations dotted modestly across the state. He dwelt on the poverty that was the lot of the reservations and of the meager district budget. With few white priests to carry on the work of the church, Indian leaders were trained to be helpers, catechists, and lay readers to carry out the morning prayer services and to teach. As the cathedral congregation well knew, he told them, there were few Indian priests who served their people. One was Vine Deloria Sr., whom the St. John's congregation had graciously helped in the past, and others included Harold Jones and Andrew Weston, sitting with the delegation from Pine Ridge.

Seated facing the congregation, Harold could look across the sea of faces and see that the bishop's words touched them.

Instead of the anthem that Sunday, a Dakota hymn was printed in the bulletin, to be sung during the offering. When the time came to sing, the organ swirled into a fortissimo of sound, playing through the entire melody with embellishments that made it barely recognizable, then pushing in the soft pedal to give an accompaniment for nine voices. The voices, Harold was proud to note, drowned out the organ as they bravely sang the familiar and loved verses of "Guide me, O Thou Great Jehovah."

Later at the coffee hour, Harold lost track of his friends. All of them became small islands, isolated from the rest by groups of parishioners congratulating them on the singing, asking questions about reservation life, and showing such genuine and uninformed interest that Harold decided the wisest course of action was to invite a delegation to visit St. Julia's. "But not until the repairs and additions are made!" He added firmly, "So it will be safe for you to sit down and so we can ring the bell to welcome you."

Dean Roberts proposed that those interested in learning more should meet together in the parish house late on the following Tuesday afternoon. To Harold's surprise, they were met by a large group, many more than the vestry members or Social Concerns Committee, who were the officials appointed to visit. It was agreed that the cathedral should continue sending $750 as before to Pine Ridge each year, but it would be earmarked for the work at St. Julia's and doubled to $1,500 the first year for initial expenses.

"Well!" exclaimed Eddie Iron Cloud when the smiles and nodding heads around the circle confirmed the good news. "If they can do so much for us, we should pledge to do something too." He paused to calculate what it could be. "There are eleven families in St. Julia's Mission. Only one of them is not receiving welfare, but I'm sure every one of those families

can raise one hundred dollars in a year's time." A spontaneous burst of applause from the cathedral members greeted that announcement.

Dean Roberts seemed to be waiting for something. He turned to Bishop
Gesner. "And what can we expect from the bishop of South Dakota?" he
asked innocently.

The bishop cleared his throat. "I suppose we can find another $750
somewhere," he agreed. Another round of applause erupted. The project
was assured.

By fall of 1954 the new building, including a bell tower, was almost
completed, all achieved by the work of the local people of Porcupine. Again
came lunch-basket sales, popcorn and sandwiches, cake and pies, rummage sales, quilting parties, and impromptu ball games. A feast, almost ri-
valing the Niobrara Convocation's in size, brought visitors from other reservations, who donated to the project they had heard about and now could
witness for themselves. It was certainly hard work. On Cheyenne River
Reservation, water had been easily available. At Porcupine there was only
one pump, but the women pitched in to fill and refill three oil barrels,
keeping them moving back and forth to the site of the new foundation,
where the men mixed and poured cement.

Dean Roberts, his wife, and the vestry were invited to the promised celebration. It was a time of rejoicing and feasting, with the oil drums
pressed into service again as pots for cooking sides of beef over wood fires.
Women leaned into the steaming pots to bring up large chunks of meat,
which was then cut and placed beside corn, fry bread, *wasna, wojapi,* slices
of pie, and generous pieces of cake. The guests from Denver shook their
heads in disbelief over the heaping plates offered to them. Balancing a
plate in one hand and a brimming coffee mug in the other, the guests
moved warily to the benches, where they could sit and enjoy the feast. Delegations from the nineteen missions on the Pine Ridge Reservation also
attended to help St. Julia's congregation welcome the honored guests.

While the setting sun poured gold over the sky, the Name Ceremony,
so seldom enacted in those days, gave Dean Roberts the name Wanblee
Wohitika, (Courageous Eagle), with a headdress and a peace pipe to take
home as a reminder of the gratitude of the people on Pine Ridge Reservation.

St. Julia's had a new beginning. From it, as Harold had hoped, other missions were stimulated into action.

✄ + ✄

The awakening of a new spirit of hope among the missions gladdened Harold's heart, but the dry, windy distances between them didn't change. He saw little of his family as he traveled many miles each day in his old, complaining car. To help pay for more frequent repairs on the engine and tires, gasoline, and food, Blossom again returned to teaching. Norma quickly took up with the old friends and cousins she had left behind and was happy at school and play. Hardly a day went by when she didn't bring one of her friends home to share supper or, in some cases, to find a temporary refuge for a week or more. Through all of their married lives, Harold and Blossom shared their home with young people who needed a place to stay for a time. In Pine Ridge visitors of all ages on their way to the clinic, on shopping trips into town from the ranch lands, or on their way to conduct business with the Indian agency office, stopped by for a chat, a meal, or an extended visit. It was the accepted pattern of reservation life, and Blossom and Harold opened their doors to receive these visitors in need.

The lonely journeys across the prairies gave Harold time to think about their debts. Both Blossom's and Harold's college years had been completed through loan programs, and the debts remained outstanding even after eighteen years. Added to them were food bills, clothing bills, and the constant cost of repairs on the old car. One night, without any apparent cause, the car coughed and died, leaving Harold stranded on a thin ribbon of road where he waited until early dawn before another car appeared on its way to the town of Pine Ridge. A worried Blossom was waiting for him. Hiring a tow truck to bring in the car for repairs added more to the debts. The tires, he was told, were too worn to stand up to the coming winter and must be replaced. Even more debts.

✄ + ✄

In September a request came to attend the annual meeting of the super-intending presbyters of the Indian reservations at the Cathedral Hall in Sioux Falls, 250 miles from Pine Ridge. With the car's engine freshly tuned, Harold decided that he could reach Sioux Falls in plenty of time for a 2 P.M. meeting if he left by 6 A.M. He was careful to fill a gallon jug with water. The "old girl" was beginning to complain about the heat generated on long trips and needed a cooling drink now and then. Twice Harold pulled off the road when he noticed that the landscape through the wind-shield was wavering. He used up the water and at the third stop needed to wait what seemed an interminable time before he could slowly and cau-tiously continue to the cathedral.

The meeting was already in progress when he entered the room, dusty and tired. He couldn't help but notice a quick exchange of amusement among his fellow priests, all white men, as he entered. "Typical Indian," the looks said to him. "He still keeps Indian time in spite of his seminary training."

Harold was reminded of those frustrating years of being tested in ways and at times that were so unfair. He seethed. But it was not worth venting his irritation to explain why he was late. With some difficulty, he turned his attention to the ongoing discussion.

All of the reports showcased the same problems: poverty; hardships of weather, alcohol, and isolation; waning interest in the church. In his re-port, Harold mentioned St. Julia's good fortune and the pilgrimage to St. John's Cathedral in Denver. He told of Eddie Iron Cloud's response to the cathedral gift and how the people of St. Julia's rallied to meet the terms of his promise. Again came smiles, not sly this time but openly admiring. One of the priests remarked, "You must know how to accomplish mir-acles. How do you get that kind of steady giving from your people? All we can manage is a one-shot gift, usually right out of the pocket, or none at all."

As the day wore on, Harold felt that the others began to forget his In-dian blood or perhaps were less conscious of his presence as they relaxed into camaraderie and reminisced about their reservation experiences. He joined in the laughter at many of the tales, adding his own stories. But some remarks left him sick at heart.

"We have a couple of old codgers who have been lay reading for years. You'd think after repeating the same passages from the Bible for the hundredth time they wouldn't stumble over the pronunciation, but it's a sure thing that there's going to be 'weeping and gunashing of the teeth' at 'Judg-ment day.'

"Do you think I can train old Fred to remember to put out the candles at the end of a service? And that dismissal prayer he uses in Dakota goes on and on. I'll be blessed if I know what all he's talking about."

"Does it annoy you to have the whole congregation sitting with bowed heads while you preach to them? I can pour out my soul and get no sign that they are taking it in. They might all be asleep, except that they stand up at the right time when it's over."

Harold felt the old anger surging. These were all good men; of their own accord they had chosen to come to the reservations. Why hadn't they been given some kind of cultural training to help them better understand the people they came to serve? From their vantage point, even the finest elder churchmen and women would appear untutored. Harold, though, knew those Indian people to be devout and humble Christians, saints of God, steeped in a spiritual sensibility that these white men might never learn.

Resentment still burned in Harold that evening as he began a rapid walk around the cathedral grounds after supper. His head was bent, his hands thrust into his pockets when he felt a clap on his shoulder. He looked up to find Dr. Barbour striding to catch up with him.

"A walk after dinner clears the brain, eh, Harold?"

"Yes, sir." The appellation came from force of habit and recalled the grim confrontations he had once had with this clergyman, whose smile was affable now. Over the years, Harold still recalled those eyebrows raised in astonishment over the stupidity of the young seminary student.

The careless remarks of the superintending presbyters that afternoon had reopened old wounds. This man had chaired the meeting, and he could have put a stop to them. Quite suddenly, Harold found his fear drain away. He stopped and faced Father Barbour. The priest was an old man now, his once dark hair white. His step, though, was as firm as ever and so was the set of his chin.

Harold's voice sounded hard and unnatural. "Dr. Barbour, you and these other men are here to guide our people. You've known the Dakotas for many years. Yet you can still joke about our customs, and when we work hard to meet the standards you set in the church, you knock us down.

"Why, Dr. Barbour, did you try to prevent my ordination to the diaconate? Why did you prevent me from receiving my seminary degree, and why did you bring your influence to bear to delay my ordination to the priesthood for two years? The seminary found me capable. I met the requirements for graduation, but when I came home to the reservation you imposed one delay after another. Why?"

The look of amazement on the priest's face made Harold realize that his own face was burning and his fists were clenched. He unclenched them and took a deep breath.

Father Barbour said nothing for what seemed a long time, then he nodded in agreement. "That's right, Harold. You came out of a humble background, although, thanks to your grandparents, with more understanding of the church than most. But we felt—I was not alone in this—that the seminary was in the process of spoiling you. You were unique to them, you know. You were going to be their first Indian graduate. They elected you class president, heaped honors on you until even you, modest as you may have been to start with, must have developed an oversized ego. We couldn't have that, you know. Yes, we needed your gifts and your new knowledge, but we couldn't stand the chance of your taking on airs and thinking you stood as high as those who had been serving your people faithfully for so many years while you were still a young lad. Yes, Harold, we really were out to fry you."

Harold blinked at this frank admission. After a pause he asked, "And when did you find you could stop? Someone decided to appoint me a superintending presbyter."

Doctor Barbour's laugh broke the tension. "I have to admit that ten years of watching you handle some pretty desperate situations and taking hardships with the Lord's own precious gift of cheerfulness made me realize that you were made of the real stuff after all. It is a little late, Harold, but that makes it more genuine. I apologize for the way we fried you. We weren't prepared for anyone like you, I guess."

This upright man of unbending dignity reached out and clasped Harold's hand. He looked fully into Harold's eyes, and his own eyes were kind and tired.

Harold's ire dissipated. He could now see this incomprehensible monolith of his more youthful years as an elderly man with failings. A man of strength and sharp intellect, a man who towered above other men in certain ways but who could be wrong and could even know humility. He was, in fact, a fellow human being and, viewed from this new standpoint, could be sincerely admired.

Harold slept well that night. He woke the next morning feeling that some heavy thing had slipped away, a heaviness he had not been entirely aware of until it was gone. He faced the day with a new lightness of spirit.

❧ + ❧

That lightness was freshly tried on the way home by another engine breakdown and another expense for having the car towed into the nearest town for a new part. When a few days later the car broke down beyond repair, Harold took the bus back to Sioux Falls to ask Bishop Gesner's help in buying another car. The bishop refused, claiming that the entire District of South Dakota was experiencing financial problems. He advised Harold to save for a new car. Harold felt it no use to explain that there was no bank in Pine Ridge and that he and Blossom had never opened an account anywhere.

Ever since their wedding day, they had faced debts. Some of the same debts still hung over their heads, dwarfed now by an accumulation of many more. When he listed them to see just how much they owed, the amount came to something over four thousand dollars, two years salary. The list of their creditors—colleges, grocers, gas stations, clothing stores, a personal loan or two—was frighteningly long, and yet the Jones family was supposed to set an example of how life in God's service could be lived. All Harold could see stretching ahead through the years was more debt until finally creditors would lose patience. Then what? This was no way for Blossom and Norma to live. He needed a car, or his work could not go on. Harold prayed, "Lord, you have an answer for me. Help me to see what it is."

Before he left Sioux Falls that day, he emptied his pockets and put a down payment of twenty-five dollars on a brave-looking, elderly Chevrolet from a used-car lot recommended by the bishop. He was wearing his collar and had a note of recommendation from the bishop under the official letterhead. The car's eight-year-old engine had a soothing sound as Harold drove back home without incident.

Was it the Lord's answer, or was it a temptation to try him that a letter came in the mail the following month from the bishop of North Dakota, his old seminary friend Richard Emery? The bishop invited him to be vicar of a church in Mandan. The Mandan congregation was all white, but as the Bishop pointed out, many Indian people lived there, and a number of Indians from Standing Rock Reservation visited the little city. Feeling they hadn't stayed long enough at Pine Ridge, Harold and Blossom politely declined the offer.

As the long, cold winter months began and the "new" car coughed, sputtered, and died in the midst of blizzards, both Harold and Blossom had second thoughts. Harold admitted, "I can't be of any use to our missions if I can't get to them. I can't be of any use to you either, Blossom, if I can't pay the bills. I'm writing to Dick to ask him to keep me in mind for some other vacancy he might have. I think I wouldn't say no to any place, no matter how difficult, if we could go to it long enough to get our debts paid." Before Harold had a chance to reconsider his decision, Bishop Emery telephoned and invited the three of them to visit in Fargo for two days "so we can talk things over."

The bishop of North Dakota met the Jones family at the Fargo airport and drove them to the house, where his wife Alice had dinner waiting. For Harold it was a happy reunion with his old friend, and Blossom and Alice took to each other immediately. No word was mentioned about the reason for their journey until Dick kindled a fire and they brought their coffee cups into the living room. Then the bishop said, "Harold, Holy Trinity Church in Wahpeton is going to need a new priest. Father Oxnam has been there a long time, and he has told me he would like to leave. The congregation doesn't know this yet. They are very much attached to him, and he has put off telling them. My thought is that we all go tomorrow night to their annual meeting. They have dinner first, but after that's over and the business meeting is in progress, he will announce his resignation. Before the people go into shock about it, I will announce that I have waiting in the car outside a very fine man who can take on the work when Father Oxnam leaves. Then I will come to the door and call you all inside so they can meet you and decide for themselves. How about it?"

Harold was stunned. This was the old Dick, telling tall tales with a straight face. He answered the bishop's absurdity with a slap of the knee and a hearty laugh.

Bishop Emery shook his head. "I'm serious. There's a fair-sized Indian school in Wahpeton, and your coming would be a great lift to the students. To the staff too. Oxnam has done what he could for them, but that was very little. Understandably, his work has been with the citizens of Wahpeton and of Breckenridge, just across the Red River in Minnesota. The congregation is almost equally divided between the two towns.

"It's a good, solid mission church, Harold, and some new blood will be good for it, though they may not see it that way at first. What do you think?"

Preposterous. A white congregation with a Santee priest.

"I'm a South Dakota Indian," Harold reminded him gently.

An instant of silence followed, and then Bishop Emery's laugh filled the room. "You old scalawag! The last eighteen years haven't done a thing to improve your cautious nature. Of course, they'll want you once they meet you. And," he added, "if they don't like the looks of you, they'll take you just so they can have Blossom and Norma."

Harold, Blossom, and Norma silently waited in the dark car outside Holy Trinity Church the next evening. Golden light glowed from the basement windows beneath the church. They could imagine what was going on. The clatter of dishes cleared away; the filling of coffee cups; next would be the secretary's reading of the minutes; a pause for their acceptance; the reading of committee reports to be discussed and voted pro or con. It was getting colder. Harold reached under the blanket and rubbed Blossom's thin ankles. He turned the key in the switch to run the engine for a bit of warmth.

Father Oxnam's announcement would, of course, come last. Then what? It just might blow up in his face. More time passed. Norma was opening the car door to have a peak through the window when a shaft of light crossed the snow and the lengthened shadow of an arm motioned them toward the door.

Bishop Emery took hold of Harold's elbow as he ushered them into the warm hall. "I've told them about you," he whispered. "Now I'll introduce you. They are pretty shaken by Oxnam's resignation."

"I feel like an owl being wakened by the daylight," Harold muttered to Blossom and Norma. "I can't make my eyes stop blinking."

"Never mind." Blossom's teeth were chattering. "Look around you. Other eyes are blinking too."

Harold did. No smiles greeted them, only serious looks, the sound of discreet blowing into handkerchiefs by men, and tears glistening on several of the women's faces.

Harold instantly forgot his own discomfort over this bizarre situation. These people were upset. They loved their priest. The evening was harder on them than it had been for the three Joneses shivering outside.

The bishop's booming voice cut through the muted sounds. "I would like you all to meet the Reverend Harold Jones and his family." Then he turned to Harold. "I have given them a rundown of your qualifications and experience, but perhaps there is something you might like to add? I am, of course, resting the final decision of a call with the congregation. They have had my recommendation."

What could Harold say to a grieving crowd? Their gaze turned upon him. Was it hostile or simply very sober? He looked back at them for a long moment, wordless at first, and then he heard himself voicing his own doubt.

"You know that my heritage is different from yours. I'm an Indian. Blossom and Norma are Indians. If you should call me to be your priest, I would come on one condition and that is that you call me as a person, not as an Indian called by white men. If we can work together as fellow human beings and on that basis alone, I would be willing to ask my bishop in South Dakota to release me so that I could come to serve you."

There were some whispers and nods of approval as the senior warden looked about the room. Finally he spoke. "We have made a good choice, and so have you. Welcome, Father Jones, Blossom, and Norma, to Wahpeton!"

Before they left for home the next day, Bishop Emery asked Harold to list his outstanding debts. The District of North Dakota would pay them all, subtracting a small portion of his monthly checks until the amount was covered, if and when the Jones family agreed to move to Wahpeton, he said.

A week later, Bishop Gesner received Harold's news with regret but understanding.

Their good-byes at Pine Ridge brought the now familiar tugging at their hearts, with a slight difference this time. This move would take them away from reservation family and friends and into a different world—white society.

12

ACROSS CULTURES

1956–1968

It was June 1956. For the long ride from Pine Ridge to Wahpeton, Harold sold the ailing car for junk and with half of his last month's salary bought an old Pontiac, which, the dealer assured him, was in better condition inside than outside. It boasted a rebuilt engine, which won his heart by responding immediately to the touch of foot on starter.

As they drove to Wahpeton, they were surrounded by fresh green prairies under a blue sky. Spring winds, softer than the summer or winter winds, played over the grass, turning it into a pale green ocean that swept against the dark gold of a land polka-dotted with new corn plants. Overhead flew geese, calling to one another in their sweeping, changing dance, happy to be back for summer.

Norma, now nearly fifteen, had been weeping silently in the back seat of the car but did manage to utter small cries of admiration as they drove past colts, testing their long legs with brief gallops up and down the hills.

"How can you stand to leave all this, Daddy?" Norma demanded. Through weeks of packing and farewells, Harold had been asking himself that same question. The struggle against mounting debts, higher each year and now threatening to engulf them, was the sole reason they were leaving this harsh but lovely land.

He was taking his family to live among white men and women, many of whom, he assumed, thought of Indians as stoic and did not understand the unwritten rules by which Indian people lived. As they began their journey away from the reservation, he felt he was taking the family into something akin to exile.

At the end of their journey, they found the vicarage in their new home of Wahpeton. It was a well-built house with a furnace and running water. The windows faced a pleasant street, along which stretched other homes the size of the vicarage, each with its small garden and lawn. After the seemingly unlimited space of the prairie, the patch of green grass and prim fence comprising their backyard seemed fit for only half a clothesline.

The District of North Dakota had arranged to ship their furniture, which now awaited them. Some members of Holy Trinity Church had already set up the furniture and made ready the beds. In such a well-built, rather spacious city house, their furniture appeared diminutive and inadequate. Harold looked at Blossom quizzically. She caught his thought and laughed. "No matter. We can add what we need gradually. In the meantime, it'll be easy to clean house."

A shopping trip the next day turned into a sight-seeing tour of Wahpeton and its sister city, Breckenridge, across the river in Minnesota. "Population of Wahpeton, 6,500," Harold read, and as they crossed the bridge, "5,000 in Breckenridge. That sounds like a reasonable number of people to learn to know. They can't all be Episcopalians. Did you know that North Dakota is the smallest district in terms of population in the country? Dick Emery told me that in round numbers there are only 4,500 Episcopalians in the whole of North Dakota. But look!" Harold drew to the side of the bridge cautiously. "I'd forgotten. Do you see what I see?" At the answering silence from Blossom and Norma, he pointed to the river. "Look at the current! It's moving up, not down. This is the Red River. It's the only river I know of in the country that flows north. North Dakota is famous for that. And look at it go!"

❧ + ❧

Very quickly after the school term began, the quiet vicarage overflowed with white guests who trooped home after school with Norma. At Holy Trinity, Harold and Blossom quickly found a group of people willing to cooperate in whatever projects their new leadership might propose.

Wahpeton Indian School was Harold's first concern. Four hundred children from fourteen Indian tribes were enrolled there, including the Ojibwes and the Sioux, who were traditional enemies. Some of the children were orphans, and many came from broken homes where alcohol had made life unbearable. The position of Director of Religious Education was an inherited part of the work of the vicar of Holy Trinity, giving Harold the opportunity to visit the school, meet its superintendent, and arrange to hold weekly Bible classes there. After a few sessions, the sea of small faces became a group of distinct individuals to him. Despite tribal differences, the children had poverty in common. The school furnished books, paper, and pencils, but missing were the small necessities of life—brushes, combs, tissues and cough drops, hats and mittens. Also lacking was the inestimable pleasure of a spare dime to spend occasionally at a candy store.

Harold discussed the children's situation with the superintendent and with his approval applied for help through the Christian Children's Fund. Initially, the fund aided 25 children, but in a short time, 168 of the neediest children had sponsors who sent them five dollars a month and pledged to remember birthdays and Christmas. The school formed its own bank so the children could learn to deposit their money, draw checks, and budget spending throughout the month. At first none of them thought of using any of the precious gift for stamps to send off letters of thanks to their sponsors, so Harold's own paycheck had to stretch to cover this new expense until the children understood better their lesson in saving.

Although the desperate squeeze of meeting personal debts was over for Harold and Blossom, they soon realized that Holy Trinity Church had its own debts and needed projects to finance them. The vicarage was not yet paid for, some repairs were needed on the church building, and the young people, a lively crowd, had plans that required money. Organizing for money-raising projects was obviously not new to Harold and Blossom. Capitalizing on the skills of the congregation, they first developed a plan to open the church hall for occasional suppers. Many in Wahpeton and Breckenridge turned out at the invitation of Holy Trinity "to give the housewives a night out." Another project was an auction, offering both funds and fun. Downtown businesses in the two towns could advertise through their donations, and every family of Trinity, no matter how poor, brought at least one article to sell. With a little encouragement, the Players Guild, which combined talents of both Breckenridge and Wahpeton, began rehearsals and from two performances proudly presented Harold with proceeds of ninety dollars.

Money was not the only need he found at Holy Trinity. It worried Harold that the Indian children, who came to church in a large group and returned to the school for their dinner as soon as the service was over, never had an opportunity to mingle with the rest of the congregation. They were very shy, and most attempts to be friendly with them met with downcast eyes and frowns. The practice of having individual families sponsor members of the confirmation class had worked well on the reservation, and Harold thought it was worth trying here too. Blossom and he spent time going over lists of the Indian children who were preparing for confirmation. By now they knew their congregation well enough to be able to pair each child with a member of the white congregation who would act as a sponsor.

Some first encounters would be painful, Harold assumed, remembering his own childhood. He found that as he encouraged his classes of Indian boys and girls to respond to their confirmation sponsors, he was at the same time encouraging himself to trust more fully in the acceptance and good will of the white congregation.

The sponsorship program worked and in ways Harold had not anticipated. Alice Horned Eagle appeared in a new white dress for the occasion, her eyes shining. It was the gift of her sponsoring family, the Burks, who even stood behind her as the bishop placed his hands on her head. Franklin Two Hearts, kneeling beside her, had Mr. Shaw standing behind him. Harold knew Mr. Shaw to be a taciturn, lonely old man, but his eyes were brimming when Franklin's turn came. Weeks later on his birthday, Franklin proudly showed Harold a new watch, a gift from his sponsor and new friend. And so it went. With each year more friendships between sponsors and students, the white congregation and the Indian children, were formed.

❧ + ❧

One day in the early fall, Harold put on his clerical collar and drove around the two towns to meet the other clergy. He pointed out the need for Bibles for the religious education classes. Several of the churches of other denominations made this special need their project. An unintended result of Harold's calls was an invitation to join the town's Ministerial Association; before long, he also became a member of Kiwanis and the Masonic Lodge. Before many months passed, he was appointed to the Department of Christian Social Relations of the District of North Dakota and became the chairman of the Episcopal Commission on Indian Affairs.

Harold was not too surprised when Blossom announced proudly at supper one night that she was starting work herself the following week. "I'm going to be an accountant at J. C. Penney's," she said blandly. Norma and Harold chuckled and Blossom joined them, but she continued to nod her head positively. "I mean it," she told them. "It's this new law about minorities being hired, I think. When the manager saw me, he thought I was his answer to the government fact sheets. I told him I'd never kept any accounts except our own, but he just smiled and said I had an 'intelligent face' and he was sure I could handle the books."

For one month, Blossom tried hard but unsuccessfully to unravel the mysteries of business accounts. "It's hopeless, Harold," she confessed finally. "I'm going to get the whole store in trouble if I keep on. Mr. Harris is such a patient man, he should have fired me the first week."

Blossom gave up that job, but by year's end she was working as a shoe-store clerk for sixty-five cents an hour. The owner was a local man who had established his own business. He soon came to depend on Blossom to keep the store open while he went on buying trips. On these occasions, Blossom confided to Harold, she would pretend that the store was hers. "I like the good smell of leather when I open the boxes," she confessed. "It's like the smell of saddles and cattle. And I like to please people with the kinds of shoes that I bring them. It's a nice feeling to see the pleasure in customers' faces. And," she noted, "it's a good feeling to have the owner trust me with his business."

❧ + ❧

Once the Jones family became used to life in Wahpeton, time passed quickly. Except for Norma's change from a little girl into a young woman, Harold and Blossom would hardly have measured that time in years. Norma began high school in Wahpeton as a sophomore, a suspicious and unwilling young one who was accepted so quickly by her classmates that she had no time to dwell on her old South Dakota life. She graduated with honors in 1959.

+

"Hal, don't you think this church's facilities are too small?" Bishop Emery asked during his official visit to Holy Trinity Church in 1959. "Why, you can't possibly squeeze all those children into such tiny Sunday school rooms. How about me approaching the United Thank Offering (UTO) for a grant? You're ministering to a minority group, y'know, and," he added with a grin, "you are one of them. That gives me a handle for asking. Let me come down for a special meeting next month to talk this over with your folks."

Thirty of the Holy Trinity congregation gathered to meet with the bishop. Bishop Emery reported that he had talked with an architect, who estimated $105,000 for the building project. "I think the UTO would approve a grant of $45,000, $40,000 for building a church and $5,000.00 for purchasing land," he said. "But these are matching grants. The people of Holy Trinity would have to raise the same amount. What do you think?" he asked.

The congregation weighed and debated several issues. Their doubts, fears, dreams, frustrations, and enthusiasm reminded Harold of other days, other churches. Their overall positive reaction launched a new series of extra bazaars, pledging, and memorial gifts. The Women's Guild, ever a hardworking group, raised money to buy new kitchen equipment—stoves, refrigerator, table, chairs—important items that memorial gifts would not cover. By 1961, the new building was constructed at a new site, its nearest neighbor the North Dakota School of Science. The church was built in English cottage style with its parish hall underneath, providing plenty of space for Sunday school rooms as well as a good-sized meeting hall and the vicar's study. The organ and the stained glass windows were carefully transported to the new location. When the old, beloved window of the Good Shepherd was safely installed, someone saw to it that a light was turned on from inside so that it would shine for passers-by to see.

As the bishop predicted, with more room to grow the church did prosper. By the spring of 1963, the once small mission felt brave enough to host the annual meeting of the entire Convocation of North Dakota. Wahpeton Indian School was featured, and arrangements were made through Fort Yates on Standing Rock Reservation to adopt Bishop Emery as a Sioux. "Leading Eagle" became his Indian name, and at his adoption ceremony Indian dancers performed in a splendid whirl of feathers and beads.

❧ + ❧

During the building years, Norma entered North Dakota State School of Science. Her advancement to higher education did not interrupt the family's routine since she continued to live at home. The house resounded as usual with the voices of the young people who gathered in the kitchen and living room, making the Joneses' home their hangout. Added now to the usual crowd of Norma's friends were some newcomers from the School of Science.

One student at the school became a favorite of Harold and Blossom. Bill was a Sioux from Lower Brulé Reservation in South Dakota. He was an intense, shy Indian, who confessed that he could feel comfortable with them but that when the demands of college became too great he would find the nearest bar and drink himself into oblivion.

One evening Blossom heard a scuffling sound at the front door. She opened it to find Bill staring at her with glazed eyes. By the time Harold arrived home from a meeting, Bill was sound asleep on the living-room couch. "He told me that he was drunk," explained Blossom in a low voice, "which I certainly could see, and that if he went back to his dormitory they would kick him out, which they certainly would, so he came here to see if we would let him sober up first." All night and through the next day, Bill slept, waking and hastily leaving the house when Norma and three college friends came in from class.

The next day Bill returned to apologize, and Harold had a chance to talk with him. His story was familiar, one that Harold thoroughly understood. Bill felt alienated from his classmates but not particularly because he was an Indian—Wahpeton people were accustomed to Indians—and not particularly because his classes were too hard. He liked science, and he liked being a surveyor's helper. His problem was money. Bill was so desperately poor he had nothing besides two pairs of worn jeans and two old shirts to wear and no money to pay the coming graduation fees and other expenses most students automatically managed.

Harold had walked the road of poverty himself for a long time, and he wanted to help Bill. He turned to his old friend Bishop Emery, who wrote Harold a check for one hundred dollars to cover Bill's expenses. When graduation day arrived, Bill had a new suit. More importantly, with the new suit and the backing of understanding friends, he gained more self-confidence. A few months after graduation, he left Wahpeton for a job in Aberdeen, South Dakota, and eventually enlisted in the Air Force. Before leaving the country for England, Bill returned to visit Harold and Blossom and told them of his plans to get married and move overseas. Years later he returned to North Dakota and studied for a degree in engineering at Fargo.

In 1960 Wahpeton Indian School offered Blossom a teaching job. Her years of teaching on the reservations made her an ideal candidate, but unfortunately she had graduated with a certificate, not the degree required for the position. Their offer did prompt her to become a night matron in the girl's dormitory. Now that Norma was older, Blossom missed being with children, so she left the shoe store to join the staff of the Indian school. At first, the nights seemed very long. For Blossom, though, the work was easy, and the young girls responded to her concerned attention.

One night Harold and Norma were awakened by the rattle of a key in the lock and stealthy footsteps. He reached for his bathrobe and looked at the clock. It was 1 A.M. Blossom was in the living room, talking to a small girl whose shoulders were hunched as she shivered with cold. Patting up the cushions on the couch, Blossom murmured a small stream of comforting words.

"Ruby is spending the night here, Harold," she explained, taking him aside and looking at him steadily. "She's reached the point where she can't stand school a minute longer, so I thought she should get away from it. It's all right," she reassured him. "Mr. Wellington knows. I woke him to tell him. I'm going back to my job, but she will be fine right here with you and Norma. And," she turned back to Ruby, "tomorrow morning you can sleep as late as you want to. You won't have to get up for classes."

Later Blossom explained to Harold and Norma that she had been making her rounds that evening when she heard persistent squeaks from bedsprings in one corner of a dark room. When she went in, the sound stopped but began again soon afterward. She went into the room again and leaned over a little girl, who seemed to be fast asleep. As Blossom straightened the covers, lifting them more closely around the child's neck, however, she discovered that Ruby was fully dressed.

"I can't stand it here any longer," the little girl whispered desperately in the darkness. "I'm going to run away."

"She meant it too," Blossom told Harold. "I could tell that nothing I could say would change her mind, so I just told her I'd help her run."

Harold grinned. "So you brought her here."

"Yes, and if she stays awhile, I believe she'll be able to think more clearly."

It took Ruby less time than Blossom expected. By the next morning, she remarked almost wistfully, "I guess I'd better go back. I left my little sister there, and she'd miss me too much if I left for good." When Blossom prepared to go to work the next evening, Ruby left with her.

At lunch the next day, Harold took Blossom's hand. "Children do come and go through this house in a steady stream, don't they," he said thoughtfully. "And do you know who may be leaving us next? That Norwegian boy, Jerry, visits every chance he gets lately to see Norma. I guess she's forgotten her impression of white boys—too anemic. Remember?"

"Not this one," Blossom observed. "He's a strapping young man with rosy cheeks and golden hair. I don't wonder that Norma's drawn to him. And have you noticed lately what a beautiful daughter we have?"

May 25, 1963 was Norma and Jerry Pederson's wedding day. The seven years between 1956, when the Jones family arrived in Wahpeton, and 1963 comprised Norma's transition from childhood to adulthood, which the parish had shared. Now the women in the congregation joined in preparations for the wedding. They transformed the church into a flower garden, and the young girls who attended her looked like flowers too in their soft green and pink dresses.

The house now felt very empty. The wedding seemed to close a very dear chapter in the Joneses' lives. But not a complete ending—the young couple would be coming back to live in Wahpeton. Harold and Blossom cherished the hope that they would grow old right there and have the pleasure of watching their only daughter become a middle-aged matron herself, with children of her own. A strange and perhaps premature thought just now, but something to anticipate.

❦ + ❦

If 1963 held moments of great satisfaction and joy, 1964 held one of the saddest. February 23 began like most winter Sundays at Holy Trinity Church. The short walk from the car to the church door gave Blossom, who was having some trouble with asthma, all she wanted of the blustering wind. It whipped up the snow and flung it into the faces of all who dared be outside, then whirled into small cyclones along the path to the door.

Blossom allowed Harold to help take off her boots inside the vestibule. "I'm so glad this isn't a day you have to travel anywhere," she said. "After the service we'll have a good hot dinner and spend the rest of the afternoon watching the snow through the windows." Uninterrupted days together were rare, but this kind of weather assured an afternoon of peace.

At the first bite of dessert, the telephone rang.

"Oh, Harold, can't we let it go?"

"No," he answered, putting down his napkin. "This will only take a minute." The voice across the wire sounded small and far away. He pressed the receiver closer to his good ear. "I can't quite hear you. Will you tell me again who this is?" The name was garbled, but the message came through with terrible distinctness.

Harold looked at the phone in disbelief. Blossom asked who it was, but he couldn't answer. Slowly returning the receiver to the hook, he sat, unable to move or think. Blossom came to stand next to him, but he could only stare at her.

The words sounding distant to his own ears, he repeated what he had just heard. "Our bishop is dead." Then, gaining a little more voice, he went on. "Dick was killed by a train. So were Ed Bigelow and Pam. Alice wasn't. She must have stayed home. But two of the Bigelow children were killed. The other three must have been in the very back of the van, and they may survive okay. A young student was among the dead too." He rehearsed the news, slowly, sifting through it until it began to seem real.

Five days later the cathedral in Fargo overflowed with mourners, who traveled over ice-coated roads and through high drifts of snow from every part of the state. Harold recalled the days when Dick Emery had been appointed to be the missionary bishop of North Dakota. There were thirty-one congregations, only four self-supporting and two others aided at the time; in the mission field, six of twenty-one church buildings had been closed; just nine priests (one Indian) were serving the church in North Dakota. By the time the bishop died, there were eight fully self-supporting parishes. Bereft of that source of energy—that strong, loving presence never far away and always supportive—Harold felt lost and sad. How did Alice manage to sing in the choir, raising her voice in praise to the Lord, as she faced her own great loss?

During the funeral service, his thoughts returned to Easter Sunday when Dick had shared their service at Holy Trinity. In his sermon he had assured them, "Christ is risen from the dead! We, too, can enter into that resurrection. Easter represents the victory of love over hate, life over death." Words that had threatened to become perfunctory had sounded sharply and intimately relevant. "We too can enter into his resurrection," Harold murmured to himself.

Weeks later, Harold was able to think more clearly about the accident and assess his sense of loss. He was again sitting with Blossom, who was knitting. Harold closed a book he was reading and stretched, feeling that something within him was coming to rest at last.

"Do you know how much I feel I owe to Dick Emery?" he asked her quietly. "My debt began way back in seminary days, when that driving energy of his stirred us to form an athletic league. As I think of it now, those hours in the gym and on the field worked off animosities and frustrations that could get pretty explosive among some of us students. And what would have happened if he hadn't made a way for us out of that burden of debts? It has taken awhile, but now they're all paid up—something we accomplished ourselves through his personal trust and support.

"But you know, Blossom, he did something else for me. I can see now that he challenged and helped overturn my feelings of self-pity. Pity that others couldn't appreciate me because I was an Indian, part of a conquered race. I was proud of being an Indian, proud of my heritage, and yet at the same time I held deep inside the same kind of belligerence toward the white people that I thought they might be harboring against me."

"And often were," Blossom murmured.

"True," Harold went on. "But that shouldn't have been *my* problem. If I'd had the right kind of confidence that I really was a child of God, as Dick kept trying to remind me, I'd have saved myself a lot of internal calluses. I've found that the soul builds up some protective layers over tender spots, just as the body does. By bringing us to this place and surrounding us with a caring white congregation, he must have known that the bruises wouldn't need calluses anymore."

Blossom's needles kept clicking. "Either way, callused or smooth, I love you," she said simply.

❧ + ❧

The new Bishop, George Masuda, came from a parish in Billings, Montana. To Harold's delight, his old piano-playing seminary friend, Chilton Powell, now bishop of the Diocese of Oklahoma, flew to Fargo on January 14, 1965, to preach at the new bishop's consecration service. During the next three years, Harold found the new bishop to be a loving and caring pastor to his clergy and a man with considerable organizational skills. The church in North Dakota recovered from the shock of its loss and resumed its growth. With satisfaction, Harold watched as the new bishop focused on the struggling Indian missions throughout the state. Bishop Masuda's concern stretched beyond North Dakota into Harold's old territory of South Dakota, where there were many Indian mission congregations.

A new program of training Indian people for ordination as well as offering classes for lay workers in the Episcopal Church was taking root at Standing Rock Reservation, within the District of North Dakota, and it served the people of South Dakota as well. This program came under the oversight of both bishops. In the days of Harold's grandfather, many devout Indian men were ordained to serve their people as priests. Now, because of rigid educational requirements, there were only nine native clergy in both states, most of them older men.

The promising new Dakota Leadership Program was criticized by some, mainly non-Indians. Some felt that without traditional education, the quality of the whole priesthood of the church might erode. Many people felt that, with the growing resurgence of traditional Native religion in the 1960s, the days of Indian clergy were vanishing. Such critics believed that devout Indians with leadership ability should help in local mission churches but leave the sacramental functions to fully educated priests. Every ordained clergyman must know the Greek Bible, argued some of the older white priests, especially one who was a professor of religion at the University of North Dakota. The Dakota Leadership Program, however, maintained that English would do as well as, if not better than, Greek as the second language for the Dakota and Lakota peoples, who already spoke their own language. Bishop Masuda called on Harold to demonstrate this point.

Christ Church, Mandan, was host to the District Convention in September of 1968. Its special theme was "The Dakota People," and more Indian missions then usual sent delegates. Harold's heart was warmed by the attendance of old friends from Fort Yates and Cannon Ball. His own part was to preach in Dakota at the closing service.

"Be as fluent as you wish," Bishop Masuda advised him with a twinkle in his eye, and Harold worked hard to bring back the old, natural fluency of his mother tongue.

It was a surprise tactic—nobody knew that Harold was to speak in Dakota. Those who understood leaned forward to catch his words; those who didn't leaned back to enjoy its melodious sound as Harold used his deepest voice to carry the point. Occasionally, he stole quick glances in the professor of religion's direction and to his delight finally saw him shake his head and break into a broad smile.

❧ † ❧

The new bishop also made a totally unexpected point in another direction. In the sacristy before the service began, Bishop Masuda asked Harold with unaccustomed abruptness, "How would you like to be the vicar of Good Shepherd Mission in Arizona? New York called me to ask if I thought you might take the position. I will talk with you about it after the service." Later, the bishop added that the Home Department of the national church in New York considered Harold to be a fine candidate to tackle a difficult situation at the church in Navajoland. Characteristically, the bishop showed no personal emotion for or against Harold's decision.

Harold's immediate reaction was self-doubt. Did the bishop want to get rid of him? Had Holy Trinity begun to feel that twelve years of Harold was enough, so they were asking for a change? He talked with the senior warden later in Wahpeton. "You've refused other calls," the senior warden reminded Harold, "Why let this one upset you?"

It was true. In 1962 the national office had urged him to come to New York to serve as Executive Secretary for Indian Work, but he could not accept the thought of leaving Blossom alone in the city while he traveled all over the country. Harold had also refused calls to serve in Minnesota, Wyoming, and even in Hawaii. The people of Holy Trinity had known about the offers and felt secure that their pastor would stay with them. He and Blossom were content and happy in their ministry.

"What do you know about the Navajos anyway?" the senior warden asked. "They might tomahawk you down there or maybe use a pair of sheep shears on you. Stay here with us."

Harold laughed with him, but his uneasiness continued. What was he being asked to do? And why?

Five days later he received a call from the New York office. The situation sounded urgent but still lacked some crucial details. "It's just an unbeliev-ably mixed-up situation down there," Harold was told. "Too complicated for a telephone conversation, but Gerald OneFeather will be getting in touch with you in a day or two, and maybe he can give you a more com-plete picture. Please don't say no until you've heard it all."

Harold felt frustrated. Why all this mystery, and why *me?* he thought. Where was God in this calling? Holy Trinity kept him busy. Norma and Jerry were about to deliver their second child. And just why did white people continually group all Indian people together in their thinking? The Navajos were a completely separate nation. A white man would be ac-cepted as readily as a Santee Sioux.

Gerald OneFeather, another South Dakota Sioux, was the trouble-shooter for the Home Department of the national church. He had been one of Blossom's and Harold's Sunday school boys in Oglala and now was married to a beautiful Navajo girl. Of all people, Gerald should be the one to unravel this mystery, and he invited the Joneses to Arizona to see the sit-uation themselves.

The cheerful voices of the congregation coming out of Sunday morning service still echoed in Harold's ears as he and Blossom headed for the air-port in Fargo. As they later left the plane in Gallup, New Mexico, they spotted Gerald at once, impressive in his sombrero as he stood behind the crowd that was pressing forward to greet other passengers. His Western shirt and blue jeans, broad, strong shoulders, and imperturbable expres-sion looked familiar.

As Gerald drove them in his station wagon, he began to unravel the first strand of the story of Good Shepherd Mission.

"The people down here are mostly shepherds. For centuries they've owned their own flocks, and that means they must stick with a wandering kind of life, living in hogans while the sheep graze off the land, then mov-ing on when the flock needs more grass. State lines between New Mexico, Arizona, and Utah mean nothing. The Navajo Reservation crosses state lines, but all the Episcopal mission work is under the Diocese of Arizona.

"About a century ago the Episcopal Church built the first hospital of any kind on the reservation. Later they built a school for Navajo children so they could learn English and other things that the white man feels are important for everybody to know, things that these people couldn't learn when they were following sheep all the time. The church built the school at Fort Defiance, where I'm taking you. It's been a good school, and over the years the people have come to accept it and count on it for their children. There's a home for orphaned children there too.

"Some years ago the Reverend David Clark and his wife—they used to be in South Dakota on the Crow Creek Reservation—came down here. Didn't you work with them there? Under their guidance, Good Shepherd became one of the outstanding missions of the Episcopal Church.

"The wealthy grandfather of a young priest who came to work with Father Clark furnished the money to build a large and impressive church and rectory beside the school—all of which you are about to see.

"It was a fine gift. But it takes money to maintain it. When the Clarks left, another priest came, and he fell in love with a Navajo girl, left his family, married her, and joined the Mormon Church. That shook up the congregation, and things began to fall apart.

"There's been a good man here since, but to pay the mounting bills, the rectory and some of the buildings were rented to some sisters—not an Episcopal order but seemingly close to it in beliefs and life style. It seemed to be a devout group of women who took over the running of the school and made the rectory their headquarters.

"You'll be meeting Ruby Bates, a fine English woman who has taught at the school for the past twenty years. She has hung on, about the only one who has. She can fill you in on the story if I leave anything important out.

"Very soon after the order took over, they began having trouble paying their teachers' salaries. First, they began paying the Navajo teachers in bits and pieces. Next, the order announced that they were closing the elementary school and opening a college. That caused a big—but silent—uproar. You'll find that the Navajo people burn silently to a white heat before they explode, not like us Sioux with a shorter fuse.

"Anyway, Ruby began some investigating and reported her findings to the Bishop, who ordered the sisterhood to leave. The sisters, however, claimed that they had never signed a contract and were not obligated to go. They barricaded themselves in and finally, when they knew the jig was up, they left and took everything with them. They stripped the place of furniture, dishes, drapes, and linens and left some tremendous bills in the local stores as well. That all happened just about a month and a half ago. You'll be seeing the whole dismal picture for yourselves."

By the time the tale ended, Gerald had turned from the paved road onto a gravel one leading toward the great wall of rock they had been approaching as he talked. "Window Rock," he told them. "Good Shepherd Mission is just five miles away in the town of Fort Defiance."

As they climbed from the car with its tinted windshield, Harold momentarily flinched at the brightness of the sunshine. How clear the air was! The cluster of buildings, the fences, even the shapes of the few people sitting and standing in the midst of the scene looked as if they were painted on a brown canvas with unusually bright colors.

They followed Gerald along a narrow walk leading to the deserted rectory. "Don't let this throw you," he warned as he turned the key in the heavy door. "This house was quite a palace when it had its furniture and drapes. Now it just reminds me of a ghost hotel." Dusty and deserted, it reminded Blossom of an old Western movie set.

Next he led them to the imposing stone building that was the mission church. "*Mission* church!" Harold chuckled. "Why, Gerald, this could swallow up both cathedrals in North and South Dakota, with room left over." Stepping from the dazzling sunlight into the interior, Harold needed time for his eyes to adjust and see the beauty unfolding around them. The tall windows of breathtaking blues, reds, greens, and crystal sent rainbows across silent pews. The shafts of colored light shone on the carved stone altar and the hanging cross.

"You've probably heard about the famous jeweled chalice," Gerald said. "It's safely locked away in the sacristy between Communion services. But there hasn't been one for quite some time now. Of course, except during tourist season, the local congregation fills about two pews. You can see why the New York office is tearing its hair over this place. Pretty unique it is, not like the kinds of problems we've handled from the Dakotas, eh? Even the faithful handful here at Good Shepherd are bitter about the church renting out its buildings."

For five days the Joneses stayed in Arizona, meeting with the ad hoc committee and talking with Ruby Bates, a forthright lady, whom Harold and Blossom liked immediately. She had witnessed the incredible events Gerald OneFeather had told them about.

"It's a terrible place and a wonderful place," Ruby confessed to them. "I love it deeply, and it simply defeats me at the same time. It so desperately needs help. I can't see this place being shut down, but that may be just what will happen. Then what will become of all the dear children who depend on the school?"

Before leaving the area, Harold and Blossom flew to Phoenix to meet with the bishop and council. After hearing Ruby's account and seeing her devotion to the Navajo people, they were drawn to the situation and very close to accepting New York's request to move to Fort Defiance.

The meeting with the bishop and council almost changed their minds. They grilled Harold about measures he might use to improve what in their eyes was obviously a hopeless situation. "Anything involving these Indians is hopeless," was the unspoken message that Harold felt he received from the meeting.

This time that implicit supposition angered him. In tones as brittle as theirs, he asked at last, "What's the use of our coming here if you don't want to carry on a program to develop leadership among the Navajo people? I'll stay in North Dakota."

Members of the council who had remained silent spoke up then, and their tone was conciliatory. They assured him that the mission's outstanding bills would be shouldered by the diocese and yes, of course, the kind of leadership training Good Shepherd had tried to promote in the past should be reestablished. "Harold Jones was recommended to us by the national office" said a seemingly influential council member, "so Harold Jones is our man."

With reluctance, Harold, with Blossom in accord, agreed to become the vicar of Good Shepherd Mission. One of the deciding factors in Harold's mind was that the dry climate would be good for Blossom's health. She had suffered in the dampness of Red River Valley.

❧ + ❧

It was October 9, 1968, twelve and a half years since their move to Wahpeton. When Harold announced his decision to the Holy Trinity congregation the following Sunday, at first the people wouldn't believe him. The Joneses' move was made even more difficult by the birth of a new granddaughter on October 25. The little girl was as dark as her brothers were fair, with a fringe of long brown hair and the rosy golden skin of a Dakota Indian.

"She'll be another beauty queen like her mother and grandmother," Harold predicted after his first long look at her. Tenderly he lifted her in a tightly rolled blanket from her mother's side. The act brought back a rush of memories—Pine Ridge, holding the little sons whose lives had been so brief. But this child was strong. He felt the pulse of life as the dark, unseeing eyes gleamed up at him. "My daughter," he said to Norma, "you have been God's instrument in bringing back to us the two boys we lost in this little one, another daughter like yourself. We thank you, and we praise God."

A whirl of farewell dinners and tearful good-byes ensued, accompanied by packing and moving, this time by van. Once again Harold helped Blossom into a car, climbed in beside her, and closed the door decisively. The temptation to remain with beloved family and friends in Wahpeton was met. They were on their way to Arizona.

Along the way, they stopped to see Kenny, who lived with his wife and eleven children in Rosebud, South Dakota. Kenny worked as a heavy-equipment operator in the construction and repair of dams throughout the area. Then they visited friends in the town of Mission and on the Pine Ridge Reservation. Who knows, thought Harold and Blossom, when they might see those dear faces again? A prophetic thought: It would be the last time they saw Kenny, who died three years later.

This leave-taking was not like the previous times they had been forced to part with friends and family. Moving to Wahpeton from the reservation had been hard enough. Living among white men and acting as their priest was a prospect that had brought Harold anxiety, but to go into the territory of an unfamiliar Indian tribe so far from home seemed foolhardy. Was it really God's finger that pointed them there?

No reproach was spoken, but in the eyes of Blossom's family and especially among the older men and women on the reservation whom Harold knew and loved, the message was clear. "Why do you leave us? Aren't there enough problems right here for you to deal with?"

Harold kept asking himself these questions, and yet there was that inescapable call: "COME."

13

NATIVE
STRANGER

❧ + ❧
―――――
1968–1971

On November 15, 1968, Harold and Blossom arrived in Fort Defiance, Arizona. They by-passed the large rectory and were grateful to find a small, comfortable house provided by the Diocese of Arizona. Ruby Bates had let the movers in and was there to greet them in person.

The cold of Arizona penetrated in a way unlike the windy, frigid air of the Dakotas. Harold found a thermostat and heard with satisfaction the purr of a motor starting up somewhere. After a few minutes, they set to work opening boxes and arranging furniture, immersing themselves in a necessary first task that always eased the pangs of moving.

While Harold worked in the bedroom, Blossom opened boxes in the kitchen. The kettle, two cups, and a can of tea appeared at last; she was calling Harold to share a break with her when the doorbell rang. "Aha!" Harold called to Blossom. "Here comes the welcoming committee! Have you enough cups unpacked for them too?"

He climbed out from among boxes and went to join her at the front door. A severe-looking white man stood at the door. "For a welcoming committee, that man has a mighty peculiar expression," Blossom murmured, her hand still resting on the doorknob.

"You're the new minister here at Good Shepherd?" the man asked abruptly.

"Yes, I am." Harold nodded. "Won't you come in? My wife has just made some tea."

The caller held out a paper and waived it in their faces. "This here bill is for eight hundred bucks. It's been due for two months. When is it going to get paid? Church or no church, business is business. We want our money now!" He paused. "Where are them ladies who used to live at the big house? They're the ones that charged all this stuff."

Harold's heart sank. Already the problems were surfacing. "I don't know about this," he explained carefully. "And I don't know what happened to the women. But give me the bill, and I'll find the right person to pay it."

The grocery bill led a procession of other bills, some arriving by mail, others hand delivered by irate collectors. One came from a hardware store, another from a bank in New Mexico demanding back payments on a five thousand dollar loan for two cars purchased under Good Shepherd's name. The largest was from a printing company, which announced it was time to start paying for an eleven thousand dollar printing press delivered over two months before but which was nowhere to be seen.

When a real welcoming committee appeared later in the day, Harold asked for a fuller picture of the mission's debts. Not many Navajos joined that first welcoming committee. Ruby was there, along with a young white priest named James Thompson and two or three people whom the Joneses had not yet met. The small group appeared to be in shock, with no real answers for him or for themselves. The debts were gigantic, the mission very small, and the diocese was baffled by the whole situation.

"Now what will *this* do for our image?" Ruby's laugh had a note of despondency. There seemed no way out except to dissolve the school and close the mission. "But they couldn't do that," she quickly reassured herself. "The church can't leave the Navajo people now. It wasn't the people's fault that this awful thing happened. As usual," she protested, "it's the Indians who are the innocent victims."

The rest of the welcoming committee sat silent, their eyes studying the floor or the ceiling.

Hopeless it certainly looked. But behind the immediate financial crisis was a more fundamental problem. Why weren't the Navajos turning out to greet them? How could this monstrous problem have developed without their being aware and taking steps to prevent it?

Harold recalled the directive from the national church office: "develop church leadership among the people." Where to start? He knew little about these people. He sighed involuntarily. Jim Thompson, the young priest sitting beside him, sighed in response and then straightened up. "You can count on me, sir, to help in any way I can. I've had some training in business and finance, if that's where you might need me, and I can help with services at the mission." Jim explained that he had been sent by the national office to assist in getting things in order.

The young priest's offer seemed to turn the mood. "Of course," Ruby interjected. "We will help in any way we can." The others nodded.

The loaves of bread and small fishes had just been offered. Harold felt his spirit responding. "Thanks!" he said, smiling. "We can move through this."

After the meeting, he reviewed the situation and formulated a strategy with Blossom. The priority, he felt, was to learn more about the Navajo people. Second, he needed to discover natural leaders among them. Third, and most difficult, that leadership had to be persuaded to encourage people to work together toward common goals.

☘+☘

During the first week in Navajoland, Harold, sometimes by himself, sometimes with Blossom, drove far into the desert to visit the hogans of Navajo sheepherders. Quickly he learned that the people were proud, unbending in their pride as "the People," and most spoke no English. The old ones didn't read or write in Navajo either. The young ones depended entirely on the mission school to teach them English and to learn about the rest of the world beyond the Navajo nation.

Harold, accompanied by Father James Thompson, began traveling among the four congregations that constituted Good Shepherd, helping the wardens to learn about bank accounts and record keeping and organizing a corps of eight interpreters willing to be called upon, night or day. Classes were organized for the teaching of the written Navajo language so that more people could take part as lay readers in the services.

In homes where someone was ill, Harold sometimes met Navajo medicine men, the traditional spiritual advisors and healers to whom people turned in times of trouble. There were still traditional healers among Harold's people; in fact, they had been gaining a new popularity on and off the reservation in the 1960s. Many Dakotas and Lakotas, however, had struck a balance, sometimes uneasy, sometimes not, between Christianity and their older cultural practices. Little of this balance existed in Navajoland. Many Navajos, it appeared to Harold, regarded Christianity as a curious set of beliefs associated with whites and therefore suspect like most of mainstream white culture. Christianity was fine as long as it didn't interfere with traditional Navajo customs. Many of "the People" listened politely, stoically, but their suspicions of Christianity—no matter whether the missionary was Indian or not—were quite deeply rooted.

❧ ✝ ❧

The churchwomen's meetings resumed. Blossom attended but returned home early more than once. "Nobody bothers to explain anything to me," she complained. Once she began to understand a few words of Navajo, Blossom made a few timid suggestions about possible projects, but nobody seemed to hear the outsider; the Navajo women continued to chatter and laugh as if she had not spoken. Finally, she could stand it no longer. One day, Blossom boldly stood up during the women's meeting and told them that everyone would do much better working on some project together instead of gossiping.

They ignored her.

But they did finally listen to one of their own. Blossom befriended a young Navajo woman named Edith who spoke English and had lived for some time outside of the reservation. Edith suggested that she propose Blossom's ideas for projects to the Navajo church women and that Blossom, an outsider, stop trying to lead the group and devote her energy instead to working with the women as a fellow member.

It worked. Soon the parish hall hummed with activity. A project as simple as saving trading stamps soon netted the church new lamps, a refrigerator, stove, curtains, and other articles to fill the empty rectory. Broken chairs were repaired through the help of a class taught by a county extension worker with materials and tools provided by the mission. The women's group began to accept Blossom, communicating through smiles, signs, and broken English, helping her to learn their language, and laughing with her at her mistakes. As she grew closer to the Navajo women, she discovered that some were quite conversant in English.

Another church project was selling Christmas trees. To investigate its feasibility, Harold drove Blossom far across the desert country while the wind blew and snow swirled about them. The firs grew in a remote area, far from the main stretch of road, and as they drove, the fallen snow grew deeper. It was exhilarating and evoked fond memories of Dakota winters.

It took much longer to return home with their tree than planned. To their amazement, the whole community of Fort Defiance was very upset by their expedition. "You're not used to these storms in our country!" one grandmother scolded them. "I was just sending my son out to look for you. Snow on the roads can make travel dangerous, and there are cliffs along the way!" Harold and Blossom apologized for the worry they had caused. It was heartening, however, that their new parishioners were beginning to care about the Native strangers in their midst.

When the Women's Guild president asked Blossom to take over a rummage project, she almost refused. Always, it seemed, wherever they went, the time-consuming task of rummage became part of their lives. Still, without rummage, the Jones family itself would have gone without some important items. The Navajos likewise lived in real poverty and needed rummage. To be asked to take charge was proof that she was now trusted. The job required strict fairness when Blossom distributed rummage all across the reservation. She made sure that an assistant was present with her whenever the shipments arrived, and they both kept careful records of what came in and where it was sent.

❧ + ❧

It didn't take more than three or four visits among the four missions to convince Harold that Navajo young people needed attention most. Sixty-five percent of the one thousand parishioners of Good Shepherd were twenty-one years old or younger. While those in the world surrounding

Navajoland grew up with radios, televisions, movie theaters, newspapers, department stores, and supermarkets, many of the Navajo children appeared to live as their ancestors had lived. The stark beauty of desert and wide sky, the life cycle of sheep, family legends and beliefs passed on orally from generation to generation were what they knew.

Some aspects of mainstream American culture, however, had penetrated the Navajo community, among both young and old. Alcoholism was a longstanding problem, as it was in many other Indian communities. In Father Jim Thompson's home, Harold met Steven Plummer, a young Navajo who had struggled with the disease. He was an earnest young man, willing and able to do any task, who now served as an interpreter and a lay reader. Through the year, Harold used Steven to interpret on many of his calls. He saw how people responded to the young man, and he learned to depend upon Steven's knowledge of customs and guidance when approaching people. One day Steven came to the Joneses' home to ask how a Navajo might become a priest. "I used to hang around the Navajo Inn, where there's a bar," Steven told Harold and Blossom. "When I got so drunk I couldn't stand up any more, the Bailey Thompsons—they were church volunteer workers—would come and get me and take me home with them to sober up. They did a good job on me. Now I want to be able to preach to my own people and give them the good word."

The first step in Steven's preparation for ministry had to be more education. Harold arranged for Steven to enroll in Farmington Junior College and then at Cook Christian Training School in Tempe, Arizona. Steven persisted in his studies, eventually graduating as a B student. During vacations, Steven threw himself into the developing programs for youth on the reservation, organizing baseball and soccer teams and supervising camping trips and later bus excursions to Disneyland and national parks.

With the agreement of Father Thompson, Steven Plummer, Ruby, and other hardworking members of the staff, Harold ended the traditional visits of outside teachers and youth, who had come for many years to teach summer vacation Bible school at Good Shepherd Mission. "We must be self-reliant," he insisted. "There are enough of us here to teach our children in their own language." Yet the congregation would still benefit from contact with outside young people. To those places from which the volunteer teachers and youths had come in previous summers, the church sent invitations to dances, cookouts, and field trips, asking them to share in activities with Navajo young people. Some came, and new friendships were formed.

The mission youth also became involved in the mission's finances. As part of the mission's new effort to take responsibility for its own welfare and manage its finances, Harold had insisted that it pay its share of the annual diocesan assessment that all churches throughout the diocese were expected to pay. Harold felt it important that the young people should take part in meeting this community obligation, so the youth group was assigned one thousand dollars of the assessment to pay. As in the old days of Niobrara, when Harold's grandmother had proudly watched a young boy present the youth offering for a cause, so now a delegate was elected among the Navajo youth to present their annual offering for the support of the Diocese of Arizona. This simple gesture both startled and educated the Diocesan Council. Harold also required the youth group to send a representative to the monthly meeting of the Navajo Mission Council, thereby drawing them closer to the church community.

❧ + ❧

Another problem Harold faced was the attitude of many Navajos toward death. Behind the mission was a cemetery that needed upkeep: some of the crosses and headstones were leaning, and weeds grew so tall that the plot looked more like a field than a graveyard. Nobody seemed to care for the cemetery, yet the people were certainly not lacking in love and respect for the dead. Blossom's Navajo friend Edith advised against attempting to restore the cemetery, claiming that the Navajos believed that the graveyard was full of the dead, whose spirits might haunt anyone spending much time there. Harold also encountered this aversion to the dead. One day he passed a burning hogan; a group of men and women stood at a distance, watching as the flames consumed it. "That's the home of a woman who just died," Father James Thompson explained. "Neighbors are afraid that if it stands, her spirit will come back to haunt it. Nobody will want to live there, so it's best to burn it down."

The circumstances of a Navajo girl named Maggie provided an opportunity for Harold to challenge the power of this belief about the dead. Maggie lived with her mother on the edge of the desert in a hogan. She had quickly learned English at school and had joined Steven as one of the interpreters for services and church meetings. Soon she was baptized and like Steven participated in the youth group activities.

When her mother became very sick, Maggie cared for her day and night for several weeks. When the mother died, Maggie was sitting beside her, holding her hand. The Navajo traditional healer predicted that Maggie too would die within the year because she had opened herself to the influence of her mother's spirit by touching her at the moment of death.

Harold counted on Maggie continuing to live—it would disprove the prediction and show the community the power of an alternative set of religious beliefs. All of Fort Defiance watched and waited, treating Maggie with special kindness because her days were numbered. A month, then two months passed. Maggie suddenly became very ill with meningitis.

Harold was determined that the child would not die. Navajo magic was strong, he readily acknowledged, having himself encountered the power of the *yuwipi*, still strong for non-Christian Dakotas and Lakotas. He believed that Jesus the healer was stronger, however. Blossom began calling other church members in all four congregations in order to organize a prayer vigil.

Harold went to Maggie's bedside, taking her hand and placing his other hand on her burning forehead. Her eyes were closed, and she made no sign that she knew he was there. The young Indian nurses in the corridor didn't say anything, but Harold knew by the way they stood nervously in a small cluster outside of the room that their studies had not erased long-standing cultural beliefs. He invited the nurses to pray with him; two approached and shyly joined him in Maggie's room.

Harold closed his eyes, and for a moment, no words came. Then the familiar words from the prayer book formed on his lips. "I lay my hands upon you in the name of our Lord and savior Jesus Christ, beseeching him to uphold you and fill you with his grace, that you may know the healing power of his love."

He continued to pray fervently. "Gracious Father, be here with your child, Maggie. Drive from her all that is evil, all that is amiss. Restore wholeness within her. Nourish her with thy love. May thy peace fill her heart. Spare her to us, Lord, and stay with her through all of the years to come on this earth. When she is old, bring her into thy everlasting kingdom. We ask this for her, and for the sake of her Navajo people, in the name of thy son, Jesus Christ."

She was healed, he was now confident. Peace filled Harold's heart as he looked down at Maggie, and he was acutely conscious of God's presence. Maggie was safe in his keeping, and anxiety was needless. Even Harold's eagerness to prove to the Navajo people that God was all-powerful was needless. Maggie was in God's hands, and God would carry her from now on.

"Come away now, girls." A cool professional voice summoned the young nurses from the bedside. "The last thing Maggie needs is a crowd around her bed. We're putting a quarantine sign on her door. If you come in here, you will find a mask in the cupboard outside the door." Her voice was severe as she turned to Harold. "That goes for you too."

"Thanks, Lord," Harold spoke silently as he left. "Your care is at work."

Maggie's fever broke during the night. She was very weak but regained consciousness the next day. Little by little, her strength returned.

❧ ✝ ❧

Back in South Dakota, Bishop Conrad Gesner was preparing to retire. He had been bishop for over twenty years; from 1954 into the mid-1960s, he had been the sole bishop in that huge district. In 1964, he asked for assistance, and Lyman C. Ogilby was appointed bishop coadjutor, and as such, would automatically succeed the diocesan bishop after his death or retirement. Ogilby had been bishop of a diocese in the Philippines and had resigned so that a native Filipino could be elected to take his place.

Bishop Ogilby brought to South Dakota a wealth of experience, along with an affinity for Native peoples. His strong support for Indian causes turned some of the white congregations against him, especially after he argued that a young Indian accused of murdering a white woman was not given a fair trail. After a few years, he resolved to follow his own example by resigning soon after Bishop Gesner's approaching retirement so that a

Native American could be elected in his place if the district wished. Bishop Gesner announced that he would retire at the District Convocation in 1969, at which time his successor would be elected. Ogilby would preside at that convocation and then resign after the new bishop was consecrated. This occasion would be the first time that the church in South Dakota could elect its own bishop. As a missionary district receiving financial assistance from the national church, its bishop was appointed by the House of Bishops. The General Convention, however, had recently voted to abolish these distinctions. Former missionary districts became dioceses and were thus empowered to elect their own bishops.

Harold was on the long list of candidates nominated for the election, but he quickly withdrew his name. His work in Navajoland had barely begun. "My name must have been submitted by one of our Indian friends," he remarked to Blossom, "but I have no illusions that an Indian could be elected in South Dakota for many years to come."

It was no secret that when Bishop Gesner announced his forthcoming retirement, he began quietly preparing young Walter Jones to take his place. Walter's birthplace was Winnipeg, Canada, but he had already given almost ten years of his ministry to the Districts of North and South Dakota, and his love for the Indian people was unquestioned. Walter was on the district staff, and in the past year as Bishop Gesner became less sure of his eyesight, Walter drove him around the state. Harold loved young Walter, an energetic, winsome man, standing six feet three inches, who exhibited great sensitivity in his work with Indian congregations. Of all the white priests nominated for bishop, Walter was certainly the most qualified.

Walter himself telephoned the joyful news of his election to Harold and Blossom. "I want to have my consecration in June during the 1970 Niobrara Convocation at Pine Ridge," he exclaimed. "And you both must come for it!"

Their two years in Navajoland were so full of new experiences that Niobrara seemed like a beloved part of the past. Letters, telephone calls, and one visit to Fort Defiance had been the only links with Norma, Jerry, and their little ones during those years.

❧ + ❧

Harold and Blossom returned from Niobrara to busy months at Ft. Defiance. Visitors began arriving for shared youth trips and projects. Rummage had to be unpacked and sorted. The women had been waiting for Blossom to do the final collecting and pricing of all the articles of driftwood, stone, plastic, and paper that they had been busy fashioning into salable knickknacks during the winter months. These items would be displayed on tables, along with traditional wool rugs and hangings, carved silver and turquoise jewelry, paintings, and beadwork. Such traditional, expensive, and lovely works of art would be admired and perhaps bought by tourists, and the less expensive, smaller items might also attract some shoppers.

The furniture-repair project had been popular, and classes continued in the parish house. One day as Harold was starting off on one of his journeys, he met one of Blossom's fellow pupils toiling up the walk, a chair balanced on top of her head. She was breathing hard, and her lined face was streaming from the heat. She murmured a respectful greeting to Harold. Harold looked at her aghast. "Aren't you Helen Chee? And don't you live out at Sawmill? That's fifteen miles from here. Did someone give you a ride?"

The woman wiped drops of perspiration from her forehead with the back of her hand and grinned. "No, Father, I walked."

"How did you keep from getting too tired on such a hot day as this?"

Helen replied by lifting the chair from her head and setting it down beside her. "Like this," she said, plumping wearily onto it. "Every time I needed to rest, I put my burden down and sat on it."

Harold looked at her with admiration. "That's good advice for all of us. With women like you for grandmothers, Helen, the future of the Navajo Nation is secure."

❧ ✝ ❧

By the end of two and a half years, Harold realized that it was impossible for him alone to reach out to the thousand communicants scattered across the vast deserts of Arizona and New Mexico. He approached the bishop to ask for an assistant. It was an auspicious time to do so. The tremendous debt that Good Shepherd confronted at the time of Harold's and Blossom's arrival had been whittled down to half, a feat that proved the bishop wrong about the abilities of "the People" to carry their own burdens. The bishop listened to Harold's request and nodded. He recommended Ned Moore and his wife, Charlotte, who had served in South Dakota among Indian people and had inquired about openings in the Southwest. The Moores agreed to come and would arrive before the end of the year.

✼ + ✼

In South Dakota, Bishop Walter Jones also confronted an impossible situation—serving ninety congregations by himself. At the first Diocesan Convention after his election, he pleaded that a suffragan bishop be elected, a suffragan being an assisting bishop who does not automatically succeed the diocesan bishop on his death or resignation. He asked that since the majority of these ninety congregations were Sioux, a Sioux priest should be chosen to fill the position. The bishop reminded the delegates that since the Dakota Leadership Program had begun several years before, the first Dakota men to be trained had passed their canonical exams and were busy serving on the reservations. Any one of these men could be nominated—if the convention favored Bishop Jones's request.

Names of white priests from other states as well as from South Dakota joined the long list of nominations, including, at Walter's request, the names of the recently ordained Sioux priests. Harold's name was added to the list.

The South Dakota district paper, which the Joneses received each month, reported events at home. Harold read the convention issue aloud to Blossom as she drank her tea after lunch.

"It just may be that with Walter's charm and persuasiveness, the convention delegates may begin to see another side to mission work," Harold remarked one afternoon. "They've watched the training program in action and are beginning to see results there. But to suggest that a bishop be elected from among the Indian people in South Dakota still sounds incredible to me. Just the same, the mere suggestion opens the possibility of bringing church leadership back to our own people."

Next came a call from the election committee, who asked for Harold's permission to put his name on the ballot. The caller said that it was proper protocol to notify the bishop of Arizona about the nomination also. That thought pleased Harold. Arizona, like South Dakota, was cautious about the kind and amount of leadership it allowed the Indian populations to assume. The news of Indian names on the ballot would be a wholesome shock to the Diocese of Arizona. After the phone call, Harold became so engrossed with religious education programs starting up with the new school year that he all but forgot the elections in South Dakota.

Harold arrived at his office one late afternoon, hot and dusty after a long journey covering three of the four mission stations.

The telephone rang.

A jumble of voices greeted him. "Hello," Harold repeated more firmly. At last, a recognizable voice answered him—Jerry, his son-in-law.

"Good evening, Bishop Jones. I am calling for Bishop Jones."

Other voices began calling out congratulations. Harold could hear faint whistles and shouting in the background.

"What's happening up there?"

"You just happened." This time it was Vine Deloria Sr.'s deep voice that answered. "You were elected suffragan bishop on the first ballot. You could have had plenty of competition but didn't. There's no doubt who is first choice. God bless you. He has chosen you for an important job."

When Harold replaced the receiver, the silence of his office closed around him. He slipped from the chair onto his knees. He had no words to say. God needed no human words, but again he felt himself in the presence of God, caught up, dust, weariness and all; a small being, an infinitesimal part of God's creation somehow briefly singled out and called into his presence.

Never would he able to completely express, even to Blossom, the impact of the news. Somehow, God in his unspeakable love had made his presence known and transformed Harold's whole being. To be loved and accepted by God was to make his service the only thing that really mattered. And to be accepted by the people of South Dakota, both white and Indian! Incredible!

When Harold rose, the sky was already blazing with sunset colors. Blossom would be wondering where he was. He found her alone in the kitchen.

She looked at him, and her voice was strained. "What is it?"

He led her to a chair and pressed her shoulders until she sat down. "Is something the matter?" she asked anxiously. "Is Norma all right? The twins, Jana?"

Harold chose his words carefully. "Everyone is fine. I have been talking to Jerry. There will be another Bishop Jones in South Dakota."

He watched her closely. What did her startled look mean? Suddenly she burst into tears. "Oh, Harold!" was all she could say as she flung her arms around his neck.

✄ + ✄

Telling Blossom was much easier than breaking the news to the four Navajo congregations. Three years had merely scratched the surface of all that needed to be done through a ministry at Good Shepherd. Short as it was, though, the roots of friendship and trust were growing. Yet when a proud, secretive people open their hearts to you, they do not lightly watch you walk away from them. Harold knew this, and his heart was heavy when he announced the news in church the following Sunday.

A chilly silence settled over the congregation. After the service, some people nodded curtly, some not at all as the congregation passed him at the door. Did he imagine a gleam in the eye of the Navajo matron who three years earlier asked him why he had left his own people?

"Something has got to be done, Harold," Blossom declared firmly after two days of downcast eyes and inaudible greetings. "They really think you're a traitor. I don't look forward to the Women's Guild meeting tonight."

It was, as Blossom predicted, a dismal time. Harold went with her, hoping that some members might be willing to ask questions so that he could share what this election meant.

"We didn't think when you came that you would desert us so soon," the guild president chided gently, but her remark opened up more bitter reproaches bordering on anger.

"What about the projects we have begun?"

"What about the old folk you visit?"

"Who will preach?"

"Who will take the rummage project?"

Some of the remarks were made in Navajo, some in English. Harold had no answers for these questions, at least no answers that could satisfy the women. He saw Blossom stand up. Was she going to scold them?

She spoke coolly, quietly, so that they had to stop talking in order to hear her. "You ladies," she said, "have had all kinds of priests come here to serve your congregations. You have had some very good ones and some that were not so good. But you never, never before have helped train a priest to become a bishop. You can be proud of yourselves and of Father Harold Jones. What he has learned from you and what you have learned from him will be very helpful to him as he begins his new work as an assistant bishop to his own people, work that God has now called him to do."

When Blossom sat down, another silence ensued, less icy this time as the women considered her points.

Blossom's small speech coupled with the arrival of the Moores a month before the Joneses were to leave for South Dakota lessened the sting of departure. Harold was comforted as he watched the same people, once so suspicious of newcomers, welcoming the Moores with smiles. Three short years seemed to have erased the feelings of hurt and suspicion that Harold and Blossom had been sent to heal.

Harold learned later that it was Ned Moore's suggestion that the four missions join together to buy Harold's new vestments. Through the first weeks of October into November, the congregations worked to raise the money for "the best vestments money can buy!" as the treasurer of the guild told him.

The best would come from England, costing a total of six hundred dollars. The check the group presented to Harold was for one thousand dollars. "You must keep what is left over," said the guild president, "to buy something for your home that you and Blossom can remember us by."

It was a memorable day when the samples of colors arrived for the new chimere, the flowing robe that fitted over the white garment with puffy white sleeves. "This is a decision we must share!" Blossom announced firmly. "Tomorrow is the women's meeting, and we will ask them which color they think you should have."

And so it happened. Blossom summoned Harold from his office the next day to come and stand in the center of the large circle of women while some of the men stood and watched. "We have looked them all over," Blossom said, fingering the handful of samples. "But we need to see which shade of purple, as they call these reds, looks best with your skin."

Harold chuckled as he pivoted slowly, holding first one then another of the squares of soft material under his chin. All faces were turned on him intently. The first piece, a deep shade of real purple, brought a unanimous shaking of heads. The next caused a few nods, and so it went until he came to the fifth piece, a brilliant red, and all nodded in unison and applauded. Next came the measuring of length and girth and shoulders, careful work accompanied by laughter and calls of encouragement from the watchers. After Harold sent the order by airmail, the whole Episcopal community of Navajoland waited with him impatiently for the big box containing the finished chimere. When it came, surprisingly quickly, it was perfect in every detail, to the satisfaction of all. Harold tried on his vestments at another "showing," explaining each piece, the history of its use, and its function.

Early in December of 1971, Father Moore was instituted as the new vicar, and by the fourteenth an exhausted Harold and Blossom climbed into their car to follow the moving van as far as Gallup, New Mexico. There, in a hotel, they lifted their coffee cups in a toast to one another and wearily fell into bed. It was their thirty-fifth wedding anniversary.

14

IN THE LIGHT

※+※

January 11, 1972

Driving from Gallup to Cheyenne, Wyoming, the next day allowed Harold and Blossom time to unwind. Three years was, indeed, a brief time to spend among the Navajo people, but when it came time to leave, Harold found that his love for "the People" was strong and deep. Packing had been interlaced with loving farewells and speeches heard and given with hugs and tears unconcealed on both sides. In South Dakota, he knew, there would be more, equally emotional encounters of welcome. The long wind-swept stretches of road in between, traveled with only each other for company, were a godsend.

On the evening of December 16, 1971, they arrived in Rapid City, South Dakota, where Norma and Jerry awaited them. One day and night with the twins and Jana would be sufficient for the grandparents, Norma had thought, so she had reserved a motel room for the remainder of their visit before the trip to Sioux Falls. Bishop Walter Jones had asked for Harold to be at Dexter House, the diocesan headquarters, by the third of January.

In Sioux Falls the days between January 2 and January 11 were filled with activity. The time included a trip for Harold to McLaughlin, where he preached at the ordination to the priesthood of his good friends Innocent GoodHouse and LaVerne LaPointe, both of them graduates of the Dakota Leadership Program. For Blossom it meant addressing the last announcements of the consecration sent out to friends. Every evening heralded a dinner party, meeting, service, or all three.

Blossom was writing one afternoon, making the most of the fading winter daylight, when three cars drove into the Dexter House drive. Sixteen Navajos strode up the walk and rang the bell. Before she could run down to meet them, she heard the startled voice of the secretary, suddenly swept into a circle of silent, dignified, and colorful people. Blossom hesitated briefly on the landing to admire them. Silver jewelry, heavy with turquoise, gleamed in the light; the shawls wrapped around their shoulders were bright, patterned in deep blues and oranges and reds. Their faces looked as chiseled as the rocks of Navajoland until they caught sight of her and broke into smiles. The dignified silence erupted into a tumult of happy voices.

With the arrival of the Navajo delegation, life took on a dreamlike quality for Harold and Blossom. Could all these things really be happening? Soon after their Navajo friends arrived, the whole group climbed back into their cars to follow the Joneses to the airport to meet the Moores and Ruby Bates, Pauline Dick, Madge Sagodie, Phoebe Cleveland, Mrs. Ivanita, and Steven Plummer. Steven had flown up from Cook School at Harold's request so that he could read the gospel lesson in his native tongue at the service.

That evening, the last before the consecration, the visitors from Arizona gathered with Harold and Blossom in Dexter House. Blossom ordered pastries and made two large urns of coffee and then two more. The hall rang with laughter until late in the night. Somehow, the bitter cold of a January night, the sound of the wind rattling the windows, and the crackle of the fire laid in the old hearth seemed to draw them all closer than ever. Harold looked long and lovingly at the faces that had grown so dear to him over the past three years. Three years? It seemed that they had always been friends, even as he knew that they always would be.

❧ ✝ ❧

Early in the afternoon of the consecration, the atmosphere was electrified with the excitement of people arriving and greeting one another from every direction. Bishop Gesner had already arrived from Massachusetts, where he was now living. Bishop Harte from Arizona and Bishop McNairy of Minnesota were on hand, and smiling faces and outstretched arms greeted Harold at every turn. Old friends from Sisseton, Waubay, Fort Thompson, Cheyenne River, Chamberlain, Belle Fouche, Deadwood, Little Eagle, Pine Ridge, Standing Rock, Wakpala, and Santee had come to share this event. Seeing his old friends brought Grandmother and Grandfather Holmes to mind. Grandmother's dream had been for Harold to become a priest, and Grandfather's example had been that of a holy, humble priest. Even at this moment, Harold only wished to become like his grandfather.

Being consecrated a bishop would bring a new dimension to his calling to the ordained ministry—not a higher one, but a different, more expansive one. Now he would be required to represent his people among the other bishops of the church around the world. Now his vision for his own people would have to stretch to include all peoples.

Harold was grateful for the hour he could spend with Bishop Walter Jones in his quiet office, soothed by the gentle voice and warm eyes of the younger man. Not long ago, Walter himself had gone through a consecration. Now he rehearsed what was to come for Harold.

"We have to make a few concessions for the television presence," he said. "We'll wait until the announcer has made his explanation of the service. He will give a brief history of your ministry and explain why the service will be held in three languages. He will also say that the offering will be given to you as the beginning of a discretionary fund." He paused. "Did I remember to tell you that, Harold?

"He will name the consecrating bishops and explain that Kent FitzGerald is a layman and that he is preaching the sermon as chairman of the National Committee on Indian Work of the Episcopal Church. He'll talk about the three choirs—Roman Catholic, Lutheran, and Episcopal—and about the Presbyterian bell ringers.

"You know, Harold." Walter leaned back in his chair and looked at Harold as if seeing him anew. "If I were part of the television audience, I think I'd be impressed by the list of names on the program. Presiding Bishop Hines, of course, and Hanford King, bishop-elect of Idaho, and then great names like the Reverend Wilbur BearsHeart, Evelyn Bergen from Rosebud, Steven Plummer from Fort Defiance, the Reverend Noah BrokenLeg from Mission. Probably the viewers won't realize how many 'firsts' go with this event. First American Indian bishop; a first Navajo soon to be ordained deacon; one of the first women to stand in the pulpit and read a lesson, your good friend Evelyn Bergen; and Communion offered in a Roman Catholic cathedral to Anglicans and other denominations; the uniting of several church choirs . . . "

Harold held up his hand. "Only Almighty God can bring me through this night." The familiar words of the old hymn "Amazing Grace" took on new meaning for him: "'Tis grace that brought me safe thus far, and grace will lead me home."

❧✝❧

As they were being driven to the cathedral that night, Harold reached for Blossom's hand. He looked at her, the dance in their eyes continuing for them as it had for his grandparents, and murmured, "This night will bring another big change in our lives, but you must be beside me in all that lies ahead."

Despite Walter's preparation that afternoon, Harold was stunned when he glimpsed crowds of people filling the pews. Ushers with quiet efficiency were bustling clergy participants in the service to one area, choir members to another, escorting people down aisles, and searching out empty seats. Already a bright light for television cameras played across the pews from the temporary scaffolding in the right front corner of the great church.

An usher suddenly appeared beside Blossom, offering his arm and whisking her away before she had time to do more than look back and smile. Harold watched as the two of them walked the length of the aisle to the front pew. Then it was his turn to be led off to the vesting room, where all the bishops were gathering, their red robes scattered like bright poppies on a field of snow. The vesting room was crowded and cheerful with voices and laughter as old friends greeted one another. Harold's old seminary friend, Chilton Powell, who was now bishop of Oklahoma, waved from across the room. Presiding Bishop John Hines, chief bishop of the Episcopal Church, and Kent FitzGerald stepped out of the crowd to greet him. Their plane had landed in Sioux Falls just two hours before, they said, and they were thankful, what with the cold and snow, to be on the ground in

time. The warm pressure of Bishop Hines's hand in his own somehow relieved a portion of Harold's tension. He had not realized that his own
hands were clenched until he needed to reach out with them. Harold
squared his shoulders, took a deep breath, and became, to his surprise,
more an observer than a participant in this great pageant of the church.

The sacristy door opened, and slowly the many priests, deacons, bishops, and other participants began to fall into line, following the dictates of
the arm motioning them into the body of the cathedral. His own familiar
vestments felt very comforting to Harold. Someone else was taking care of
those bright new ones. He savored the combined scents of melting snow
on fur, sweet blend of perfumes, burning candles, and even a whiff of
wood smoke carried on the coats of those freshly arrived from the reservations—the good smell of living, breathing human beings, his longtime
friends.

The faint voice of the announcer was followed by a triumphant burst of
sound from the organ, joined by a thousand voices.

> The church's one foundation is
> Jesus Christ her Lord . . .
> *Okodakiciye kin*
> *He Jesus Christ Ahan . . .*

The procession moved forward, through the five verses of that hymn
and the five verses of another of his favorites: "Jesus shall reign where'er
the sun doth its successive journey run." The procession traveled the
length of the aisle to the chancel and passed the front pews where Blossom
and Norma were standing. Harold, with his son-in-law, Jerry Pederson, beside him, was directed to seats in a choir stall, fairly well out of public view.
Jerry, as a member of the Standing Committee of the diocese, was to be an
official presenter, along with Bishops Harte of Arizona and McNairy of
Minnesota.

At the last notes of the hymn, Jerry and his fellow presenters stood up.
They surrounded Harold and piloted him to the presiding bishop's chair.
They then joined in saying:

"Reverend Father in God, the clergy and people of the Diocese of South
Dakota, trusting in the guidance of the Holy Spirit, have chosen Harold

Stephen Jones to be a bishop and a chief pastor. We therefore ask you to lay your hands upon him and in the power of the Holy Spirit to consecrate him a bishop in the one, holy, catholic, and apostolic church."

Then came the testimonials. Harold was pleased to have so many of his Indian colleagues in South Dakota taking part in the ceremony. Young Martin Brokenleg, priest of Holy Apostles Church in Sioux Falls, served as master of ceremonies. Father Andy Weston of Eagle Butte read the Certificates of Consents of all of the Standing Committees in the Episcopal Church, while his old friend Frank Thornburn (a non-Indian) read the consents of all of the bishops.

After the presentation of these testimonies, Harold was called on to make his solemn Declaration of Conformity. "In the Name of the Father, and the Son, and the Holy Spirit, I, Harold Stephen Jones, chosen bishop of the church in South Dakota, do promise conformity and obedience to the doctrine, discipline, and worship of the Episcopal Church." Under the vaulted roof, his voice was strong.

The presiding bishop then spoke: "Dear friends in Christ, you have heard the testimony given that Harold Stephen has been duly and lawfully elected to be a bishop of the church of God to serve in the Diocese of South Dakota . . . Is he worthy?"

"*He ikipi!*" "*Haw!*" "*Han!*" "He is worthy!" The answer came in a great thunder.

Silently, with downcast eyes, Harold acknowledged this trust. "You know, Lord, that I am not worthy, except as you cleanse and guide me," he prayed silently. He was an observer no longer. His whole being was caught up in this outpouring of grace.

Fervently he prayed with the people as Father Wilbur BearsHeart led the Litany for the Ministry. "That you will inspire all bishops, priests, and deacons with your love, that they may hunger for truth and thirst after righteousness . . . That you will bless our brother Harold Stephen . . . and pour your grace upon him, that he may faithfully fulfill the duties of this ministry, build up your church, and glorify your name . . . that you bless his family and adorn them with Christian virtues."

Evelyn Bergen rose from her place among the robed clergy and stepped into the pulpit. Evelyn Bergen, the daughter of a priest and friend of Harold's childhood; he remembered her with flying pigtails and a streak of mischief that matched his own. Evelyn was reading Isaiah, wonderful words that never failed to bring tears to his eyes and that had brought him comfort so long ago. "The Spirit of the Lord God is upon me; because the Lord has anointed me. He has sent me to bring good tidings to the afflicted . . . to comfort all who mourn . . . to give them a garland instead of ashes, . . . the mantle of praise instead of a faint spirit." (Isaiah 61:1–3)

With a great thrill of sound, organ and voices sang out. "O be joyful in the Lord all ye lands: serve the Lord with gladness and come before His presence with song."

Harold stopped his own singing to listen, and a great peace filled his heart. He wished that he might stand this way, always, forgetful of everything else except the presence of God and in the company of fellow worshippers.

"First Timothy, chapter three, verses one through seven." It was the clipped voice of Hanford King, reading from St. Paul. After another hymn, the beloved, young voice of Steven Plummer, reading from the Gospel of John, filled the cathedral with the sound of a language few would understand. Harold turned his head to find the small group of Navajos proudly standing together, almost lost in that great company except for a vivid splash of color. Harold imagined the pleasure they were feeling. He had been theirs for a little while, but Steven was bone of their bone, a true Navajo, and the first soon to be ordained deacon and priest.

After Steven, another Indian, Kent FitzGerald, entered the pulpit. He was an Ojibwe and had accepted a job most Indians, including Harold, shunned because it meant they must live in New York City, working with the National Committee on Indian Work. The television lights were turned directly on him now. Like all faces belonging to the older generation of Indian people, his face bore the marks of pain endured. Kent FitzGerald was wise, shy, a little sad but also full of compassion, humor, and dedication. Shy he might be, but he readily agreed to give this message at Harold's consecration because he knew it would be the time and place to speak out to many he would not otherwise reach. But Harold knew, as he watched Kent stand up to face this great throng of dignitaries and strangers, that he could do so only after earnest prayer for strength.

"This is an occasion for great joy," Kent FitzGerald began. "An occasion for sober reflection. It says in the most meaningful way possible that American Indians have something of great value to bring to the life of the church; and this election occurred in a state where Indian people still suffer from a wide range of injustices. South Dakota is not alone in bearing this kind of burden. Every state, city, town that has a sizable minority population caught in the cycle of continuing poverty bears its own burden . . . The election of Harold puts the reputation of the Episcopal Church on the line. All across the country people have eyes on South Dakota and on the Episcopal Church and on what the performance of the church will be. Will it be a challenge to the other denominations and states with Indian populations and other racial groups?"

The faces of the congregation were blurred in the darkness beyond the bright lights turned upon Kent. But Harold could tell from the listening silence that Kent's mild manner was able to convey some truths, which, spoken more vehemently, might not have been accepted.

Kent's voice rose, and he slowly enunciated. "The greatest gift of the white man to the Indians was the gospel of Jesus Christ. But one thing marred that. The message was brought clothed in the white man's culture.

"When Jesus was accused by his own people of associating with the wrong people and preaching in a way that distressed the devout Jews, his answer was, 'I have come not to destroy but to fulfill the law.' The first missionaries to the Indian people forgot that saying, and the Indian law and ways of worship were replaced by the dominant culture."

Harold's mind traveled back to his boyhood days and the tales Grandfather told. Funny tales that made them all laugh but there was sadness and darkness in them, too. There were jokes on himself and on his brother priests as they ran head-on into social customs of the dominant society and made, what seemed to non-Indians, some ridiculous mistakes.

Kent's voice continued, "This law and way of worship of the Indian people were not meant to be destroyed. They were a deeply religious people. Religion was the center of their lives. They started the day with a song of praise. They had a deep sense of stewardship toward the earth and all living things. They believed in the worth of the spirit. 'Lay not up for yourselves treasures—Love one another. Seek ye first the Kingdom of God.'

Many things taught to them by Christians corresponded to their beliefs. These messages converted the Indians by the thousands. A large number of native priests were raised up, and the people gladly heard their message.

"But while the message was so gladly and quickly received, the white culture was rejected, and those who accepted it did so under duress because of the government structure that would control and dominate their lives over the next seventy-five to one hundred years. Indian people in many places still question the kinds of values proclaimed by the dominant society.

"Now, after one hundred years, there comes a growing awareness of the Indian way of life. More study of old Indian ways is being made and put into books for the young to read. Indian people have been waiting to share their insights and their spiritual sense with the greater body of the church.

"These kinds of tensions between racial groups are not uncommon. They are rampant throughout the world and bursting into violence and destruction. Many people are asking what is the role of the church in the world in which we find ourselves today, and are trying to redefine the church's mission. Although it needs to be defined in words, a more meaningful definition is that set by example; an example we set by the way we live, how we treat our fellow man. By what you have done here . . . you have begun a new definition of mission, which people can see and which people throughout the world are waiting to see."

When Kent finished, he gathered up his papers and stepped back into the shadows. The congregation he had addressed was from many backgrounds: Indian and white, rich and poor, official and private citizen, oppressor and oppressed. He had rolled out grim facts and lessons of history before them but then closed on a prophetically hopeful note.

The prelude to a favorite hymn rolled from the organ, high in the balcony. The congregation rose.

> God of the prophets, Bless the prophet's sons . . .
> *Tuwe nahanh wacinyapi sni kin*

Singing to God in two languages at once, Harold knew that God understood them equally and was pleased with the blending of them on his earth.

During the singing of the last verse, Harold rose and walked to the chancel steps where Bishop Hines stood. In a strong voice that could be heard by people in the farthest pews, the presiding bishop posed the questions that Harold had read and reread searchingly, testing himself and his own will through them since his election two months before. "Will you fulfill the peoples' trust in your obedience to Christ, be faithful in prayer and study, preach boldly the gospel of Christ, nourish the people through prayer and celebration of the sacraments with them. Guard the discipline and faith of the church, join in the government of the whole church with brother bishops, guiding and sustaining the priests and deacons and all other ministers in the church?" Now Harold answered them with conviction. "I will . . . by the grace given me."

Again came the exciting jumble of two languages and one creed as the congregation joined in the confession of faith, led by Harold.

> I believe in one God, the Father Almighty,
> Maker of heaven and earth.
> *Wakantanka wanjina, Ateyapi Iyotan wasaka,*
> *mahpiya maka iyakna, Qa taku wanyaagpica sni*
> *kin owasin Kage cin, he wicawida.*

"Come Holy Ghost our souls inspire," sang the presiding bishop.

"And lighten with celestial fire," sang the choirs and congregation. It was an age-old chant, sung by Christians from generation to generation at the time of consecrations.

> Teach us to know the Father, Son,
> And thee, of both, to be but one,
> That through the ages all along,
> This may be our endless song:
> Praise to thy eternal merit,
> Father, Son, and Holy Spirit.

From their places in the chancel, the ten bishops came to join Bishop Hines as he commenced the consecration prayer. Harold knelt as they stood circling him, placing their hands on his head.

"Pour out, now, upon Harold Stephen the power of that princely Spirit whom you bestowed upon your only son, Jesus Christ, with whom he endowed the apostles and by whom your church is built up every place to the glory and unceasing praise of your name." The prayer continued, asking for the Spirit's guidance and strength in all his life ahead. The eleven pairs of hands on Harold's head did not seem a heavy weight. Instead, they seemed to burn with a kind of heat that flowed through him. He rose unsteadily to his feet, with the assistance of both Bishop Gesner and Bishop Walter. He felt both weak and yet strong. The red robe was brought forward and laid on his shoulders. Then he stood alone with Bishop Hines, who presented him to an applauding congregation.

Facing the congregation, with arms outstretched, Bishop Harold Jones proclaimed, "The peace of the Lord be always with you." "And with your spirit," rolled back the response from the people.

With the exchanging of the peace among the congregation, a happy kind of confusion ensued. Harold managed to step down to Blossom and Norma, hold them closely for a moment, and to give Blossom a kiss. He knew his voice was too unsteady to say what he wanted to say. But he knew from her eyes that she understood that without her love and faith and help, he would not be here.

Minutes later he was holding the paten, the plate of bread, the offering of Christ's body. With the other bishops and priests, Harold served it to the thousand and more who had come to be there with him on this cold winter night. Beloved faces, every one of them. Old ones and young ones from every stage of his life, mingling all together, coming up to share the holy gifts that Harold was privileged to offer them. These were the visible folk. He also knew that his own mother, grandmother, and grandfather, his two lost sons, and Kenny were present too, rejoicing with him. In his gracious and loving way, God had brought the whole of Harold's life together so that every part of it was represented in this time of great happiness. God in this glorious gathering demonstrated what his kingdom was like, and he had called Harold, a Dakota, to serve his own people and all mankind as an apostle in his church.

EPILOGUE

Harold Jones thus began his service as suffragan bishop of South Dakota. News of the consecration of the first Native American bishop traveled across the country, and he received many invitations to speak outside of the diocese. He had difficulty declining those requests. Even though he felt he could serve God and his people by accepting them, he knew that his time and energy must be used first in ministry in his own diocese. As Bishop Walter had insisted at Harold's election, he was to share in serving both white and Indian congregations and those obligations would keep him busy.

A sudden stroke ended this phase of his work in the fall of 1972, just months after his consecration. For a few years Harold was an invalid, with Blossom as his nurse. His recovery has been remarkable, and except for the cane that he carries for balance, there is no sign that he has been ill. Although he officially retired in 1976, the church still calls on him for assistance, and he is still invited to represent his people at national services and meetings of the Episcopal Church.

Harold was in the midst of recuperating in February 1973 when a group of Indian militants from the American Indian Movement (AIM) took over the historic community of Wounded Knee in a symbolic act of protest. Their grievances were against what they felt to be a corrupt tribal government on Pine Ridge, supported by the United States. While his illness prevented involvement at that time, he later expressed mixed feelings about

AIM and its methods. Harold sympathized with their protests against tribal corruption. As a witness to racism himself, he was also outraged by such gross anti-Indian acts as posting signs in neighboring Nebraska that read "Indians and dogs keep out," or the incident where an Indian was murdered and his body kept in the trunk of a car for three days. Yet in keeping with his commitment to the Christian way of reconciliation, Harold opposed the confrontational tactics of AIM, which seemed at times to escalate violence. He was moved by compassion for those people and communities he had served, torn with conflicting views over AIM, and frustrated by his inability to serve as a moderator and reconciler in that time of crisis.

Blossom passed away in 1989.

Harold lived alone for some time in their house in Rapid City, but in 1996 he accepted the invitation of his daughter and son-in-law, Norma and Jerry Pederson, to live with them in Chandler, Arizona.

SUGGESTED READING

Raymond A. Bucko
Martin Brokenleg

We suggest the following materials for readers who wish to gain deeper insights into the historical and cultural context in which Bishop Jones and his family lived. We also have provided works by other Dakota and Lakota authors so that the reader might attend to the rich multiplicity of voices of these peoples.

The Dakotas and Lakotas have produced a significant number of authors since the nineteenth century. Charles Eastman, a Santee doctor who served at Pine Ridge during the Wounded Knee massacre, authored a considerable amount of material on Dakota life, philosophy, and religion, including reflections on the relationship of Christianity to Dakota belief (1915, 1977, 1980, 1991a, 1991b, 1991c) and works coauthored with his Anglo-American wife, Elaine Goodale Eastman (1990). Elaine Eastman also wrote her own reflections on life among the Dakota and Lakota (1891, 1945, 1978). Luther Standing Bear was a Lakota who wrote autobiographical works as well as reflections on Lakota culture and life at boarding school (1975, 1978, 1988a, 1988b). Gertrude Simmons Bonnin (Zitkala-Ša), Yankton, wrote about her own life as well as about Dakota culture and mythology (1985a, 1985b). Marie McLaughlin, a Santee from Devil's Lake, also wrote stories told by her people (1916).

Ella Deloria was a relative of Philip and Vine Deloria, who are mentioned in this book. She wrote various works on the Dakota people, including various ethnographic pieces while working with anthropologist Franz Boas (1926, 1927, 1954, 1961), a general work on the lifeways of the Dakota and Lakota people (1944), and a charming novel of traditional Indian life at the time of contact with Europeans

(1988). This anthropological tradition is also continued today by Lakota Beatrice Medicine (1969a, 1969b, 1976, 1978, 1979, 1981, 1983, 1985, 1986, 1987, 1988).

Vine Deloria Sr., an Episcopalian priest, has written a reflection on Native Christianity (1987, 1995 [recorded narrative]), and his son, Vine Deloria Jr., has also written on theological topics (1969, 1977, 1979, 1983, 1996, 1999). Vine Deloria's son Philip has written on history and identity of Native peoples (1998). For information on the Deloria family, see Bruguier 1989, 367–78.

Virginia Driving Hawk Sneve is a contemporary Lakota writer who has authored work on the mission history of the Episcopal Church among her Dakota and Lakota relatives (1977b), an autobiographical work (1995), and works on stories and other Indian topics (1972a, 1972b, 1974a, 1974b, 1977a, 1978, 1993, 1997; 1975 [with Ernest L. Schusky]; 2000 [with Paul Sneve]). Delphine Red Shirt has recently published her autobiography, which considers both Christianity and Native religion (1998). Other reflections on Christianity by Lakota people include works by Sr. Marie Therese Archambault (1995, 1996, 1998), Mercy Poor Man (1987), and Emerson Spider Sr. (1996). James Treat has brought together a variety of Native voices from different tribes and traditions in his anthology on Native Christianity (1996), and Sergei Kan writes on the importance of seriously studying American Indian Christianity (1999: xxiii–xxv).

In addition to works by Native authors, Protestant and Catholic missionaries have produced a significant amount of material about their experiences with the Dakotas and Lakotas. These writings include works by the Pond brothers (1854, 1857, 1880, 1889, 1893, 1986), Stephen Return Riggs (1869, 1872, 1880a, 1880b, 1880c, 1894) and his wife, Mary Buel Riggs (1928), Thomas L. Riggs (1958), and John P Williamson (1918). Works by early Episcopalian missionaries include the autobiographies of Bishop Henry Whipple (1899), Bishop William Hare (1873), and Bishop Ethelbert Talbot (1906). Father Vine Deloria Sr. has written on his views of Christianity (1987) and Father Martin Brokenleg has written on counseling youth at risk and on Lakota cultural practices (1990 [with Brentro and Van Bockern], 1993 [with Middleton], 1998). Sarah Olden produced the only other biography of a native Episcopalian priest, Philip Deloria (1918). All three of these priests figure in Jones's narrative. For a bibliography of works translated into Dakota by various missionaries, see the Dakota Bibliography (1880).

Reflective works by early Catholic missionaries who worked with the Dakota and Lakota include those of Monsignor Ravoux (1890), Fr. Louis Goll, S.J. (1940), Florintine Digmann, S.J. (n.d.), Henry Westropp, S.J. (n.d.), and Gontran Laviolette, O.M.I. (1944). More contemporary accounts of both mission experience and cultural observations among the Lakota have been created by Fathers William Stolzman (1986a, 1986b), Paul Steinmetz, S.J. (1970, 1984a, 1984b, 1990, 1998a, 1998b), Robert Hilbert, S.J. (1987), Stephen Huffstetter, S.C.J. (1998), Michael Steltenkamp, S.J. (1982, 1993) and layman Ron Zeilinger (1990). Fr. Don Doll, S.J. has done extensive photo documentation of reservation life (1976 [with Alinder], 1994, 1996). Works that specifically examine the Episcopalian missions to the Dakota and Lakota include a missionary handbook (1925), the Swift Bird account (1926), Alexander (1994), O. Anderson (1988), Burleson (1911), Hare (1926), Lane (1914), Wilkins and Wilkins (1959), Wolff (1989), and Woodruff (1934). *Spirit of Missions,* a journal that recorded information about the Episcopal Church missions from 1836 to 1939, is a rich source of data for the Dakota missions. For a list of articles on Episcopalian activity on the Dakota and Lakota missions from 1862 to 1897, see, specifically, Woodruff 1934, 597–603.

There is also a significant amount of scholarly literature on Christianity and the missionization of the Dakota and Lakota people (Barnds 1969; Barton 1919; Blegen 1934; Clow 1982; Duncan 1990; Duratscheck 1943, 1947, 1985; Enochs 1996; Forbes 1977; Gates 1935; Gilkerson 1961; Hancock 1905; Holler 1984, 1995; Howe 1911; Karolevitz 1980; Kessler 1989; MacPeek 1973; Markowitz 1987; McLaren 1996; Parker 1962, 1964; Peterson 1980, 1982, 1983; Peterson and Kessler 1989; Rice 1998; Smith 1992; Stahl 1989; Sterling 1956; Thompson 1992; Vecsey 1999; Willand 1964; Young 1958a, 1958b, 1963). A considerable number of hymnals have been published in Dakota and Lakota by various Christian denominations (1899, 1914, 1919, 1927a, 1927b, 1929, 1946, 1951, 1962, 1964, [1965?], 1972, 1979, 1986, 1991, 1993; see also Hunt 1899, 1907; Renville 1842; Riggs and Williamson 1863). Finally, novels in which missionaries and questions of mission influence among the Dakota and Lakota figure include Boyles and Boyles (1910) and Hong (1983).

While the current volume and Sarah Olden's biography of Philip Deloria are the only instances of "as-told-to" works involving Christian Dakota or Lakota ministers, Lakota people have produced a plethora of narratives in this genre that focus on traditional lifeways. The most famous of these accounts are based on narration by the nineteenth-century spiritual leader Nicholas Black Elk (Brown 1953; Neihardt 1961; see also DeMallie 1984; Neihardt 1951). Contemporary narratives have also been collected and edited by Ron Theiz (1994 [with Young Bear]), Thomas Mails (1991; 1979), William Lyon (1990), and Richard Erdoes (1972 [with Lame Dog]; 1990 [with M. Crow Dog]; 1993 [with Brave Bird]; 1995 [with L. Crow Dog]).

Historians who have written on the Dakotas include Gary Anderson (1984,

1986, 1988 [with Woolworth]), Ruth Landes (1968), Roy Meyer (1968, 1993), Chester Oehler (1959), and Doane Robinson (1967). Mary Eastman also recorded early experiences among the Dakotas (1849, 1970). Historical material on the Lakotas includes works produced by Royal Hassrick (1964), George Hyde (1937, 1956, 1961), James Olson (1965), Catherine Price (1996), and Mari Sandoz (1961). Books specifically about Wounded Knee include works by James McGregor (1940), David H. Miller (1985), James Mooney (1991), William and Marla Powers (1994), and Robert Utley (1963).

Anthropologists who have written on the Dakotas include James Howard (1980, 1984), Ruth Landes (1968), and Alanson Skinner (1919). Early anthropological studies of the Lakotas include the work of James Owen Dorsey (1889a; 1889b; 1891a; 1891b; 1894; 1897), James Mooney (1991), James Walker (1905, 1914, 1917, 1980, 1982, 1983), Wilson Wallis (1947), and Clark Wissler (1904, 1905, 1907a, 1907b, 1912). Works on the Lakotas by contemporary anthropologists include Raymond Bucko, S.J. (1988; 1998), Raymond DeMallie (1977 [with Lavenda], 1982, 1983, 1984, 1987, and 1987 [with Parks]), Elizabeth Grobsmith (1974, 1979, 1981a, 1981b), Marla Powers (1986), William Powers (1975, 1982, 1986, 1987), Ernest Schusky (1975), and Michael Steltenkamp, S.J. (1993).

The following resources will be of interest to individuals who wish to pursue further research using mission documents: the archival holdings at the Archives of the Episcopal Church, Austin, Texas; the South Dakota Protestant Episcopal Church Diocesan Archives; Center for Western Studies, Augustana College, Sioux Falls, South Dakota; Marquette University, Milwaukee, Wisconsin; Gonzaga University, Spokane, Washington; the archives of the South Dakota Conference of the United Church of Christ at Yankton College, Yankton, South Dakota; the South Dakota State Historical Society in the Historical Resource Center, Pierre, South Dakota; the Indian Rights Association Papers, Pennsylvania Historical Society, Philadelphia, Pennsylvania; the American Missionary Association Archives at Fisk University, Nashville, Tennessee; the American Board of Commissioners for Foreign Missions Papers at the Houghton Library, Harvard University, Cambridge, Massachusetts; the Papers of the General Council of the Congregational and Christian Churches of the United States, housed in the Congregational Library, Boston, Massachusetts; the Minnesota Historical Society, St. Paul, Minnesota; the Lake Mohonk Conference manuscript collection at Haverford College, Haverford, Pennsylvania; and the Presbyterian Historical Society, Philadelphia, Pennsylvania. The majority of these archival locations are listed in Richmond L. Clow (1982, 65). (I am also indebted to Mark Thile for supplementary listings.) Additional sources can be found in articles detailing archival holdings by Edward Hill (1981), Joseph Svoboda (1983), Harry Thompson (1992), Philip Batin and Mark Thiel (1984), and Alan Schwartz (1983).

HYMNALS AND PRAYER BOOKS

1914. *Sioux Indian Prayer and Hymn Book.* Cincinnati: Jos. Berning Printing.

1919. *First Complete Catholic Sioux Hymnal.* Fort Yates ND: Benedictine Missionaries.

1927a. *Lakota Wocekiye na Olwan Wowapi: Sioux Indian Prayer and Hymn Book.* St. Louis: Central Bureau of the Catholic Central Verein of America.

1927b. *Sioux Prayer Book.* St. Francis SD: Jesuit Fathers at St. Francis Mission.

1929. *Lakota Wocekiye na Olowan Wowapi (Sursum Cordia): Sioux Indian Prayer and Hymn Book with an Appendix of English Prayers and Hymns.* St. Louis: Central Bureau of the Catholic Central Verein of America.

1946. *Wakan Cekiye Odowan: Hymns in Dakota and English for use in Niobrara Deanery.* Sioux Falls SD: Niobrara Deanery.

1951. *Wakan Cekiye Odowan qa Okna Ahiyayapi Kta Ho Kin: Hymnal with Tunes and Chants According to the use of the Episcopal Church in the Missions among the Dakotas of the Missionary District of South Dakota.* Pierre SD: State Publishing.

1962. *Niobrara Wocekiye Wowapi: The Niobrara Service Book from the Book of Common Prayer of 1929.* Philadelphia: Bishop White Prayer Book Society.

1964. *St. Joseph Okolakiciye Ta Olowan.* Marty SD: School Print Shop, St. Paul's Indian Mission.

[1965?]. *Lakota Song Prayers.* Eagle Butte SD: All Saints Church.

1972. *A Lakota and English Hymnal For Use in Sioux Communities.* Pine Ridge SD: Holy Rosary Mission.

1979. *Hymnal: South Dakota Catholic Congress—For Catholic Societies.* Pine Ridge SD: Holy Rosary Mission.

1986. *Owacekiye Ymni Olowan.* Oglala SD: Our Lady of the Sioux Church for the South Dakota Catholic Congress.

1991. *Niobrara Wocekiye Wowapi: The Niobrara Prayer Book: Services for Trial Use in the Episcopal Church.* Sioux Falls SD: The Niobrara Deanery of the Diocese of South Dakota, S.P.C.K. and the Diocese of SD.

1993. *Olowan: Catholic Hymns and Prayers among the Lakota Sioux—Catholic Wocekiye na Olowanpi Lakota Kin Wicopeya.* Pine Ridge SD: Holy Rosary Mission.

Hinman, Samuel D. 1865. *Ikce Wocekiye Wowapi. (The Book of Common Prayer).* St. Paul: Pioneer Printing Company.

―――. 1869. *Odowan (Hymns)*. Philadelphia: McCalla & Stavely.

Hunt, Rev. Jerome, O.S.B. 1899. *Katholik Wocekiye Wowapi: Prayers, Instructions, and Hymns in the Sioux Indian Language*. Fort Totten ND: Catholic Indian Mission.

―――. 1907. *Prayerbook*. St. Michael's Mission ND: St. Michael's Mission.

Renville, Joseph. 1842. *Dakota Dowanpi Kin. Hymns in the Dakota or Sioux Language*. Boston: Board of Commissioners for Foreign Missions, printed by Crocker & Brewster.

Riggs, Stephen Return, and John P. Williamson. 1863. *Dakota Odowan: Hymns in the Dakota Language*. New York: American Tract Society.

ADDITIONAL SOURCES

Albers, Patricia, and Beatrice Medicine, eds. 1983. *The Hidden Half: Studies of Plains Indian Women*. Lanham MD: University Press of America.

Alexander, Ruth Ann. 1994. Gentle Evangelists: Women in Dakota Episcopal Missions, 1867–1900. *South Dakota History* 24 (3–4): 174–93.

Anderson, Gary Clayton. 1984. *Kinsmen of Another Kind: Dakota-White Relations in the Upper Mississippi Valley, 1650–1862*. Lincoln: University of Nebraska Press.

―――. 1986. *Little Crow: Spokesman for the Sioux*. St. Paul: Minnesota Historical Society Press.

Anderson, Gary Clayton, and Alan R. Woolworth, eds. 1988. *Through Dakota Eyes: Narrative Accounts of the Minnesota Indian War of 1862*. St. Paul: Minnesota Historical Society Press.

Anderson, Owanah. 1988. *Jamestown Commitment: the Episcopal Church and the American Indian*. Cincinnati: Forward Movement Publications.

Archambault, Sister Marie-Theresa. 1995. "Back to Back": Roman Catholicism among the Brulé at St. Francis Mission, South Dakota. Master's thesis, University of Colorado, Boulder.

―――. 1996. Native Americans and Evangelization. In *Native and Christian: Indigenous Voices on Religious Identity in the United States and Canada*, edited by J. Treat. New York: Routledge & Kegan Paul.

―――. 1998. *A Retreat with Black Elk: Living in the Sacred Hoop*. Cincinnati: St. Anthony Messenger Press.

Barnds, William J. 1969. The Ministry of the Reverend Samuel Dutton Hinman, among the Sioux. *Historical Magazine of the Protestant Episcopal Church* 38 (4): 393–401.

Barton, Winifred. 1919. *John P. Williamson: A Brother to the Sioux.* New York: Fleming H. Revell.

Batin, Philip C., and Mark G. Thiel. 1984. *Guide to Catholic Indian Mission and School Records in Midwest Repositories.* Milwaukee: Marquette University Libraries.

Blegen, Theodore C. 1934. The Pond Brothers. *Minnesota History* 15:273–81.

Boyles, Kate, and Virgil D. Boyles. 1910. *The Spirit Trail.* Chicago: A. C. McClurg.

Brentro, Larry K., Martin Brokenleg, and Steve Van Bockern. 1990. *Reclaiming Youth at Risk: Our Hope for the Future.* Bloomington IN: National Educational Service.

Brokenleg, Martin. 1998. A Native American Perspective: "That the People May Live." In *Preaching Justice: Ethnic and Cultural Perspectives,* edited by C. M. Smith, pp. 26–42. Cleveland OH: United Church Press.

Brokenleg, Martin, and David Middleton. 1993. Native Americans: Adapting, Yet Retaining. In *Ethnic Variations in Dying, Death and Grief: Diversity in Universality,* edited by D. P. Irish, K. F. Lundquist, and V. J. Nelsen, pp. 101–12. Washington: Taylor & Francis.

Brown, Joseph E. 1953. *The Sacred Pipe: Black Elk's Account of the Seven Rites of the Oglala Sioux.* Norman: University of Oklahoma Press.

Bruguier, Leonard R. 1989. A Legacy of Sioux Leadership: The Deloria Family. In *South Dakota Leaders: From Pierre Chouteau, Jr., to Oscar Howe,* edited by H. T. Hoover and L. J. Zimmerman. Vermillion: University of South Dakota Press.

Bucko, Raymond A., S.J. 1988. The St. Francis Community New Year's Dance. *European Review of Native American Studies* 2 (2): 25–28.

———. 1998. *The Lakota Ritual of the Sweat Lodge: History and Contemporary Practice.* Lincoln: University of Nebraska Press.

Burleson, Rt. Rev. Hugh L. 1911. *The Conquest of the Continent.* New York: Domestic & Foreign Mission Society.

Clow, Richmond L., ed. 1982. Autobiography of Mary C. Collins, Missionary to the Western Sioux. *South Dakota Historical Collections* 41:1–66.

Dakota Bibliography. 1880. *Minnesota Historical Society Collections* 3 (1870–1880): 37–42.

Deloria, Ella C. 1926. Dakota Mourning Customs. *Indian Notes* 3:295–96.

———. 1927. Oath-Taking Among the Dakota. *Indian Notes* 4:81–83.

———. 1929. The Sun Dance of the Oglala Sioux. *Journal of American Folklore* 42:354–413.

———. 1944. *Speaking of Indians*. New York: Friendship Press.

———. 1954. Short Dakota Texts, Including Conversations. *International Journal of American Linguistics* 20:17–22.

———. 1961. Some Notes on the Santee. *Museum News of the W. H. Over Museum* 22:1–7.

———. 1988. *Waterlily*. Lincoln: University of Nebraska Press.

Deloria, Philip J. 1998. *Playing Indian*. New Haven CT: Yale University Press.

Deloria, Vine, Jr. 1969. *Custer Died for Your Sins; an Indian Manifesto*. New York: Macmillan.

———. 1977. Confusion of History: A Review Essay. *Historical Magazine of the Protestant Episcopal Church* 46:349–53.

———. 1979. GCSP: The Demons at Work. *Historical Magazine of the Protestant Episcopal Church* 48 (March): 83–92.

———. 1983. *God Is Red*. New York: Dell.

———. 1996. Vision and Community: A Native American Voice. In *Native and Christian: Indigenous Voices on Religious Identity in the United States and Canada*, edited by J. Treat. New York: Routledge & Kegan Paul.

———. 1999. *For This Land: Writings on Religion in America*. New York: Routledge & Kegan Paul.

Deloria, Vine, Sr. 1987. The Establishment of Christianity among the Sioux. In *Sioux Indian Religion: Tradition and Innovation*, edited by R. DeMallie and D. Parks. Norman: University of Oklahoma Press.

———. 1995. Father Vine Deloria: Sioux. In *To Be An Indian: Oral History*, edited by J. H. Cash and H. T. Hoover. St. Paul: Minnesota Historical Society.

DeMallie, Raymond J., Jr. 1982. The Lakota Ghost Dance: An Ethnohistorical Account. *Pacific Historical Review* 51:385–405.

———. 1983. Male and Female in Traditional Lakota Culture. In *The Hidden Half*, edited by P. Albers and B. Medicine. Lanham MD: University Press of America.

———. 1984. *The Sixth Grandfather: Black Elk's Teachings Given to John G. Neihardt*. Lincoln: University of Nebraska Press.

———. 1986. The Sioux in Dakota and Montana Territories: Cultural and Historical Background of the Ogden B. Read Collection. In *Vestiges of a Proud Nation: Ogden B. Read Collection of Western Art*, edited by R. J. DeMallie and R. B. Hassrick. Burlington VT: Robert Hull Fleming Museum.

———. 1987. Lakota Belief and Ritual in the Nineteenth Century. In *Sioux Indian Religion: Tradition and Innovation*, edited by R. DeMallie and D. Parks. Norman: University of Oklahoma Press.

DeMallie, Raymond J., Jr., and Robert H. Lavenda. 1977. Wakan: Plains Siouan Concepts of Power. In *The Anthropology of Power: Ethnographic Studies from Asia, Oceania, and the New World,* edited by R. Fogelson and R. Adams. New York: Academic Press.

DeMallie, Raymond J., Jr., and Douglas R. Parks, eds. 1987. *Sioux Indian Religion: Tradition and Innovation.* Norman: University of Oklahoma Press.

Digmann, Florintine, S.J. N.d. History of St. Francis Mission, 1886–1922. Manuscript in Archives of St. Francis Mission. Saint Francis SD.

Doll, Don, S.J. 1994. *Vision Quest: Men, Women, and Sacred Sites of the Sioux Nation.* New York: Crown.

————. 1996. *Vision Quest: Men, Women, and Sacred Sites of the Sioux Nation.* Omaha: Magis Press. CD-ROM.

Doll, Don, S.J., and Jim Alinder, eds. 1976. *Crying for a Vision: A Rosebud Sioux Trilogy 1886–1976* Dobbs Ferry NY: Morgan & Morgan.

Dorsey, George A. 1906. Legend of the Teton Sioux Medicine Pipe. *Journal of American Folklore* 19:326–29.

Dorsey, James Owen. 1889a. Camping Circles of the Siouan Tribes. *American Anthropologist* 2:175–177.

————. 1889b. Teton Folk-Lore. *American Anthropologist* 2:143–58.

————. 1891a. Games of Teton Dakota Children. *American Anthropologist* 4:329–45.

————. 1891b. The Social Organization of Siouan Tribes. *Journal of American Folklore* 4.

————. 1894. A Study of Siouan Cults. *Bureau of American Ethnology, Annual Reports* 11:351–544.

————. 1897. Siouan Sociology. *Bureau of American Ethnology, Annual Reports* 15:205–44.

Duncan, Kunigunde, ed. 1990. *Blue Star: The Story of Corabelle Fellows, Teacher at Dakota Missions 1884–1888.* St. Paul: Minnesota Historical Society Press.

Duratschek, Sister Mary Claudia. 1943. *The Beginnings of Catholicism in South Dakota.* Washington: Catholic University Press.

————. 1947. *Crusading Along Sioux Trails: A History of the Catholic Indian Missions of South Dakota.* New York: Grail Publications.

————. 1985. *Builders of God's Kingdom: The History of the Catholic Church in South Dakota.* Yankton SD: Diocesan Publication, Sacred Heart Convent.

Eastman, Charles A. 1915. *The Indian Today: The Past and Future of the First American.* Garden City NY: Doubleday, Page.

———. 1977. *From Deep Woods to Civilization: Chapters in the Autobiography of an Indian*. Lincoln: University of Nebraska Press.

———. 1980. *The Soul of the Indian: An Interpretation*. Lincoln: University of Nebraska Press.

———. 1991a. *Indian Heroes and Great Chieftains*. Lincoln: University of Nebraska Press.

———. 1991b. *Indian Boyhood*. Lincoln: University of Nebraska Press.

———. 1991c. *Old Indian Days*. Lincoln: University of Nebraska Press.

Eastman, Charles, and Elaine Goodale Eastman. 1990. *Wigwam Evenings: Sioux Folk Tales Retold*. Lincoln: University of Nebraska Press.

Eastman, Elaine Goodale. 1891. The Indian Girls in Indian Schools. *Homemaker* June: 199–205.

———. 1945. The Ghost Dance War and Wounded Knee Massacre of 1890–91. *Nebraska History* 26:26–42.

———. 1978. *Sister to the Sioux: The Memoirs of Elaine Goodale Eastman, 1885–91*. Edited by K. Graber. Lincoln: University of Nebraska Press.

Eastman, Mary. 1849. *Dahcotah; or Life and Legends of the Sioux around Fort Snelling*. New York: John Wiley.

———. 1970. *The Romance of Indian Life*. Upper Saddle River NJ: Literature House.

Enochs, Ross. 1996. *The Jesuit Mission to the Lakota Sioux: Pastoral Theology and Ministry, 1886–1945*. Kansas City MO: Sheed & Ward.

Erdoes, Richard, and John Lame Deer. 1972. *Lame Deer, Seeker of Visions*. New York: Simon & Schuster.

Erdoes, Richard, and Leonard Crow Dog. 1995. *Crow Dog: Four Generations of Sioux Medicine Men*. New York: HarperCollins.

Erdoes, Richard, and Mary Brave Bird. 1993. *Ohitika Woman*. New York: Grove Press.

Erdoes, Richard, and Mary Crow Dog. 1990. *Lakota Woman*. New York: Grove Weidenfeld.

Forbes, Bruce David. 1977. Evangelization and acculturation among the Santee Dakota Indians, 1834–1864. Ph.D. diss. Princeton Theological Seminary, Princeton NJ.

Gates, Charles M. 1935. The Lac qui Parle Indian Mission. *Minnesota History* 16:133–51.

Gilkerson, Peggy. 1961. Missionary rivalries among the Santee Sioux. Master's thesis, Harvard University.

Goll, Louis. 1940. *Jesuit Missions Among the Sioux*. St. Francis sd: St. Francis Mission.

Grobsmith, Elizabeth S. 1974. Wakunza: Uses of Yuwipi Medicine Power in Contemporary Teton Dakota Culture. *Plains Anthropologist* 19 (64): 129–33.

———. 1979. The Lakhota Giveaway: A System of Social Reciprocity. *Plains Anthropologist* 24:123–31.

———. 1981a. The Changing Role of the Giveaway in Contemporary Lakota Life. *Plains Anthropologist* 26:75–79.

———. 1981b. *Lakota of the Rosebud: A Contemporary Ethnography*. New York: Holt, Rinehart & Winston.

Hancock, Rev. Joseph W. 1905. Missionary Work at Red Wing, 1849–1852. *Minnesota Historical Society Collections* 10, pt. 1:164–78.

Hare, Rt. Rev. William H. 1873. *Annual Reports of the Missionary Bishop of Niobrara*. New York: Bible House.

———. 1925. *Indian Tribes and Missions: A Handbook of General History of the North American Indians, Early Missionary Efforts, and Missions of the Episcopal Church*. Hartford ct: Church Missions Publishing Company.

Hassrick, Royal. 1964. *The Sioux: Life and Customs of a Warrior Society*. Norman: University of Oklahoma Press.

Hilbert, Robert. 1987. Contemporary Catholic Mission Work among the Sioux. In *Sioux Indian Religion: Tradition and Innovation*, edited by R. DeMallie and D. Parks. Norman: University of Oklahoma Press.

Hill, Edward E., comp. 1981. *Guide to Records in the National Archives of the United States Relating to American Indians*. Washington: National Archives and Records Service, gsa.

Holler, Clyde. 1984. Black Elk's Relationship to Christianity. *American Indian Quarterly* 8 (1): 37–49.

———. 1995. *Black Elk's Religion: The Sun Dance and Lakota Catholicism*. Syracuse ny: Syracuse University Press.

———, ed. Forthcoming. *The Black Elk Reader*. Syracuse ny: Syracuse University Press.

Hong, Edna H. 1983. *The Way of the Sacred Tree*. Minneapolis: Augsburg Publishing House.

Howard, James H. 1980. *The Dakota or Sioux Indians: A Study in Human Ecology*. Lincoln: J & R Reprints.

———. 1984. *The Canadian Sioux*. Lincoln: University of Nebraska Press.

Howe, M. A. DeWolfe. 1911. *Life and Labors of Bishop Hare, Apostle to the Sioux.* New York: Sturgis & Walton Co.

Huffstetter, Stephen, S.C.J. 1998. *Lakota Grieving: A Pastoral Response.* Chamberlain SD: Tipi Press.

Hyde, George E. 1937. *Red Cloud's Folk: A History of the Oglala Sioux Indians.* Norman: University of Oklahoma Press.

———. 1956. *A Sioux Chronicle.* Norman: University of Oklahoma Press.

———. 1961. *Spotted Tail's Folk: A History of the Brulé Sioux.* Norman: University of Oklahoma Press.

Indian Tribes and Missions: A Handbook of General History of the North American Indians, Early Missionary Efforts, and Missions of the Episcopal Church. 1925. Hartford CT: Church Missions Publishing Company.

Kan, Sergei. 1999. *Memory Eternal: Tlingit Culture and Russian Orthodox Christianity through Two Centuries.* Seattle: University of Washington Press.

Karolevitz, Robert F. 1980. *Bishop Martin Marty: The Black Robe Lean Chief.* Yankton SD: Sacred Heart Convent.

Kessler, Sr. Ann, O.S.B. 1989. First Catholic Bishop of Dakota: Martin Marty, The Blackrobe Lean Chief. In *South Dakota Leaders: From Pierre Chouteau, Jr., to Oscar Howe,* edited by H. T. Hoover and L. J. Zimmerman. Vermillion: University of South Dakota Press.

Landes, Ruth. 1968. *The Mystic Lake Sioux: Sociology of the Mdewakantonwan Santee.* Madison WI: University of Wisconsin Press.

Lane, Elizabeth H. 1914. *Handbook of the Church's Mission to the Indians in Memory of William Hobart Hare, An Apostle to the Indians.* Hartford CT: Church Missions Publishing Company.

Laviolette, Gontran. 1944. *The Sioux Indians in Canada.* Regina SK: The Marian Press.

Lyon, William, and Wallace Black Elk. 1990. *Black Elk: The Sacred Ways of the Lakota.* New York: Harper & Row.

MacPeek, Gertrude A. 1973. "Tall Oaks from Little Acorns Grow": The Story of St. Mary's Episcopal School for Indian Girls. *Daughters of the American Revolution Magazine* 107 (5): 392–98.

Mails, Thomas E. 1991. *Wisdom and Power.* Tulsa: Council Oak Books.

Mails, Thomas E, and Dallas Chief Eagle. 1979. *Fools Crow.* Garden City NY: Doubleday & Co.

Markowitz, Harvey. 1987. Catholic Mission and the Sioux: A Crisis in the Early

Paradigm. In *Sioux Indian Religion: Tradition and Innovation*, edited by R. De-Mallie and D. Parks. Norman: University of Oklahoma Press.

McGregor, James Herman. 1940. *The Wounded Knee Massacre from the Viewpoint of the Sioux*. Baltimore: Wirth Brothers.

McLaren, Darcee. 1996. Living the Middle Ground: Two Dakota Missionaries, 1887–1912. *Ethnohistory* 43, 2:277–305.

McLaughlin, Marie L. 1916. *Myths and Legends of the Sioux*. Bismark ND: Bismark Tribune.

Medicine, Beatrice. 1969a. The Changing Dakota Family and the Stresses Therein. *Pine Ridge Research Bulletin* 9:1–20.

———. 1969b. Warrior Women: Sex Role Alternatives for Plains Indian Women. In *The Hidden Half: Studies in Plains Indian Women*, edited by P. Albers and B. Medicine. Lanham MD: University Press of America.

———. 1976. The Schooling Process: Some Lakota (Sioux) Views. In *The Anthropological Study of Education*, edited by C. J. Calhoun and F. A. J. Ianni The Hague: Mouton.

———. 1978. *The Native American Woman: A Perspective*. Austin TX: National Educational Laboratory Publishers.

———. 1979. Native American Communication Patterns: The Case of the Lakota Speaker. In *Handbook of Intercultural Communication: Theories, Research and Application*, edited by M. Asante, E. Newmark, and C. Blake. Beverly Hills CA: Sage Publications.

———. 1981. Native American Resistance to Integration: Contemporary Confrontations and Religious Revitalization. *Plains Anthropologist* 26:277–86.

———. 1985. Child Socialization among Native Americans: The Lakota (Sioux) in Cultural Context. *Wicazo Sa Review* 1 (2): 23–28.

———. 1986. Contemporary Cultural Revisitation: Bilingual and Bicultural Education. *Wicazo Sa Review* 2 (1): 31–35.

———. 1987. Indian Women and the Renaissance of Traditional Religion. In *Sioux Indian Religion: Tradition and Innovation*, edited by R. DeMallie and D. Park. Norman: University of Oklahoma Press.

———. 1988. Professionalization of Native American (Indian) Women: Towards a Research Agenda. *Wicazo Sa Review* 4 (2): 31–42.

Meyer, Roy W. 1968. The Canadian Sioux: Refugees from Minnesota. *Minnesota History* 41 (spring): 13–28.

———. 1993. *History of the Santee Sioux: United States Indian Policy on Trial*. Revised edition, Lincoln: University of Nebraska Press.

Miller, David Humphreys. 1985. *Ghost Dance*. Lincoln: University of Nebraska Press.

Mooney, James. 1991. *The Ghost-Dance Religion and the Sioux Outbreak of 1890*. Lincoln: University of Nebraska Press.

Neihardt, John G. 1951. *When the Tree Flowered: An Authentic Tale of the Old Sioux World*. New York: Macmillan.

———. 1961. *Black Elk Speaks: Being the Life Story of a Holy Man of the Oglala Sioux*. Lincoln: University of Nebraska Press.

Oehler, Chester M. 1959. *The Great Sioux Uprising*. New York: Oxford University Press.

Olden, Sarah E. 1918. *The People of Tipi Sapa (The Dakotas) Tipa Sapa Mitaoyate Kin*. Milwaukee WI: Morehouse Publishing.

Olson, James C. 1965. *Red Cloud and the Sioux Problem*. Lincoln: University of Nebraska Press.

Parker, Donald Dean. 1962. *Founding the Church in South Dakota*. Brookings: History Department, South Dakota State University.

———. 1964. *Early Churches and Towns in South Dakota*. Brookings: History Department, South Dakota State University.

Peterson, Susan. 1980. From Paradise to Prairie: The Presentation Sisters in Dakota, 1880–1896. *South Dakota History* 10:210–22.

———. 1982. Religious Communities of Women in the West: The Presentation Sister's Adaptation to the Northern Plains Frontier. *Journal of the West* 21:65–70.

———. 1983. "Holy Women" and Housekeepers: Women Teachers on South Dakota Reservations, 1885–1910. *South Dakota History* 13 (3): 245–60.

Peterson, Susan, and Sr. Ann Kessler, O.S.B. 1989. Valiant Religious Women: Mothers Superior Joseph Butler, Raphael McCarthy, and Jerome Schmitt. In *South Dakota Leaders: From Pierre Chouteau, Jr., to Oscar Howe*, edited by H. T. Hoover and L. J. Zimmerman. Vermillion: University of South Dakota Press.

Pond, Gideon H. 1854. Power and Influence of Dakota Medicine Men. In *Historical and Statistical Information Respecting the History, Condition and Prospects of the Indian Tribes of the United States*, edited by H. Schoolcraft. Vol. 4. Philadelphia: Lippincott, Grambo & Co.

———. 1857. Religious and Mythological Opinions of the Mississippi Valley Tribes. In *Historical and Statistical Information Respecting the History, Condition and Prospects of the Indian Tribes of the United States*, edited by H. Schoolcraft. Vol. 6. Philadelphia: Lippincott, Grambo & Co.

———. 1889. Dakota Superstitions. *Minnesota Historical Society Collections* 2:215–55.

Pond, Samuel W. 1880. Indian Warfare in Minnesota. *Minnesota Historical Society Collections* 3 (1870–1880): 129–38.

———. 1986. *The Dakotas or Sioux in Minnesota as They Were in 1834.* St. Paul: Minnesota Historical Society Press.

Pond, Samuel Jr. 1893. *Two Volunteer Missionaries among the Dakotas, or the Story of the Labors of Samuel W. and Gideon H. Pond.* Boston: Congregational Sunday-School & Publishing Society.

Poor Man, Mercy. 1987. Christian Fellowship Church. In *Sioux Indian Religion: Tradition and Innovation,* edited by R. DeMallie and D. Parks. Norman: University of Oklahoma Press.

Powers, Marla N. 1986a. *Oglala Women: Myth, Ritual, and Reality.* Chicago: University of Chicago Press.

Powers, William K. 1975. *Oglala Religion.* Lincoln: University of Nebraska Press.

———. 1982. *Yuwipi: Vision and Experience in Oglala Ritual.* Lincoln: University of Nebraska Press.

———. 1986. *Sacred Language: The Nature of Supernatural Discourse in Lakota.* Norman: University of Oklahoma Press.

———. 1987. *Beyond the Vision: Essays on American Indian Culture.* Norman: University of Oklahoma Press.

Powers, William K., and Marla N. Powers. 1994. *Testimony to Wounded Knee: A Comprehensive Bibliography.* Kendall Park NJ: Lakota Books.

Price, Catherine. 1996. *The Oglala People, 1841–1879: A Political History.* Lincoln: University of Nebraska Press.

Ravoux, Augustin. 1890. *Reminiscences, Memoirs and Lectures of Monsignor A. Ravoux, V. G..* St. Paul: Brown, Treacy.

Red Shirt, Delphine. 1998. *Bead on an Anthill: A Lakota Childhood.* Lincoln: University of Nebraska Press.

Riggs, Mary Buel. 1928. *Early Days at Santee: The Beginnings of Santee Normal Training School.* Santee NE: Santee N. T. S. Press.

Riggs, Stephen Return. 1869. *Tah-koo Wah-kan: or, the Gospel among the Dakotas.* Boston: Congregation Sabbath-School & Publishing Society.

———. 1872. Concerning Dakota Beliefs. American Philological Association, Proceedings of Third Session.

———. 1880a. The Dakota Mission. *Minnesota Historical Society Collections* 3:115–28.

———. 1880b. *Mary and I: Forty Years with the Sioux*. Chicago: W. G. Holmes.

———. 1880c. The Dakota Mission. *Minnesota Historical Society Collections* 3 (1870–80): 115–28.

———. 1880d. Narrative of Paul Mazakootemane. *Minnesota Historical Society Collections* 3 (1870–80): 82–90.

———. 1894. Protestant Missions in the Northwest. *Minnesota Historical Society Collections* 6:117–88.

Riggs, Thomas L. 1958. Sunset to Sunset: A Lifetime with My Brothers, the Dakotas. *South Dakota Historical Collections* 29:143–51.

Robinson, Doane. 1967. *A History of the Dakota or Sioux Indians: From Their Earliest Traditions and First Contact with White Men to the Final Settlement of Them upon Reservations and the Consequent Abandonment of the Old Tribal Life*. Minneapolis: Ross & Haines.

Sandoz, Mari. 1961. *These Were the Sioux*. New York: Hastings House Publishers.

Schusky, Ernest. 1975. *The Forgotten Sioux: An Ethnohistory of the Lower Brulé Reservation*. Chicago: Nelson-Hall.

Schwartz, Alan M. 1983. Dakota Resources: Religious Archives at the Center for Western Studies. *South Dakota History* 13 (3): 261–64.

Skinner, Alanson B. 1919. A Sketch of Eastern Dakota Ethnology. *American Anthropologist* 21:164–74.

Smith, Craig R. 1992. Christianity and Lakota Tradition: One and the Same. *Witness* 75 (January): 526–27.

Sneve, Virginia Driving Hawk. 1972a. *High Elk's Treasure*. New York: Holiday House.

———. 1972b. *Jimmy Yellow Hawk*. New York: Holiday House.

———. 1974a. *Betrayed*. New York: Holiday House.

———. 1974b. *When Thunders Spoke*. New York: Holiday House.

———. 1977a. Grandpa Was a Cowboy and an Indian. In *Images*. New York: Scott Foresman.

———. 1977b. *That They May Have Life: The Episcopal Church in South Dakota, 1859–1976*. New York: Seabury Press.

———. 1978. Special Places. In *Ethnic American Women: Problems, Protests, Lifestyles*, edited by E. Blicksilver. Dubuque IA: Kendall/Hunt.

———. 1993. *The Chichi HooHoo Bogeyman*. Lincoln: University of Nebraska Press.

———. 1995. *Completing the Circle*. Lincoln: University of Nebraska Press.

———. 1997. *The Trickster and the Troll*. Lincoln: University of Nebraska Press.

Sneve, Virginia Driving Hawk, and Ernest L Schusky. 1975. *They Led a Nation.* Edited by N. J. Hunt. Sioux Falls SD: Brevet Press.

Sneve, Virginia Driving Hawk, and Paul Sneve. 2000. *Enduring Wisdom: Sayings from American Indians.* New York: Holiday House.

Spider, Emerson Sr. 1996. The Native American Church of South Dakota. In *Native and Christian: Indigenous Voices on Religious Identity in the United States and Canada,* edited by J. Treat. New York: Routledge & Kegan Paul.

Stahl, Robert. 1989. Carrying the Word to the Sioux: The Williamson and Riggs Families. In *South Dakota Leaders: From Pierre Chouteau, Jr., to Oscar Howe,* edited by H. T. Hoover and L. J. Zimmerman. Vermillion: University of South Dakota Press.

Standing Bear, Luther. 1975. *My People, the Sioux.* Lincoln: University of Nebraska Press.

———. 1978. *Land of the Spotted Eagle.* Lincoln: University of Nebraska Press.

———. 1988a. *My Indian Boyhood.* Lincoln: University of Nebraska Press.

———. 1988b. *Stories of the Sioux.* Lincoln: University of Nebraska Press.

Steinmetz, Paul B., S.J. 1970. The Relationship between Plains Indian Religion and Christianity: A Priest's Viewpoint. *Plains Anthropologist* 15:83–86.

———. 1984a. *Meditations with Native Americans: Lakota Spirituality.* Santa Fe NM: Bear.

———. 1984b. The Sacred Pipe in American Indian Religions. *American Indian Culture and Research Journal* 8:27–80.

———. 1990. Shamanic Images in Peyote Visions. In *Religion in Native North America,* edited by C. Vecsey. Moscow ID: University of Idaho Press.

———. 1998a. *Pipe, Bible, and Peyote among the Oglala Lakota: A Study in Religious Identity.* Syracuse NY: Syracuse University Press.

———. 1998b. *The Sacred Pipe: An Archetypal Theology.* Syracuse NY: Syracuse University Press.

Steltenkamp, Michael F., S.J. 1982. *The Sacred Vision: Native American Religion and Its Practice Today.* New York: Paulist Press.

———. 1993. *Black Elk: Holy Man of the Oglala.* Norman: University of Oklahoma Press.

Sterling, Everett W. 1956. Moses N. Adams: A Missionary as Indian Agent. *Minnesota History* 35:167–77.

Stolzman, William, S.J. 1986a. *How to Take Part in Lakota Ceremonies.* Pine Ridge SD: Red Cloud Indian School.

———. 1986b. *The Pipe and Christ.* Pine Ridge SD: Red Cloud Indian School.

Svoboda, Joseph G. 1983. *Guide to American Indian Resource Materials in Great Plains Repositories.* Lincoln: Center for Great Plains Studies, University of Nebraska.

Swift Bird, the Indians' Bishop. 1926. Hartford CT: Church Missions Publishing.

Talbot, Rt. Rev. Ethelbert. 1906. *My People of the Plains.* New York: Harper & Brothers.

Theiz, Ron, and Severt Young Bear. 1994. *Standing in the Light: A Lakota Way of Seeing.* Lincoln: University of Nebraska Press.

Thompson, Harry F. 1992. Dakota Resources: The Riggs Family Papers at the Center for Western Studies. *South Dakota History* 22 (1): 64–74.

Treat, James, ed. 1996. *Native and Christian: Indigenous Voices on Religious Identity in the United States and Canada.* New York: Routledge & Kegan Paul.

Utley, Robert. 1963. *The Last Days of the Sioux Nation.* New Haven CT: Yale University Press.

Vecsey, Christopher. 1999. *Where the Two Roads Meet.* Vol. 3. American Indian Catholics. South Bend IN: University of Notre Dame.

Walker, James. 1905. Sioux Games. *Journal of American Folklore* 18:277–90.

———. 1914. Oglala Kinship Terms. *American Anthropologist* 16 (1): 96–109.

———. 1917. The Sun Dance and Other Ceremonies of the Oglala Division of the Teton Sioux. *Anthropological Papers of the American Museum of Natural History* 16 (2): 51–221.

———. 1980. *Lakota Belief and Ritual.* Edited by R. DeMallie and E. Jahner. Lincoln: University of Nebraska Press.

———. 1982. *Lakota Society.* Edited by R. DeMallie. Lincoln: University of Nebraska Press.

———. 1983. *Lakota Myth.* Edited by E. Jahner. Lincoln: University of Nebraska Press.

Wallis, Wilson D. 1947. The Canadian Dakota. Anthropological Papers of the American Museum of Natural History 41:1.

Westropp, Henry Ignatius. N.d. *In the Land of the Wigwam: Missionary Notes from the Pine Ridge Mission.* Pine Ridge SD: Student Apprentices in the Office of the Oglala Light.

Whipple, Rt. Rev. Henry Benjamin. 1899. *Lights and Shadows of a Long Episcopate.* New York: Macmillan Company.

Wilkins, Robert P., and Wynona H. Wilkins. 1959. *God Giveth the Increase: The History of the Episcopal Church in North Dakota.* Fargo: North Dakota Institute for Regional Studies.

Willand, Jon. 1964. *Lac qui Parle and the Dakota Mission*. Madison MN: Lac qui Parle County Historical Society.

Williamson, John P. 1918. Removal of the Sioux Indians from Minnesota. *Minnesota History Bulletin* 2:420–25.

Wissler, Clark. 1904. Decorative Art of the Sioux. Anthropological Papers of the American Museum of Natural History 18:231–78.

———. 1905. The Whirlwind and the Elk in the Mythology of the Dakota. *Journal of American Folklore* 18:257–68.

———. 1907a. Some Dakota Myths, I, II. *Journal of American Folklore* 20:121–31; 195–206.

———. 1907b. Some Protective Designs of the Dakota. Anthropological Papers of the American Museum of Natural History 1, Pt. 2:21–53.

———. 1912. Societies and Ceremonial Associations in the Oglala Division of the Teton-Dakota. Anthropological Papers of the American Museum of Natural History 11, Pt. 1:1–99.

Wolff, Gerald W. 1989. First Protestant Episcopal Bishop of South Dakota: William Hobart Hare. In *South Dakota Leaders: From Pierre Chouteau, Jr., to Oscar Howe*, edited by H. T. Hoover and L. J. Zimmerman. Vermillion: University of South Dakota Press.

Woodruff, Brent K. 1934. The Episcopal Mission to the Dakotas 1860–1898. *South Dakota Historical Collections* 27:553–603.

Young, Gertrude S. 1958a. In the Missions. In *And there were these—*. Brookings SD: Privately published.

———. 1958b. The Journal of a Missionary to the Yankton Sioux: 1875–1902. *South Dakota Department of History: Report and Historical Collections* 29:63–86.

———. 1963. The Correspondence of a Niobrara Archdeacon. *Historical Magazine of the Protestant Episcopal Church* 32:3–15.

Zeilinger, Ron. 1990. *Sacred Ground: Reflections on Lakota Spirituality and the Gospel*. Chamberlain SD: Tipi Press.

Zitkala-Ša. 1985a. *American Indian Stories*. Lincoln: University of Nebraska Press.

Zitkala-Ša. 1985b. *Old Indian Legends*. Lincoln: University of Nebraska Press.

INDEX

⚘ + ⚘